A BAD PEACE AND A GOOD WAR

A BAD PEACE AND A GOOD WAR

SPAIN AND THE MESCALERO APACHE UPRISING OF 1795–1799

MARK SANTIAGO

UNIVERSITY OF OKLAHOMA PRESS : NORMAN

Publication of this book is made possible through
the generosity of Edith Kinney Gaylord.

Library of Congress Cataloging-in-Publication Data

Names: Santiago, Mark, 1959– author.
Title: A bad peace and a good war : Spain and the Mescalero Uprising of 1795–1799 / Mark Santiago.
Description: Norman : University of Oklahoma Press, [2018] | Includes bibliographical references and index.
Identifiers: LCCN 2018013079 | ISBN 978-0-8061-6155-6 (hardcover)
  ISBN 978-0-8061-6744-2 (paper) Subjects: LCSH: Mescalero Indians—Wars. | Indians of North America—Wars—

  1750–1815. | Nava, Pedro de—Military leadership. | Apache Indians—Wars. | Indians of North America—Wars—Southwest, New. | Mexico—History—Spanish colony, 1540–1810. | Mexico—History—Spanish colony, 1540–1810—Ethnic relations. | Mexican-American Border Region—History, Military—18th century.

Classification: LCC E99.M45 S35 2018 | DDC 972/.02—dc23
LC record available at https://lccn.loc.gov/2018013079

The paper in this book meets the guidelines for permanence and durability of the Committee on Production Guidelines for Book Longevity of the Council on Library Resources, Inc. ∞

Copyright © 2018 by the University of Oklahoma Press, Norman, Publishing Division of the University. Manufactured in the U.S.A.

All rights reserved. No part of this publication may be reproduced, stored in a retrieval system, or transmitted, in any form or by any means, electronic, mechanical, photocopying, recording, or otherwise—except as permitted under Section 107 or 108 of the United States Copyright Act—without the prior written permission of the University of Oklahoma Press. To request permission to reproduce selections from this book, write to Permissions, University of Oklahoma Press, 2800 Venture Drive, Norman OK 73069, or email rights.oupress@ou.edu.

To Dawn
Forever and always

CONTENTS

List of Illustrations ix
Acknowledgments xi
Maps xiii

Introduction 3
1. A General Irruption 10
2. Origins of Conflict 24
3. War, Peace, War 33
4. Between Two Fires 48
5. Forging a Bad Peace 60
6. Threats to Fragile Peace 76
7. Sparking the Fire 93
8. Blood and Suffering 100
9. The Cruel Season 118
10. War in Their Own Lands 133
11. Invasions Real and Imagined 148
12. The Calamities of War 166
13. Chasing the Shadow of Peace 184
    Epilogue: The Turns of History 195

Notes 201
Bibliography 225
Index 231

ILLUSTRATIONS

Figures

The Ruins of the Church at San Elizario on the Rio Grande. . . . 19
Bernardo de Gálvez. 46
Juan Vicente de Güemes Pacheco y Padilla,
  second Conde de Revillagigedo. 66
Organ Mountains, New Mexico 87
Church at El Paso del Norte 101
Granite Masses—Waco [Hueco] Mountains, Texas 137
The Capture of Trinidad, 17 February 1797 149
Miguel de la Grúa Talamanca,
  1st Marqués de Branciforte. 151
Guadalupe Mountains, Texas 168
Miguel José de Azanza Alegría, Duke of Santa Fe. 175

Maps

Interior Provinces of New Spain, 1795–1799 xiv
Mescalero War, Theater of Operations xv

ACKNOWLEDGMENTS

I AM HUMBLED BY THE INSPIRATION I HAVE RECEIVED over the years from the following friends: from the members and committed supporters of the Tucson Presidio, especially William Islas, Kirk Huelle, Mike Araiza, John Patla, Rudy Bird, Mike Starace, Tom Preselzki, Eric Thing, and most especially for the superb embrace of the spirit of historical reenacting from the inestimable Jeff Coleman. Blood, dirt, flint, and steel shrinks academic falderal to insignificance.

For not only being instrumental in founding the Tucson Presidio Garrison, but also shepherding this work to fulfillment, I am eternally indebted to Rick Collins of Tucson, Arizona, for his unfailing belief, critical eye, and scholarly insistence on verifiable truth in the presentation of this book. Rick's input was supported by his wonderful wife, Barb.

I would also call special attention to the patient and caring tutoring and mentoring I received for almost seventeen years at the Arizona Historical Society (AHS) from Pierce A. Chamberlain III, Thomas H. Peterson Jr., and Jay Van Orden. There has never been a more significant, impactful, and lasting legacy at that renowned institution than this magnificent trio of curators and historians. Yet their efforts would have proven vain if not for the wisdom and discernment of the late Sidney B. Brinkerhoff, past director of the AHS, gentleman, and scholar, who assembled, led, and supported these three *caballeros* in their quests.

In a similar vein, it would be remiss to not recall the friendship, mentoring, and paternal love showed to me by the late George Allen Brubaker, professor emeritus from the University of Arizona. He was a remarkable man.

In New Mexico, the guidance and insights of scholars and archaeologists Karl and Toni Laumbach of Las Cruces were invaluable in determining the geographical and material world of the indigenous and Hispanic peoples of the region. I am forever grateful for their friendship.

The love and support given to me by my sons Edward, Alexander, and Justin Santiago have provided me a wonderful refuge in this pilgrim life for hope in a future that includes such honorable men. I am especially grateful to Justin for agreeing to provide the cartography for this book.

Finally, I cannot express my debts for the generosity, scholarly advice, critical editing, indexing, and ever-knowing rectitude provided by my wife, Dawn Moore Santiago. All that I am and ever will be owes to her.

MAPS

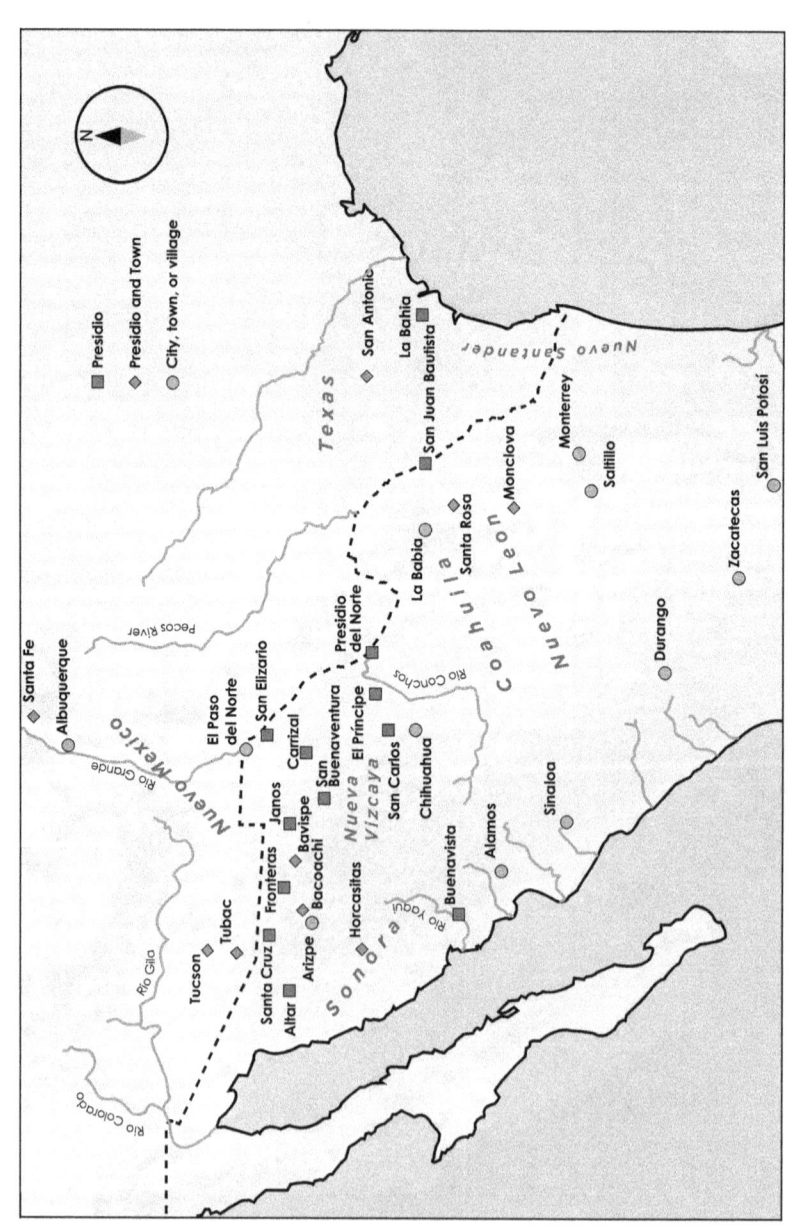

Interior Provinces of New Spain, 1795–1799. *Cartography by Justin Santiago.*

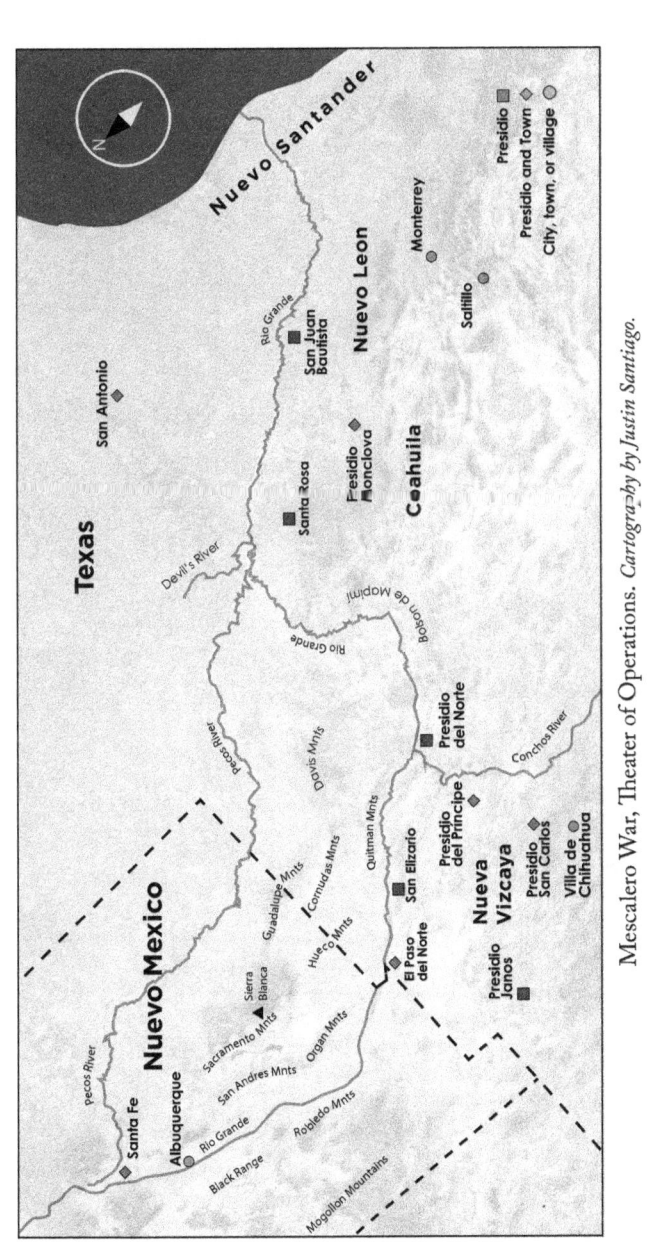

Mescalero War, Theater of Operations. *Cartography by Justin Santiago.*

A BAD PEACE AND A GOOD WAR

INTRODUCTION

IT HAS LONG BEEN A STANDARD CLAIM among borderlands historians that beginning around 1790 and lasting over the following three decades, a period of general peace emerged between the Spaniards and the many Apache groups along the northern frontier of New Spain's Interior Provinces. With the development of what some modern historians have labeled *establecimentos de paz*, or peace establishments, the long and bloody war between both peoples began to wind down into one of mutual accommodation. This era of relative peace has often been attributed to the adoption of new Spanish policies, laid down by Viceroy Bernardo de Gálvez in his *Instructions of 1786*. In these, Gálvez annunciated the strategy of alternating constant aggressive warfare against the Apaches with offers of peaceful coexistence in which the Indians would be given food and goods at what were essentially reservations, in exchange for their quiescence. This strategy of holding forth both the mailed fist of war and the velvet glove of peace was seen as a method of fostering gradual acculturation among those Apaches who entered the reservations, while continuing to attack and destroy those who refused.[1]

Among the many concepts attributed to Gálvez, one is often quoted as a particularly apt summation of Spanish dealings with the Apaches: "A bad peace with all the [Indian] nations who may ask for it will be more beneficial to us than the efforts of a good war." Within this construct, it was maintained that the Spaniards were willing to accept low levels of Apache raiding and concomitant violence because the costs, both in lives and property, were less than waging a full-scale war.[2]

Yet, was that aphorism really true? Was a bad peace really better than a good war? In one major instance it is clear that the answer was no. Beginning in August 1795 and lasting at least until the end of 1799, there was a general and sustained surge in violence between the Mescalero Apaches and the Spaniards of such a large extent that it can be fairly categorized as a particular war. The area of hostilities stretched across the central and eastern Interior Provinces, including Nueva Vizcaya, New Mexico, Coahuila, Texas, Nuevo León, and Nuevo Santander. In addition, warfare extended beyond the Spanish frontier line into the Mescalero homelands in what is now central and eastern New Mexico and West Texas.[3]

How could it be that in the midst of success in bringing the Apaches into the peace establishments, there was such a long-lasting and destructive war? Part of the answer may lie in the nature of the conflict itself and the way in which it was recorded. With only a few exceptions, the Mescalero war was waged beyond the Spanish frontier in the lands of the Apaches themselves. Thus the written reports, complaints, and demands that were produced by exasperated Spanish civil and military officials when the Apaches raided their lands, and that fill so many volumes in archives in Spain and Mexico, were simply not created.

In addition, at the same time the Mescaleros were fighting the Spaniards, most other Apache groups *were* maintaining the peace. For example, the Chiricahua Apaches to the west were for the most part relatively tranquil, with substantial numbers actively residing outside several peace establishments. Of these, the establishment at Janos has been the most studied and detailed as a result of the survival of that presidio's official archives. The abundant historical records for Janos show a situation among the *Apaches de paz* (peaceful Apaches) there and at other associated posts reflecting a fair amount of stability and implicit success, as far as the Spaniards' overall goals for the peace establishments were concerned. The condition of the establishments at the presidios of Tucson and Bacoachi in Sonora appeared to be similar, although admittedly with far less historical documentation.[4]

In the same fashion, along the eastern portion of the Interior Provinces, a general movement toward peace was also identifiable. There, significant numbers of Lipan Apaches were actively attempting to make peace with the

Spanish authorities, especially in the Provinces of Texas, Nuevo León, and Nuevo Santander. Indeed, several Lipan bands concluded formal peace treaties in all three provinces during the 1790s at the exact same time the Mescalero war was raging. Although these Lipans do not appear to have congregated into formal peace establishments, many of them did gather regularly within easy reach of several Spanish towns and presidios that came to be seen as within their "home" range.[5]

Thus, it was the Mescalero Apaches in the middle of the frontier who were the holdouts. During a period that witnessed an acceleration of the accommodation between Spaniards and Apaches elsewhere, many Mescaleros were instead engaged in open warfare. In addition, those Mescaleros who actually did gather around Spanish peace establishments have been the least documented, as records about them are relatively scarce. Immediately prior to the conflict, as many as nine hundred Mescaleros may have been affiliated with the peace establishment at Presidio del Norte. Yet the Spaniards never seem to have conducted a detailed survey and accounting of these Indians, or if they did do so, the documents have not come to light. The similarly scarce records for another peace establishment, affiliated with the Presidio of San Elizario, did include numbers of Mescaleros actually residing about twenty miles upstream at El Paso del Norte. This imprecision probably caused no small amount of confusion for both Spanish officials at the time and modern historians afterward.[6]

The scarcity of Spanish documents may be the reason the war waged between the Mescaleros and Spaniards has been largely obscured and forgotten. However, a study of the available records reveals a scale of violence between the two peoples from 1795 to 1799 that calls into question the accuracy of previous historical portrayals of a prolonged period of general peace following the implementation of Gálvez's policies. Accordingly, a reevaluation of the nature and overall extent of the general peace is called for.

In piecing together the story of this conflict, I have taken several approaches. The first is that I have designated this as a separate and discernible war. This recognition stands in contrast to the usual categorization of Spanish-Apache conflict as part of a continuous, longer, and broader war that unfolded over centuries. Indeed, the Spaniards themselves when describing this specific conflict used words such as "revolt," "uprising," and "irruption." However, these terms clearly indicate a particular point of view—namely, to paint the Mescaleros as having rebelled against a legitimate sovereignty they had previously acknowledged and agreed to accept. Furthermore, characterizing the conflict as an uprising allowed the Spaniards to paint themselves as the aggrieved party, victims of a surprise attack launched by foes whom they had treated humanely and who now treacherously returned evil for good. Finally, casting the conflict in this manner gave the Spaniards a clear legal license to undertake their operations under the guise of what they understood as the rules governing a just war. In fact, the Mescaleros *had* started the war and initiated hostilities. They *did* violate the mutual understandings at the peace establishments to which at least some of their leaders had agreed. That the Mescaleros, from their own historical and cultural perspective, may have had perfectly understandable and perhaps justifiable reasons for their actions was for the Spaniards entirely irrelevant.[7]

In addition, I have consciously attempted to write a "military history." The fact is that the mechanisms of war necessarily involve logistics, marches, tactics, combats, and body counts. To some, these details may obscure the "real" causes of conflict or may "glorify" the brutality and horror of war. However, these small, common, everyday things that occur in war constitute the very narratives that bring the tragic humanity of it to the forefront.

Knowing that Spanish soldiers or Mescalero Apache warriors moved along the same mountains and deserts we now drive and hike along helps form a human bond between past lives and our own. Further, the history of the northern frontier of New Spain between 1765 and 1821 is most particularly a military history. While many scholars seek to highlight the cultural and social complexities of the Spanish Borderlands, it was first and foremost a zone of active or potential warfare. The clearest indicator of this is the obvious fact that the Interior Provinces were made a separate *military* command under a *military* commandant general. Therefore, the military aspect is in many ways as important as or at least equal to investigations into other facets of the region's history.

This war against the Mescaleros came to my attention in a quite offhand manner. A noted translation of a Franciscan priest's critique of the Spanish peace policies during the 1790s contained a curt reference to the uprising of Mescaleros that killed almost sixty soldiers and officers outside the peace establishments at Presidio del Norte. While the author used this incident to justify his own arguments as to how the establishments should actually be operated, a telling detail was how casual, how routine, the reference was. But viewed from a military perspective, this was far from routine. The loss of so many troops in one fell swoop would have represented a major defeat of Spanish arms; indeed, it would rank as one of the largest single losses of military personnel within the Interior Provinces in the entire eighteenth century. Surely, there must be more to this story than indicated by this passing reference.[8]

Further research demonstrated that other, secondary sources maintained the characterization of this event as a transitory affair that only briefly interrupted the Spanish drive toward reaching a peaceful détente with the Apaches at the end of the eighteenth and the beginning of the nineteenth century. Yet from a military perspective, Spain (or any other nation-state) would have seen the "uprising," by contemporary standards, as intolerable. Clearly something was missing. However, by delving deeper into the primary records of the period, it soon became obvious that the Spaniards under the leadership of Commandant General Pedro de Nava y Porlier had indeed waged an impressively large-scale and coordinated campaign over several years against the Mescalero Apaches in retaliation for the original outbreak. Indeed, Nava's operations constituted one of the largest and arguably the most sustained Spanish military operations along the northern frontier throughout the entire eighteenth century.[9]

That Pedro de Nava was able to marshal this effort is evidence of the culmination of the Spanish military policies that had originated in the 1760s and had been tested, reformed, and redoubled over the following decades. Gradually, the Spaniards had honed their ability to launch large-scale campaigns across the frontier and coordinate them with smaller, more localized expeditions. Alongside the mailed fist that these operations represented, the Spaniards began after 1786 to employ the velvet glove of the peace establishments, albeit with several fits and starts. Thus, Nava and his military commanders had available to them a wide variety of tools and tactics to deal with the Apaches, many of which they were able to unleash upon the Mescaleros when war unexpectedly broke out in 1795.[10]

Yet, while the war demonstrated the high level of efficiency the military apparatus had achieved, even in the midst of the conflict, Spain's Achilles heel in the Interior Provinces was laid bare. Its constant involvement in European wars with Great Britain and France, plus the increasing danger presented by the emerging United States, made the efforts to deal with the Mescaleros and other Native peoples along the northern frontier increasingly problematic. Events in Europe, the Caribbean, and elsewhere dominated Spanish strategic policy to such an extent that Pedro de Nava and his forces were increasingly called upon to consider in their calculations the potential of British or American invasions.

This was a prospect for which Nava's men were singularly unprepared and unsuited, as they had been engaged exclusively in war against Native peoples. Thus, throughout this period, Nava found himself beset by financial constraints and strategic demands from Madrid that predictably subordinated the "minor" conflict with the Mescaleros to the greater demands of imperial defense.[11]

Still, from Nava's perspective the war against the Mescaleros was anything but minor. To allow the initial attacks to go unanswered would have threatened the entire construct of Spanish military superiority over the Apaches, even if that superiority was more perception than reality. If the Mescaleros were not punished severely, other Apaches at other peace establishments might also rise up to disrupt the fragile accommodation for which Nava and so many other Spanish officials had labored so long and so hard. As a result, Nava tenaciously continued hostilities, even in the face of calls from his superiors to focus on threats from Great Britain or the United States.

In the end, after almost four years, the Spaniards succeeded in killing, capturing, and deporting approximately 750 Mescalero men, women, and children, representing in all a high percentage of the overall tribal population. Faced with such losses, many Mescaleros returned to seeking accommodation outside the peace establishments, while others remained independent but generally quiescent in the hinterlands beyond. Nevertheless, raids and counterraids by both peoples continued to plague the region until Mexico's independence in 1821.

The story of the Mescalero war of 1795–99 may be seen, then, as a culmination of decades of Spanish effort to defeat or at least contain Apache aggression. As such, it represents an important moment in the evolution of Spanish-Apache relations: confirmation in the most brutal terms that this relationship had always been grounded, at least from the Spanish perspective, in the naked use of military power. And while it is from the Spanish perspective that much of this story is told, there are opportunities to see things from the Mescaleros' point of view as well. Unfortunately, most of the latter must of necessity be filtered through the prism of Spanish reports and documents, as there simply are no contemporary Mescalero accounts directly relating to this particular period. Although oral histories and tribal traditions do give perspective to the Mescalero worldview and their interrelationships with the Spaniards and other peoples, these are often of a general nature and do not touch upon particular events, such as the war that began in 1795. Still, the identities and roles of individual Mescaleros do appear with enough frequency in Spanish reports that it is possible to at least recognize that their actions were formed out of the milieu of their own independent volition and societal beliefs, even if these are ignored, obscured, or forgotten in the primary sources. I have attempted to include as many of these individuals as possible within this story and to bring forth the ideas and environments that impacted the course of their actions. In a similar fashion, I have also attempted to flesh out the personalities and actions of the Spanish participants in these events. The latter has proven a much easier task, in that many of the officers and not a few of the common soldiers left service records that provide personal details.

Both the detailed records of the Spaniards and the correspondingly sparse references to the Mescaleros have, for me at least, been a vehicle through which the terrible face of war, even one so little understood and so long forgotten as this, could be distilled to a recognizable, if elemental, humanity. This in itself is what makes the story of the Mescalero war and the recollection of its participants worth telling.

1

A GENERAL IRRUPTION

THE SUMMER OF 1795 found Pedro de Nava a very concerned man. As the commandant general of the Interior Provinces of New Spain, Nava was responsible for the security of the northern frontier of Spain's vast imperial holdings, stretching from the Gulf of California in the west to the Gulf coast of Texas in the east. Into this region the complexities of Spain's international rivalries had increasingly escalated. Looking east beyond the great Mississippi River, Spanish officials were genuinely alarmed by the rapidly burgeoning power of the land-hungry United States of America. Spain's perennial enemy Great Britain was locked in a worldwide struggle against revolutionary France, and Spain had formed an unnatural and uneasy alliance with the British. In addition to open warfare in the Caribbean, the conflict had seen an influx of French revolutionary ideas and propaganda calling for the liberation of Spanish America and seeking to spark nascent independence movements in Spain's colonies. In the face of these threats, the last thing Pedro de Nava needed were problems within the frontier areas under his control.[1]

Luckily for Nava, the Interior Provinces had been relatively calm for several years. Decades of warfare between the Spanish and numerous indigenous peoples of the region, especially the Apaches, had finally abated to something resembling peace. Across the wide expanse of the northern frontier, eight reservations had been set up for several Apache groups in an attempt to induce them to curtail their raiding activity. Almost two thousand Apaches were now frequenting the reservations, and a general quiescence had settled upon the area. Despite the increased costs to maintain these establishments, Nava believed they were vital to securing the peace and were more economical in the long run than large-scale military operations. Apaches still engaged in raids, but these were generally confined both in size and scale to a level Nava's subordinates could deal with. As they had for almost a decade, the Spaniards were willing to tolerate the disruptions of this "bad peace" rather than expend the resources required to decisively crush the Apaches in a "good war." Now, in the face of increasingly strident calls for cost cutting to help defray the expense of the war with France, Nava maintained that the Interior Provinces of New Spain were functioning peacefully and efficiently.[2]

A native of the Canary Islands, Nava had enjoyed a long career that had seen him rise steadily, owing more to his organizational and administrative abilities than any combat experience. Between 1781 and 1789 he had served with distinction as garrison commander of the strategic city of Caracas, Venezuela, where he attained the rank of brigadier general. The following year, he was promoted to field marshal and named commandant general of the Interior Provinces. During the next five years, Nava labored long and hard to bring a semblance of peace with the Apaches, and it appeared he had been successful.[3]

On August 6, 1795, Nava's thoughts were centered on far eastern Texas. He had received reports that a substantial group of Indians from east of the Mississippi River were seeking to settle in Spanish Texas. They claimed they were fleeing persecution from the Americans and promised to ally with the Spaniards in exchange for sanctuary. In writing to his superiors in Madrid, however, Nava questioned the veracity of these Indians and speculated that it was all a ruse. Allowing them to cross into Spanish territory might strain relations with the United States. Furthermore, permitting these Indians to settle in Texas might encourage others and lead to unforeseen consequences with Native groups already living in the region. With his eyes firmly fixed to the east, Nava confidently assured his superiors that he would act to ensure the continued tranquility of the frontier areas under his command. Unfortunately for him, on the very day he was writing his report, events were occurring in far western Texas that would make a mockery of his claims.[4]

At fifty-one years of age, Josef Urías had served as a soldier for almost three decades. A native of the old Presidio of Conchos in the Province of Nueva

Vizcaya, Urías had enlisted as a common soldier in 1768 at the age of twenty-three. Over the next twenty-eight years he rose steadily through the ranks until commissioned as an officer, becoming *alférez,* or ensign, of the Primera Compañía Volante, the First Flying Company, in June 1788. The First Volante was stationed north of the city of Chihuahua, the capital of the Interior Provinces; but like all of the *compañías volantes,* the First was designed to be a mobile force without a permanent base. Thus, they could operate throughout the frontier region. For the next seven years, Urías served in the First competently, if unspectacularly, having participated "in twenty campaigns and some *corredurías* [pursuits], and in these he had many combats with the enemy and in these he succeeded in killing two Apaches and recovering 589 animals." Overall, his superiors judged Alférez Urías as "a good officer for this war."[5]

In late July 1795, Urías found himself in command of a body of troopers from the First Volante serving on detached duty at the Presidio del Príncipe, located at the village of Coyamé, some forty miles southwest of the confluence of the Río Conchos and the Rio Grande. Toward the end of the month, Urías was informed by the post commander, Captain José de Tovar, that he had received dispatches that two small groups of Indians had raided Spanish settlements and were reportedly heading toward Presidio del Príncipe. Captain Tovar determined that Urías, given his experience, would command a detachment that would try and locate the raiders.[6]

The Indians Urías would be searching for had struck their targets several days earlier, far to the south of the presidio. On July 25, the garrison of the Presidio of San Carlos, sixty miles southwest of Príncipe, had been alerted that two parties of Indians, with four to six men each, had carried off twenty head of livestock from some ranches in the jurisdiction of Ciénega de los Olivos, more than one hundred miles farther south. Fortunately, the commander at San Carlos, Captain Antonio García de Texada, had at his disposal not only the seventy-three men of his own garrison, but also substantial detachments from the Third and Fourth Compañías Volantes, temporarily stationed at the presidio. He immediately sent out two separate squadrons in pursuit of the Indian raiders, one with twenty men from the Third Volante and the second with forty-four men from San Carlos and the Fourth Volante.[7]

The latter detachment of troopers, under the command of Alféreces Don Cayetano Limón and Don Juan Fernández, pursued one group of the Indian raiders. The tracks they followed initially paralleled the course of the Río Conchos, to the east of San Carlos, but then began to veer to the northwest, clearly making for the Rio Grande. Whether through skill or luck, or a combination of the two, the pursuing Spaniards were able to successfully follow the Indian raiders' tracks for several days.

However, despite their best efforts, the men of the Third Volante in the other detachment eventually lost the trail of their quarry. But the signs indicated this group of Indians was generally heading to the northwest, into the area where the garrison of the Presidio del Príncipe regularly patrolled. The men from the Third immediately sent word of this fact to Captain Tovar at Príncipe.[8]

By Sunday, August 2, 1795, Captain Tovar had given Alférez Urías his orders, and Urías and fifty troopers from the First Volante and Príncipe immediately rode out from the presidio to search for the raiders who were believed headed into their territory. Whether the men had the occasion to attend Mass, as was usual before their journey, is not known. As they scoured the terrain for signs, Urías and his party quickly discovered the trail of six Indians, which they immediately followed. After many hours of riding, the soldiers had covered nineteen leagues, or about forty-seven miles, heading west from Príncipe. On Monday, August 3, they arrived at the approaches of the Sierra del Carrizo, one of the numerous mountain ranges that covered the region. Though the tracks leading into the mountains indicated they were pursuing only six men, Alférez Urías's long-honed experience demanded caution. He decided to split his force, ordering a detachment of twenty-two men to guard the mules and horses of his supply train while he led the remaining twenty-eight *soldados* to reconnoiter the mountains.[9]

Among this advanced party rode soldado Nolasco Medina, a thirty-four-year-old veteran with fourteen years of service. Standing only five feet tall, with a pock-marked and swarthy complexion, an aquiline nose, black hair, and black eyes, Medina was typical of the troopers that filled the Spanish military ranks on the northern frontier. Representing a diverse variety of features from Spanish, Indian, and black progenitors, these "sons of the Country" were classified into a complex number of *castas*, or racial castes, in the rigidly hierarchical society of the time. Yet most of these soldados were sufficiently Hispanicized so that whether out of necessity or conviction, they had volunteered and been accepted into military service.

As he spurred his horse forward into the Sierra del Carrizo, Medina's military career had so far proven mostly uneventful. Born into a farming family of Nueva Vizcaya, twenty-year-old Medina on September 1, 1781, had enlisted voluntarily for ten years as a light trooper in the company of the Presidio del Príncipe. After a decade of service, he reenlisted for another ten years on June 17, 1792. During his entire career he had been involved in at least three combats that resulted in the death of eleven Apache men and women and the capture of another twenty-five men, women, and children. Still, Medina appears not to have particularly distinguished himself and, despite all his service time, he was still only a private. In the coming hours, all of that was to change.[10]

Medina and the other twenty-seven men under Alférez Urías had not ridden very far when they were suddenly ambushed. Ensconced among the rocks and outcroppings of the Sierra del Carrizo was a force estimated to contain 150 Mescalero Apache warriors. Using their superior numbers, the Apaches gradually surrounded Urías and his men. "Despite making the greatest resistance, fighting with extraordinary valor for more than one hour," Urías and his men were doomed. The Mescaleros were armed with muskets as well as bows and arrows, and given their numbers, their firepower soon began to tell. The most likely scenario is that Urías and many of his men were gradually shot down. As the number of Spaniards began to shrink, flight became the only hope for survival.[11]

Despite being wounded by gunshot, soldado Nolasco Medina had continued fighting throughout the engagement. At some point, either on his own initiative or at the order of others, Medina put spurs to his horse and rode out of the ambush. According to later reports, "he broke the circle of the Enemy . . . and was the first to warn the train." Four other wounded Spaniards followed in Medina's wake, and all reached the twenty-two men left with the supply train at the entrance to the mountains. However, the Apaches pursued the fugitives closely and now launched a second assault on the remaining Spaniards. Medina and the other survivors joined in the defense of the train, and Medina was hit again and again, taking another four wounds. The Apaches managed to capture some and perhaps all of the horses of the pack train, but Medina and the remaining twenty-six Spaniards were able to make good their escape.[12]

Within a day the survivors brought word of the disaster back to Captain Tovar at Presidio del Príncipe. Tovar immediately sent dispatch riders to Commandant General Pedro de Nava at Chihuahua City with the news. The captain then set out with a substantial body of troops and returned to the Sierra del Carrizo to recover the bodies of Alférez Urías and his men for burial. After performing this grim task, on August 8, undoubtedly in an attempt to bolster the morale of his shaken command, Tovar promoted soldado Nolasco Medina to *cabo de escuadra*, or squad corporal, a testament to Medina's wounds, if not his valor. As the presidio recovered from these losses, unbeknownst to Captain Tovar, other recent events would further darken the morale of his men.[13]

On the same day Urías's command was decimated, the second detachment of troops that had set out from San Carlos after the initial Indian raiders was still following its quarry's tracks. Over the course of a week and a half, the forty-four Spanish troopers had covered almost two hundred miles, as their two commanders pushed them relentlessly.

The senior officer in charge was actually almost twenty years younger than his subaltern. At thirty-five, First Alférez Cayetano Limón had been in the military practically his whole life. A native of the Presidio of Altar in Sonora, Limón's father and namesake was one of the most combat-hardened veterans along the entire northern frontier. The elder Limón, a mestizo from the Villa de Sinaloa, had joined the Company of Altar in 1754 while in his early twenties. Over the next thirteen years he had risen in rank from soldado, to cabo, then to sergeant, and finally obtained commissioned rank as alférez in 1767. Despite his mixed-race background, the elder Limón's ability as an Indian fighter was such that he participated in an inordinate amount of combat, so much so that his superiors described him as "excelling for war and knowledge of the field." During his thirty-five-year-long military career, the elder Limón was determined to have his two sons enter the military and advance even higher than he had himself. Both boys, Ygnacio and Cayetano, served as volunteers as soon as they were big enough to handle a musket. As they entered their teens, both enlisted as soldados, but their father petitioned that they be enrolled as officer cadets. Despite many delays, in 1787 both were eventually commissioned, with Cayetano admitted as a cadet at the Presidio of Buenavista and Ygnacio admitted as a cadet at Altar.[14]

With such antecedents, the younger Cayetano Limón fully justified his family's reputation as skilled Indian fighters, and in 1789 he was commissioned as Second Alférez of the Fourth Volante in the neighboring Province of Nueva Vizcaya. Less than six months later, Cayetano was promoted to First Alférez and for the next six years saw much action. He took part in six campaigns and many raids and pursuits, in which twenty-seven Apaches were captured, as well as being credited with killing an Indian warrior in hand-to-hand combat. Despite his obvious valor, Limón was judged by his superiors as displaying less than stellar conduct and was rated only as "a medium officer."[15]

His apparent lackluster behavior notwithstanding, Limón's aptitude for field service was unquestioned, even by his *segundo* for this operation, Second Alférez Juan Fernández. At fifty-two, Fernández was old enough to be Limón's father. Over three decades, the second alférez had ridden out on seventeen campaigns and participated in many smaller actions that had killed or captured twenty-five Apache warriors, or *gandules* as the Spanish labeled them. His superiors noted in his service record that "he was distinguished for entering at the point of the lance and killing two to the satisfaction of his superiors." Despite being much older and more experienced than Limón, Fernández appropriately deferred to Limón as his superior officer.[16]

Both veteran officers doggedly hung on to the tracks of four Indian raiders they had been chasing from the vicinity of San Carlos since late July. By Wednesday, August 5, Limón, Fernández, and their troopers had reached the banks of the Rio Grande, which marked the boundary of what the Spaniards officially regarded as their territory. Beyond the river lay the lands of the Mescalero Apaches, who had traditionally cared not a whit for the Spanish predilections for lines on a map. Such distinctions were made clear to Limón and his men when they came to the ruins of the original site of the Presidio del Príncipe, near a ford on the Rio Grande called Los Pilares. Originally constructed in 1773, fifteen years later the presidio was relocated south to the village of Coyamé, ostensibly to better protect Spanish settlements from Mescalero raids. For now, the remains of the original presidio offered a campsite and landmark that Limón and his command most likely utilized.[17]

The next day, the Spaniards crossed the river and, still following the tracks of the four Indians, headed into the nearby Sierra de los Ojos Calientes. By this time it was obvious that the four raiders were Mescalero Apaches returning to their own people. Despite this realization, Limón and his men were probably not overly concerned. Many of the Mescalero *rancherías*, or encampments, north of the Rio Grande were inhabited by *Mescaleros de paz*—peaceful Mescaleros. This was the name the Spaniards applied to those Mescalero Apaches that had agreed to settle near reservations established several years earlier. Limón and his men were in an area almost halfway between two such reservations, the first near Presidio del Norte downstream from Los Pilares about one hundred miles and the other at Presidio de San Elizario, the same distance upstream. There was a good chance the four raiders were from the rancherías of the Mescaleros de paz. Limón and Fernández may have reasoned that, as with other small raids by rogue Mescaleros de paz, they would be able to retrieve the stolen stock and leave the malefactors to be punished by their own leaders. If such reasoning did occur to the two Spanish officers, it would prove to be their bane.[18]

By the late afternoon of August 6, Limón and his troopers were searching for trail signs in the Sierra de los Ojos Calientes. He had detached ten men to guard his supply train while he and Second Alférez Fernández led the bulk of the command, thirty-two men, farther into the mountains. How far Limón and his men searched and for how long is unknown, but at approximately four o'clock, they suddenly found themselves attacked by an overwhelming number of Mescaleros, variously estimated at between three and four hundred warriors. According to later reports, these included many of the same men who had ambushed and destroyed Alférez Josef Urías and his detachment three days earlier at the Sierra del Carrizo. Unfortunately for the Spaniards, the result of this second fight would be almost exactly the same as the first.

Once again, the Mescaleros had the advantages of surprise, numbers, terrain, and most importantly a large quantity of muskets. As before, the volume of fire they were able to unleash upon the Spaniards undoubtedly proved decisive. Writing sometime after the fact, Commandant General Pedro de Nava gave a brief summation of the battle, declaring that "although the Alféreces Don Cayetano Limón and Don Juan Fernández, who commanded our Troops, made the most vigorous resistance, imitated by their people, they were killed with thirty-one soldados, having sustained the action from four in the afternoon until the coming of night, according to one [soldado] who came out to the Train with eight grave wounds, being the only one who escaped."[19]

When the unnamed sole survivor reached the ten men guarding the pack train, they all must have expected that death was imminent. However, the victorious Mescaleros did not pursue and finish off this last remnant of the Spaniards. Instead, they seem to have concentrated on stripping the dead. The clothing, muskets, pistols, swords, lances, horses, and horse gear of the thirty-three dead Spaniards would have provided much valuable booty to the Apaches. Combined with a similar amount of spoils taken from the troopers destroyed under Urías three days earlier, the Mescaleros would have garnered a significant amount of first-class weaponry and a large number of animals. This may have triggered a desire to divide up their winnings and quickly return to their homes. Whatever the cause for their not destroying the remaining eleven soldados, the Mescaleros quickly evacuated the Sierra de los Ojos Calientes.

As night fell on August 6, the small party of Spaniards appears to have remained frozen in place. However, sometime the next day they were discovered by a detachment of soldiers from the Presidio of San Elizario. This force was commanded by Alférez José Ygnacio Carrasco, but it is unclear if they were on a routine patrol of the area or if they had received prior communications from Limón and were seeking to link up with him. Regardless, Carrasco and his men were clearly shocked by the carnage surrounding them. Believing his numbers sufficient to hold his ground, Carrasco immediately sent riders back to San Elizario with a letter describing what had occurred.[20]

On August 8, Lieutenant Antonio Vargas, temporarily in command at San Elizario, was informed that riders had come in with urgent news. The messengers had ridden hard, covering almost a hundred miles in less than thirty-six hours. Upon reading the contents of their dispatches, Vargas acted decisively. He immediately dashed off a letter and sent a rider to El Paso, some twenty miles to the north, to the senior Spanish official there, the lieutenant governor of the province of New Mexico, Francisco Xavier de Uranga. In this letter Vargas succinctly described the situation: "About one thirty today I received the report given to me by the Alférez Dn José Ygnacio Carrasco, that he had found in the Sierra de los Ojos Calientes, turned into cadavers, the party of 27 men, including the officers Dn Cayetano Limón and Dn José Fernández that commanded, recovered one wounded [man], and a small number of them that he found with the train. The said report I sent at 2 in the afternoon to the Señor Commandant General."[21]

Vargas then informed Lieutenant Governor Uranga that he was going to gather his troopers and head out immediately to the Sierra de los Ojos Calientes to link up with Alférez Carrasco and "to reconnoiter the field of ruin and recover the bodies." However, given the limited number of soldiers remaining at the presidio, Vargas asked Uranga for reinforcements from El Paso's militia companies, declaring "it would be of indispensable benefit if Your Honor would order sent out to serve 40 men from your militia that can reinforce the *caballada* [horse herd] and accompany me." A short time thereafter, Vargas gathered his men and set out on his melancholy task of bringing in the remains of his brother officers and their fallen soldados.[22]

For his own part, Lieutenant Governor Uranga moved quickly. He ordered that seventy militiamen, thirty more than requested, be mustered from the four companies that served El Paso. Within a day these men rode south to Presidio San Elizario to reinforce the garrison and aid Lieutenant Vargas in his efforts. Uranga also apparently sent messengers down the Rio Grande to the ranchería of an Apache headman the Spaniards labeled as "Francisco,"

The Ruins of the Church at San Elizario on the Rio Grande, by Henry Cheever Pratt, 1852. Courtesy of the John Carter Brown Library at Brown University, John Russell Bartlett Collection.

whose people had been settled in peace outside El Paso del Norte for some time. Francisco was one of numerous *capitancillos*, or "little captains," that the Spanish recognized as the official leaders of their people. However, in many cases, these capitancillos exercised very limited authority, even among their own extended family groups. Nevertheless, Uranga needed answers, and he needed them quickly, as he struggled to assess the extent of the hostilities. It is clear that at this point neither Uranga nor Lieutenant Vargas were aware of the destruction of Alférez Urías and his detachment at the Sierra del Carrizo on August 3.[23]

On August 13, Vargas and his men returned to San Elizario, carrying with them on pack horses the now decaying bodies of Cayetano Limón and the thirty-two men of his last command. After interviewing the survivors, Vargas had certainly been told of the large numbers of Mescaleros that had launched the attack. Given this information, it was becoming increasingly clear that this situation was not confined solely to the districts around El Paso, a fact that he undoubtedly communicated to Lieutenant Governor Uranga.

Nevertheless, the greatest fear for both men remained. What would they do if the numerous Mescalero rancherías gathered near San Elizario and El Paso united and launched a coordinated attack against the Spanish settlements?[24]

While Uranga and Vargas struggled to put into focus how they would react to a worst-case scenario should the Mescaleros in their vicinity begin hostilities, Commandant General Pedro de Nava was already moving to deal with the worsening situation from a much wider perspective. He had received word of the destruction of both Urías's and Limón's detachments within several days of their occurrence. At first he was no doubt stunned by the news, that not just one but two groups of his soldiers had been ambushed, but he quickly gathered himself and began to issue orders to deal with the situation. If he did not respond quickly and forcibly, then the entire system of Apache reservations in the Interior Provinces might be threatened.

Having received no further reports of major hostilities from other areas of the frontier, Nava realized that the attacks had been confined to the Province of Nueva Vizcaya, in an area between the Presidio del Norte, at the confluence of the Rio Grande and the Río Conchos, and the Presidio of San Elizario, a two-hundred-mile-long stretch of territory. As such, the commandant general would be able to draw on forces not only from Nueva Vizcaya, but also from the neighboring provinces of Sonora in the west and Coahuila in the east. He immediately ordered that detachments from all three provinces begin to assemble at strategic locations in preparation for war. Most importantly, he summoned one of his most experienced officers to lead the operations—Lieutenant Colonel Antonio Cordero y Bustamante.

He was described as standing five feet, ten inches tall, with a fair complexion and blue eyes, "and in every part of his deportment was legibly written 'The Soldier' . . . and a body which appeared to be neither impaired by the fatigues of the various campaigns he had made, nor disfigured by the numerous wounds he had received from the enemies of his king." For more than twenty-one years, Lieutenant Colonel Antonio Cordero y Bustamante had fought almost exclusively against the Apaches. A native of the great port city of Cádiz, Spain, Cordero enrolled in the Spanish army at the age of fourteen, and the military had become his chosen vocation. When fortune brought him to Mexico and the New World, he joined the Regiment of the Dragoons of Spain, and in 1772 served in the piquet of fifty men the regiment sent to help bolster the defenses of the Interior Provinces. Service along the northern frontier quickly brought his innate leadership abilities to the fore.²⁵

Within the piquet of the Dragoons of Spain, Cordero rose from cadet to alférez, and at the end of seven years had come to be the de facto commander of the unit after the lieutenant and captain had taken inordinate amounts of leave to return to the comforts of Mexico City. But such subterfuge was alien to Cordero, and his dedication was rewarded when in 1782 he was appointed as lieutenant commandant of the Fourth Compañia Volante in the Province of Nueva Vizcaya. Two years later he was commissioned as a captain, taking command of the Presidios of San Buenaventura and Janos, where he served for more than eleven years and during which he was promoted to lieutenant colonel. Finally in 1794, Cordero was named adjutant inspector of presidios, one of the most senior military positions throughout the entire Interior Provinces.

During this time Antonio Cordero developed into one of the most effective Spanish commanders against the Apaches ever seen. Over two decades along the northern frontier, he fought in twenty-three major campaigns, nineteen of which he had commanded. As noted in his service record, these campaigns "have resulted in the death and capture of four hundred and forty-seven Enemies, the recovery of six captives, and an abundance of field goods; having had in all of these thirty-three *funciones de guerra* [combats] with them. He has made as well many other *salidas* [sallies], *corredurias* [pursuits], and *mariscadas* [raids] taking back many stolen cattle of all species." No armchair commander, Cordero led his men from the front, sharing their hardships and the dangers they faced.²⁶

Throughout his long career, Cordero became not only one of the most deadly opponents the Apaches had ever faced, but he had also developed an impressive knowledge of their language, their religion, and their culture. This knowledge was gained not just through contact with the Apaches on the field of battle, but also through an intimate association with many of them during everyday life. His familiarity with the Apaches was such that he came to understand the many nuances of what he characterized as "the cruel and bloody war which the Apaches have been carrying on for many years in the Spanish possessions." He conceded that much of the hatred was the richly deserved result of Spanish aggression. "Perhaps," he noted, "it was originated in former times by the trespasses, excesses, and avarice of the colonists themselves who lived on the frontier exercising a subordinate authority."²⁷

Nevertheless, he realized that much of the Apaches' propensity for raiding was not solely a product of their long-standing enmity with the Spaniards. There were many factors contributing to the Apaches viewing raiding as an essential part of life. The lack of an entirely dependable food supply and the competition for natural resources with neighboring peoples were ever present. But Cordero recognized that the atomistic patterns surrounding Apache leadership was a prime social factor in much of their aggressive behavior. He would later write that the Apaches were "jealous of their liberty and independence," and noted that "every family head in his own camp considers himself a sovereign in his district." This fierce independence could reach such an extent that some heads of families "prefer to live completely separated from the others with their wives and children, because thus no one disputes their leadership." Thus the behavioral constraints of many Apaches often devolved to the lowest social unit, namely the immediate or extended family.[28]

Such behavior was pervasive in Apache society, and Cordero believed it would be possible to manipulate these ever-fluid leadership patterns to the Spaniards' advantage, especially when it came to the workings of the reservations established for the Apaches de paz. It was with these groups that Cordero gradually saw the opportunity to turn them from enemies into potential allies. Capitalizing on their extreme independence, it was likely that individual Apaches, and perhaps even entire rancherías, might join the Spaniards in warring against other Apaches, if suitably supplied with food, gifts, and promises of security.

Cordero had seen for himself the effectiveness of courting individual Apaches de paz. During his many years as commander of the Presidio of Janos, he had personally overseen the reservation established for several Chiricahua Apache groups near that post. He had cultivated good relations with several capitancillos, ensuring that they were properly supplied with rations and even going so far as helping to secure the release of some of their family members who had been captured by the Spaniards. In exchange, Cordero demanded that these Chiricahua headmen lead their people in allying with the Spaniards. The result had seen the Apaches de paz acting as scouts and auxiliaries and leading Spanish punitive forces in attacking those Apaches that remained at war outside the reservations. Many of these capitancillos had provided good service for the Spanish, and Cordero noted, "These individuals and all their rancherías have been accredited for a long time in these parts with great fidelity to our alliance. They have accompanied our expeditions with vigor, carrying out the most gallant feats in the combats that have been made against their own compatriots."[29]

Still, the fierce independence and individuality among the Apaches continued to be manifest among the Apaches de paz, who just as often manipulated the Spaniards who sought to control them. Many stayed at the reservations only long enough to receive their rations before furtively exiting to continue raiding Spanish settlements. As long as such activities were maintained at a low level without major loss of life, Spanish officials were wont to overlook the transgressions. However, if a large number of Apaches left the confines of the reservations at any one time, the Spaniards were apt to label the event as a revolt or rebellion and would respond with overwhelming military force. Often severely chastened, the Apaches would routinely sue for peace, promise to remain quiet, and return to the reservations.

In 1794 Lieutenant Colonel Cordero had been forced to deal with just such a scenario himself involving many of those same Apaches he had dealt with for so long. In December of that year he noted in his annual review to Commandant General Pedro de Nava: "I passed by superior orders to subjugate the *Apachería Gileña* who had revolted, in which I succeeded in 4 months of Expeditions in reducing these Indians and having put them under submission of the Presidios, to the number of 400 souls."[30]

For Pedro de Nava, the combat experience against and intimate knowledge of the Apaches that Antonio Cordero had garnered in his lengthy career made him the perfect officer to deal with the recent attacks by the Mescaleros that had annihilated the commands of Alférez Urías and Alférez Limón. Most importantly Nava needed to know if these attacks were a localized occurrence or signaled the beginning of a general "rebellion" among the numerous rancherías of Mescaleros de paz gathered along the borders of the Interior Provinces. If it were the latter, Nava would be forced to marshal his forces for an all-out war, an expensive and unforeseen conflict that would no doubt infuriate his superiors. The answers inevitably all revolved around the complexities and subtleties of the true nature of peace with the Mescalero Apaches, and only in examining the lessons learned on how that peace had come about in the first place would Nava be able to deal with the current crisis.

2

ORIGINS OF CONFLICT

PRESIDIO DEL PRÍNCIPE, SUNDAY, AUGUST 16, 1795—Despite Sunday having been prescribed as a day of rest, this day was one of grim intensity at the post. Lieutenant Colonel Antonio Cordero had recently arrived after hurriedly gathering detachments from several other Spanish frontier companies throughout Nueva Vizcaya. Joining together with selected men from Príncipe, they were all preparing to ride out and pursue the Mescalero Apaches who had recently ambushed and killed their comrades. In the never-ending chain of violence that enmeshed them, these soldados were determined to exact blood for blood.

On the following day Cordero and his men had reached the field of battle in the Sierra del Carrizo, the site of the destruction of Alférez Urías and his command. After combing the battlefield for signs and tracks, the troopers moved out, heading north toward the Rio Grande. By August 18, they discovered the signs of a large Mescalero encampment and recognized that these were the same Indians who had annihilated Urías and his men.

Continuing to follow the course of the river northwest, two days later the men then came to the Sierra de los Ojos Calientes, where the second party of Spanish soldiers under command of Alférez Limón had been ambushed and wiped out. Here again, Cordero discovered evidence of the large encampment of Mescaleros who had carried out the attacks. Realizing the Indians had scattered into the mountain ranges north of the Rio Grande, the Spanish commander decided to head toward the Presidio of San Elizario and the nearby reservation of Mescaleros de paz.

By August 25, Cordero had reached San Elizario, where he was soon joined by significant reinforcements that had been dispatched there by Commandant General Nava. With more than four hundred men now at his disposal, Cordero was determined to track down the Mescaleros who had destroyed Urías's and Limón's commands. But first he sought the aid of Francisco, the capitancillo of the Mescaleros de paz living outside San Elizario. Francisco was able to identify many of the leaders among the Mescaleros who had joined together to attack the Spaniards, and had even seized several of the participants, who he now turned over to Cordero. Armed with this information, Cordero soon had the names of the Mescalero leaders, the number of warriors, and the mountain ranges in which they traditionally made their homes. With this knowledge, he was determined to pursue and attack them in their own country.

That Cordero and his men were able to so quickly gather such details concerning the Mescaleros who had attacked across the frontier is not surprising given the long and complicated interactions between the Spaniards and the Mescaleros de paz. For twenty years the Spaniards had been trying to convince the Mescalero Apaches to settle and make peace after almost two centuries of sporadic warfare.[1]

The ancestors of the Mescaleros were among those Athabaskan peoples gradually identified by the name Apache. The word "Apache" is somewhat obscure in its origins. One explanation holds that it derived from a term meaning "enemy" in the language of the Zuni people of New Mexico. But if the name used by outsiders and modern anthropologists for the Apaches is obscure, then when and where they first emerged into the light of recorded history, as defined in Western terms, is also rather dim. However, it is generally agreed that the people now called Apaches are within a linguistic group that entered into what is now the southwestern part of the United States no later than around 1400 A.D. and perhaps significantly earlier. Why and how they migrated into this area cannot be definitively discerned.[2]

Before the coming of Europeans to the Americas, Apaches were among the numerous indigenous peoples that ranged across the southwestern plains in what are now parts of Kansas, Colorado, Oklahoma, and Texas. Others had entered the mountain ranges of central and eastern Arizona and western and central New Mexico. Over time, the various Apache peoples developed unique societies influenced by the different environments in which they lived. Those to the east depended mainly on the ever-wandering herds of buffalo for their food and tools, while the more westerly Apaches came to depend more on the game and plants of the desert, basin, and range. The ancestors of the Mescaleros were unique in that they came to occupy an area that encompassed both bio zones. The contacts these Apache groups had with other Native peoples were constant, sometimes peaceful and sometimes violent. Trade with settled agricultural societies such as the Puebloan peoples brought the Apaches items not encountered in their own environments and linked them, however tangentially, within cultural and economic patterns that reached as far as central Mexico.[3]

As was to happen throughout the Americas, the entrance of Europeans into the Western Hemisphere was to unleash forces that forever altered indigenous societies. Microbes and diseases spread ahead of the actual physical presence of the newcomers, sometimes by decades, and devastated many Native peoples. Less deadly, but no less profound, the Europeans brought new animals and plants that began to alter the environment and reshape the cultural norms of almost all the Indian peoples. Finally, the actual arrival of the Europeans among the Native nations invariably led to conflict being unleashed on societies already staggered by unknown forces, and many times on the brink of demographic or environmental collapse.[4]

It is unknown when Spaniards and Apaches first stood against each other as adversaries. Between 1540 and 1542 Francisco Vásquez de Coronado led an expedition throughout the American Southwest, and in their wanderings the Spaniards encountered a people they called "Querechos," who were almost certainly an Apache group. A half-century later in 1598 Juan de Oñate returned to the region to conquer and establish what he termed the "Kingdom of New Mexico." Over the next twelve years, Oñate and his successors crushed the resistance of the various Puebloan peoples and imposed themselves in permanent settlements that drew on Native communities for their needs. The newcomers' insatiable appetite for goods and labor disrupted agricultural production and trade relationships among many Native groups, including the Apaches. Throughout the seventeenth century, Apache resistance to these demands led to conflict, and as violence escalated so did the Spaniards' knowledge of the Apaches. By the 1670s as mines, ranches, and towns moved out of central Mexico into the northern frontier provinces of Sonora, Nueva Vizcaya, and

Coahuila, the Spaniards encountered various groups of Apaches in each of these locations. During the course of the 1680 Pueblo Revolt and throughout the Spanish reconquest of New Mexico by 1695, violent interactions between Spaniards and Apaches increased. As the Spaniards struggled to assert their dominance throughout their northern frontier, the homelands of numerous Apache groups began to become clear for the Spaniards.[5]

By the early eighteenth century, several ethnically diverse Indian groups such as the Jumanos, Jocomes, Sumas, Mansos, and others appear to have allied or melded with the Apaches. This "Apacheization" led the Spaniards to apply the name "Apache" to a large number of peoples covering a huge swath of territory. Around 1730, the Spaniards identified Apaches as living from the plains of central Texas, along both banks of the Rio Grande from almost the mouth of the river westward through the Big Bend Country, and following the river farther north past the area around Santa Fe. Other Apache peoples occupied the drainage of the Gila River in what is now southern New Mexico and Arizona. The Spaniards would come to call the whole area *"el gran Apachería"* (the great Apache land).[6]

Eventually, the Spanish and other Western peoples would apply specific names to these Apache peoples reflecting their geographic location or cultural traits. To the east the Spanish identified the Lipan, Lipiyan, Jicarilla, Llanero, Faraón, Natagé, and Mescalero. In the regions surrounding the Gila River were the Gileño, Mimbreño, and Chiricagui. To the northwest were the Navajo, who developed a unique identity that differentiated them from the Apaches. Farthest west in the mountains of central Arizona were the Tonto and the Coyotero, also known as White Mountain Apaches.[7]

Yet despite this attempt at classification by the Spaniards, the Apaches themselves viewed their relationships quite differently. For example, many groups labeled by the Spaniards as Faraón, Natagé, and Mescalero regarded themselves as close kindred and were in fact later to be seen as the progenitors of the present-day Mescalero, despite their apparent political differences. That these nuances were often lost speaks to just how little the Mescalero were understood by outsiders. This in turn may have been the result of the vast geographical areas that these people regarded as their home.

Over the course of several centuries, the progenitors of the Mescalero gradually spread throughout the present-day American Southwest and northern Mexico.

During the Coronado expedition, the Querechos encountered by the Spaniards may have included ancestral Mescaleros, ranging along the foothills of the Rocky Mountains and spreading out into the flatlands of the Llano Estacado (palisaded plains) of what is now the Texas Panhandle. In 1598, when the forces of Juan de Oñate came to conquer and occupy the Puebloan peoples of New Mexico, they increasingly came into contact with Apache groups later recognized as Mescaleros, but to which the white men gave a variety of names. For example, one of these groups was named by the Spaniards as the Faraón Apaches, as they reputedly reminded the Spaniards of the armies of Pharaoh by their large numbers.[8]

However, as with all the Athabaskan peoples, the Mescalero term for themselves was *Indé* or a variant thereof, simply meaning "the people." Over time various rancherías of Indé were identified as belonging to a certain geographical area and were denominated as a particular band, such as the Natahéndé ("mescal people"), whom the Spaniards called Natagés; Guhlkahéndé ("people of the plains"); and the Nitahéndé ("people who live against the mountains"), who were probably the ancestors of those people living today in the Mescalero Reservation in the Sacramento Mountains. Regardless of terminology, the homelands occupied by these Apache peoples were indeed immense. By the 1650s the Spanish recognized the Faraónes as controlling large sections of north central New Mexico between the Rio Grande and the Pecos River. The Natagés ranged farther to the east and north, between the Pecos and the vast plains of the Texas Panhandle. The Mescalero proper were identified as dwelling in the Sacramento Mountains and Sierra Blanca of central New Mexico and ranging as far to the southwest as the Big Bend of west Texas.[9]

Despite the broad expanse of territory they covered, the Mescalero and their kindred all shared certain broad social characteristics. As with many other Apaches, the Mescalero lived in relatively small communities the Spanish labeled "rancherías." Usually grouped around extended families or local groups, rancherías could contain anywhere from a few individuals up to several dozen, and it was with the ranchería that individual identity was most closely connected. Generally speaking, the Apaches traced descent through both the male and female lines, but they were a matrilocal society, with married men moving to live with the families of their wives. Groups of kindred might come together at various times of the year for mutual protection, for common hunts, for harvests of wild plants or sown crops, or for religious ceremonies. Specific regions were inevitably associated as the "home" of various rancherías.

Many Mescalero rancherías lived in mountain areas that bordered relatively close to the southern buffalo plains of the Llano Estacado. Thus they were able to traverse annually into both ecological zones for sustenance and support. This allowed them to develop a combined "economy" hunting buffalo on the plains for part of the year then gathering native plants in the mountains and deserts at other times. Indeed, the Spaniards name for them, "Mescalero," comes from their great reliance on gathering wild agave, or *mescal*. They also engaged to varying degrees in widespread trading networks and occasional raiding with other Native peoples.[10]

After the Pueblo Revolt of 1680, the area controlled by the various Mescalero peoples expanded as they garnered and bred many more horses from the defeated Spaniards. At the same time, the process of Apacheization accelerated. Numerous hitherto independent indigenous groups seemed to have been absorbed by the Mescaleros and other Apaches. The result was the expansion of Mescalero territory both to the south into the Big Bend region of the Rio Grande in Texas and northern Mexico, and to the northeast into the plains of the Texas Panhandle. During this period, the Mescaleros and other eastern Apache groups such as the Jicarilla and Lipan began to dominate the buffalo-hunting grounds and riverine agricultural lands that sustained this region. But their success would prove ephemeral.[11]

At the beginning of the 1700s a new and expansive Native power emerged in the form of the Comanches. With incredible aggression, the Comanches initiated a series of wars for control of the southern plains, and their primary rivals were the eastern Apaches, including the Mescaleros. Within two generations the Comanches had crushed the Apaches and forced them southward, gradually driving them into collision with the line of Spanish settlements coming from Mexico. The Mescaleros and other Apaches were thus caught between two fires, and as a result, warfare accelerated throughout the region. Largely driven out of the southern plains, with its enormous herds of buffalo, the Mescaleros increasingly turned to the Spaniards to sustain themselves. Unfortunately this in turn accentuated several deep-seated social practices in Mescalero and Apache society in general, namely raiding for gain and for vengeance.[12]

For centuries before the arrival of the Spaniards, raiding and warfare had been part of Apache lifeways. For example, the Apaches were regarded by some of the Puebloan peoples as aggressive raiders who, although they might engage in trade, were often hostile. However, as Spanish settlements began to move northward toward the end of the seventeenth century, a new dynamic emerged. The Apaches found that the newcomer's communities provided increased raiding opportunities for food, goods, and supplies. But the most tempting prizes were the herds of horses the Spaniards brought, and these animals quickly became the favorite target of raids. By the early eighteenth century the horse became a crucial element within Mescalero and Apache society.[13]

Although they did raise their own animals, the relative proximity of Spanish settlements resulted in numerous forays by the Mescaleros and other Apaches to steal horses and raid for other goods. Inevitably, during these raids, there would be resistance from the animals' owners, and oftentimes Apaches would be killed. Such a loss in turn triggered another requisite in Apache culture—vengeance.

Like all Apaches, the Mescaleros believed that the killing of one of their people demanded retribution. If the killing had been committed by individuals from a different people, Apache customs allowed that vengeance could be unleashed collectively against "the other." Thus, for example, if an Apache were killed while raiding for horses at a particular Spanish settlement, other settlers far away that had no part in the killing could be attacked in retaliation. Among the Spaniards, it was unjust to hold one individual responsible for the actions of another. But among the Mescaleros and other Apaches, it was justifiable to exact vengeance on "the other" in a collective sense to repay the loss they had suffered. Ultimately, the convergence of these two cultural traits—raiding and vengeance—became the anvil upon which a bloody dynamic between the Mescaleros and the Spaniards would be hammered out.[14]

Hostilities between the Spaniards and the ancestral Mescalero dated at least as far back as the early 1600s. Faraón Apaches were reported to have poached horses from the Oñate expedition, and after the Spanish imposed themselves on the Puebloan peoples (many of whom had been raided by the Apaches for generations), all the communities of New Mexico became frequent targets for raiding, especially animal rustling. The Spaniards in turn used these thefts as justification for sending out slaving expeditions masked as attempts to "pacify" the Apaches. The result was a steady upsurge in violence in the region throughout the seventeenth century.

Especially hard-pressed were the Pueblo missions of Abó, Quarai, and Las Humanas. These were located in the Estancia Basin, southeast of the other settlements along the Rio Grande, near the remains of ancient lakes known as Las Salinas that yielded large deposits of salt. Apache raiding against these pueblos became so great that about 1655, the Spanish launched a major punitive expedition into the Sierra Blanca of central New Mexico. The Spaniards labeled these people as Salinero and Siete Rios, or Seven Rivers Apaches, but they were in reality Mescaleros. Spanish expeditions continued over the following decades, as did Apache counterstrikes. Then, in 1667, a prolonged drought struck the region and lasted at least until 1672. The resulting famine drove the Apaches to increase their assaults in search of sustenance, and the combination of war and natural scarcity led to the abandonment of the Salinas Pueblos during the 1670s.[15]

When the great Pueblo Revolt exploded in 1680, many Apache groups joined the insurrection and helped the Puebloan peoples drive out the Spaniards. For thirteen years the area remained free from white men, but tensions among the Pueblo peoples themselves and also between them and their erstwhile Apache allies intensified. In 1693, when Diego de Vargas led the Spaniards back into New Mexico in his *reconquista* of the territory, he was aided materially by the complexities of shifting loyalties between many of the Native peoples both Puebloan and Apache. Though such divisions allowed the Spaniards to eventually reach a mutual accommodation with most of the Pueblos, hostilities with the Apaches became a seemingly inalterable reality.[16]

By the year 1700, the Spaniards had firmly reestablished themselves in New Mexico, while simultaneously expanding earlier settlements around El Paso del Norte (present-day Ciudad Juárez, Mexico) and almost two hundred miles downstream at Junta de los Ríos, at the confluence of the Rio Grande and the Río Conchos, where the modern twin cities of Presidio, Texas, and Ojinaga, Mexico, now lay. Along this vast expanse of the Rio Grande, the Mescalero and kindred Apache peoples held sway over a vast arc that stretched along the course of the river from north of El Paso all the way south past the Big Bend, and out into the vast southern plains. In 1722, when the Spaniards established a new settlement at San Antonio de Bexar, in Texas, they conceded that much if not all of the lands between San Antonio and Santa Fe in the north and Junta de los Ríos in the south belonged to the Apaches.[17]

Yet within a decade, that control would evaporate. The onslaught of the Comanches shattered Apache control of the region. The Mescaleros, along with the Lipan and Jicarilla Apaches, were repeatedly defeated by the Comanches in an unrelenting war of attrition. In 1724 Spanish sources tell of an apocalyptic five-day battle between a large group of Apaches and the Comanches northeast of Santa Fe. The Apaches were disastrously defeated, and from that point forward, the Comanches held the initiative. Though this battle may not have represented an "Apache Waterloo," it nevertheless reflected a brutal reality. Taking advantage of the Apache practice of semi-sedentary farming along the region's rivers, the Comanches repeatedly and systematically attacked Apache settlements twice a year, inexorably diminishing their population base and restricting their ability to maintain food sources.[18]

In desperation, many Lipan, Mescalero, and other eastern Apaches tried to ally with the Spaniards for protection. Showing a remarkable grasp of Spanish intentions and methods, they played upon the religious hopes of the white men by clamoring to become Christians and to have missionaries settle among them. But it was ultimately all a momentous ruse, a vain hope that Spanish arms would succor them against the Comanches. The Spaniards, ever hopeful, in 1758 established a mission and nearby presidio at San Sabá in central Texas to shelter the Apache. But the Comanches and their allies were determined to crush this nascent alliance in the womb, and in 1759 attacked and destroyed the San Sabá mission. When the Spaniards attempted to reassert their power over the next several years, they quickly discovered that the Comanches, having acquired French muskets and ammunition, combined with their sheer numbers, held an overwhelming military advantage.

By the early 1760s, after the failure to establish missions for the Apaches, and in the face of their seemingly never-ending raids, the Spaniards decided that they would no longer attempt the religious conversion of the Apaches. The debacle at San Sabá convinced many Spanish officials that the Apaches as a whole were a treacherous and inconstant people, who had only feigned interest in Christianity to lure the Spaniards into war with the Comanches and their allies. For this they deserved to be subjected to unrelenting war. Further, to help them in punishing the Apaches, the Spaniards believed they should now actively seek common cause with the Comanches and other powerful Indian tribes and that together, they would crush the mutual enemy. Unfortunately for the Mescalero and other Apache peoples, Spanish resolve would finally be matched by the necessary means to achieve this end after almost a century of vacillating and an ineffective military strategy.[19]

3

WAR, PEACE, WAR

SIERRA DEL MOGANO, NOVEMBER 27, 1773, AT DAWN—The commander knew they were there and probably waiting for him. For more than a week he and his men had been searching the lands of the Mescalero, Faraón, and Natagé Apaches in an effort to bring them to battle. During a five-day stretch they had been plagued by a snowstorm that forced the men to dismount and lead their horses. At one point the cold was so bitter, the commander would later write, that most of his men "could not move their hands or their feet." Despite the weather, the soldiers continued their pursuit for three more days and eventually tracked a large number of Apaches heading toward the broken outcroppings of the Sierra del Mogano (the present-day Davis Mountains of West Texas).[1]

By sundown of the eighth day of their pursuit, the command had reached the mountains. They could see that the Apache trail entered into one of the main valleys, but after that they could see no farther. Numerous side canyons opened up on the valley floor, with grass- and scrub-covered hillocks and rock outcroppings leading for miles in all directions. The commander had his men make camp. There were to be no fires, and strictest silence was to be observed.

After perhaps taking some rest and eating, the commander gathered his officers and told them his plans. At dawn they would enter into the main valley following the Apaches and ride until they found them. The mountains would give the Indians the advantage of cover and a ready means of retreat. Once they entered the canyon, the soldiers would be vulnerable to attack from all sides. The commander led 150-plus soldiers. They could only guess the number of Apaches present. Combat was certain; the final outcome unknown.

With first light, the commander and his men were ready. At the head of the formation, he turned and called out a prayer, beseeching the Immaculate Mother of God, Mary Most Holy, to intercede on their behalf this day. He then led the command forward. After some time, a great number of Apaches, later estimated at some five hundred warriors, began to appear. Despite being clearly outnumbered, the commander had his men charge forward to engage them; at this point he could do little else.

Amid the shouts of men and cries of horses, combat commenced. Bows, pistols, and muskets all loosed death from a distance. As opponents drew closer to each other, lances, clubs, and swords stabbed and swung at man and beast. However, the commander and his men kept their formation together, and in a matter of moments their solidity overthrew their more numerous but scattered adversaries. Individually and in small groups, the Apaches turned their mounts and began to flee. The commander and his men stayed together and pursued those Apaches that headed down the main valley of the canyon. For what must have seemed an eternity, the command rode after the Indians, killing and wounding those they could catch up with. By the time the commander ordered his men to rein in, they had ridden more than ten miles, and the Apaches had scattered to the winds. Blown horses and winded men gasped for air and slowly made their way back the way they had come. As they retraced the route of the charge, they counted more than forty dead Apaches strewn along the path the battle had run. Of their own men, only two had been wounded, neither seriously. Few of the men could recall such a large-scale combat nor such a complete victory. The commander was delighted with the result, but, being a sincerely religious man, would always credit the victory to the intercession of the saint to whom he had prayed, la Imaculada.[2]

For Don Hugo O'Conor, knight of Calatrava, colonel of infantry in the Royal Armies, and commandant inspector of the Interior Provinces, the fight in the Sierra del Mogano remained one of the proudest achievements of his military career. Yet, as O'Conor himself well knew, the battle was far from decisive, and the enemy he had vanquished would prove as difficult to catch and kill as any foe he had ever faced. Like the teeth of the Hydra, it seemed that every enemy killed brought forth another. In the end he would never see the victory he sought.

Nevertheless, the determination shown by O'Conor to defeat the Apaches militarily was to remain the Spanish Crown's official policy for almost two decades. During this period the Spaniards would repeatedly shuffle their command structure and their commanders at the highest levels. The result would be numerous stops and starts in their military policies. However, despite the confused and erratic implementation of particular means, the end of the Spaniards remained constant—to crush the Apaches.

It had not always been so. Before the middle of the eighteenth century, the Spanish government did not have a centralized frontier policy for dealing with the Apaches. Military forces in the regions consisted mainly of independent garrisons, or *presidios*, but these were spread across thousands of miles and were controlled by a variety of governors and commanders independent of each other. However, the decentralized system came to a dramatic halt following Spain's disastrous defeat by Great Britain during the Seven Years' War (1756–1763). Having resolved to strengthen his empire against future British assaults, Spanish King Charles III set out to overhaul and consolidate the economic and military structures of his empire. Gradually, the impetus of reform and retrenchment spread as far as the northern frontier of New Spain, with profound effects on the continuing war against the Apaches.[3]

The most important development was the establishment of a unified military command over the whole frontier. This policy grew out of the recommendations of the Marqués de Rubí, one of four field marshals sent from Spain to Mexico in 1764 to institute military reforms. From 1766 to 1768 he conducted a 7,600-mile inspection of Spain's northern frontier, after which he compiled a comprehensive plan for dealing with the region. Realizing that Spain controlled much less territory than she claimed, Rubí advocated a radical reorganization and retrenchment of the frontier zone between the Gulf of California and the Gulf of Mexico, known as the Interior Provinces of New Spain. Within this region the presidios of Spanish soldiers would be repositioned in a vast arc following the irregular course of the Rio Grande and a line approximating the thirtieth parallel. More importantly, the presidios and other military forces within the Interior Provinces would all be placed under a unified military command to coordinate operations against hostile Indians, especially the Apaches.[4]

In 1772, Charles III largely adopted Rubí's plans and instituted the famous *Regulations for Governing the Interior Provinces of New Spain*. The Regulations of 1772, as they came to be called, entrusted this new policy of centralization to the previously mentioned Colonel O'Conor, who was appointed first commandant inspector of the Interior Provinces. O'Conor was an Irish exile with more than twenty years of military experience in Europe and the Caribbean, and who had served as the governor of Texas. O'Conor had actually taken up his duties provisionally in 1771 while still awaiting formal authorization from Spain. Establishing his headquarters in the Villa de Chihuahua in the central province of Nueva Vizcaya, he soon encountered a variety of problems that would plague him throughout his tenure. One of these was the constant opposition from many of the provincial governors on the northern frontier, who resented the limitations placed on their authority by the new regulations. But of much greater concern to O'Conor was the constant raids and violence the Spaniards laid at the feet of numerous Apache groups along the northern frontier. Among these, none were to prove so difficult to deal with than the Mescaleros.[5]

The Bolsón de Mapimí was a vast inland sink surrounded by a string of mountain ranges into which several rivers emptied. Over eons, much of the water disappeared, leaving a desolate desert basin that plunged in a great arc below the Big Bend of the Rio Grande. During the seventeenth and early eighteenth centuries, Spanish settlements moved up to the basin until they surrounded it on three sides. To the west the Province of Nueva Vizcaya and to the east, the Province of Coahuila pushed to the edges of the bolsón and joined together on its southern border. To the north the Rio Grande marked the bolsón's limit.[6]

Beginning in the 1730s many Mescaleros and other eastern Apaches began to push through the bolsón and raid Spanish farms, ranches, and villages, before disappearing the way they had come. The Spaniards were often totally surprised by these raiders so far from the frontier, and were just as often unable to muster military forces quickly enough to stop them. Even when the Spaniards occasionally managed to thwart the Apaches, the raiders would quickly retreat into the bolsón, where their knowledge of the terrain habitually confounded their pursuers. For the Mescaleros and other Apaches, the Bolsón de Mapimí offered a virtual open door through which they could penetrate deep into Nueva Vizcaya, Coahuila, and other Spanish provinces without encountering any military forces. For the Spaniards the bolsón was a dagger at their heart.[7]

The threat posed by Mescalero access to the Bolsón de Mapimí would prove one of the major obstacles that Commandant Inspector O'Conor would attempt to overcome. As called for by the Regulations of 1772, the creation of the presidial line across the northern frontier was planned to deter Apache transits across the Rio Grande into the bolsón. But to ensure that no enemy were left behind the line, for several months in 1772 and 1773 O'Conor had his forces sweep the Bolsón de Mapimí from south to north. Although they encountered only a few Apaches, the Spaniards succeeded in clearing the region of potential enemies, and one Mescalero ranchería pushed out of the bolsón even negotiated for peace with O'Conor and agreed to settle near El Paso.[8]

With this preventive operation completed, O'Conor next turned to actually establishing the presidial line. Moving from east to west, he would eventually reconnoiter almost the entire frontier from Texas to the Gulf of California to form the new cordon of seventeen presidios. To cover the Bolsón de Mapimí, O'Conor positioned a total of six presidios along the Rio Grande between El Paso and the eastern end of the Big Bend, where before there had been only two. Most of these were directly across the river from lands frequented by the Mescaleros.

To guard the frontier during this massive relocation, O'Conor also undertook a series of attacks across the Rio Grande into the Apache homelands. In November 1773 one of these into the Sierra del Mogano resulted in a singular victory for Spanish arms, with O'Conor's men killing forty-two Apaches, almost certainly Mescaleros. Yet despite this and other strikes, Apache raids continued unabated along the northern frontier. Indeed, O'Conor's movements probably triggered more violence, as losses suffered by the Apaches invariably demanded revenge, according to their cultural mores.[9]

O'Conor also began to implement with greater frequency the policy of deporting captured Apaches from the frontier. There had existed previously the widespread practice of prisoner exchanges between the Spaniards and the Apaches. However, beginning in 1773 the Spaniards increasingly employed the tactic of permanently exiling Apache prisoners of war. Many captured Apaches were dispatched in chain gangs, or *colleras,* to Mexico City. There, they were routinely sent on to Veracruz and then to Havana, Cuba, where they were set to work on that city's massive fortifications. Although typically sentenced to a term of ten years, none would ever be allowed to return to their homelands.[10]

In addition, O'Conor believed that larger and better-coordinated Spanish attacks in the Apache homelands would be the key to ultimate victory. As a result in 1775, he began organizing a massive offensive against the Apaches. He planned for eight Spanish columns, totaling two thousand men, to attack the Apache homelands in a series of three consecutive envelopments from east to west, all the way from the Gulf Coast of Texas to what is now southeastern Arizona. Spanish regulars, presidial soldiers, citizen militiamen, and Indian allies were all to take part in the assault. The central envelopment in O'Conor's plans covered most of what is now southern New Mexico and west Texas, and was primarily designed to strike against the Mescaleros.

To complete this encirclement, four separate contingents were to converge on the Sacramento Mountains, the traditional heartland of the Mescalero. Captain Francisco Bellido, commander of the Presidio of San Elizario, was to sweep into the Sacramentos from the southeast. José Antonio de Arrieta, the lieutenant governor of New Mexico, would lead a force from El Paso and attack from the southwest. Two other Spanish contingents from Albuquerque under New Mexico Governor Pedro de Medinueta would enter the Sacramentos from the north.[11]

O'Conor launched his "general campaign," as he termed it, in the late summer of 1775, with the Irishman himself setting out on September 7 to attack the Gileño and Mimbreño Apaches. After numerous pursuits and a few engagements, by late October he had completed his planned movements and had reached the Rio Grande. In his diary, O'Conor noted that when he arrived at the river on October 20, "I found the Captain of the Presidio of San Elizario Dn Francisco Bellido and the Lieutenant Governor of the Pueblo del Paso del Rio Norte with the detachments under their command who informed me that they had retired from the Sierra Blanca." The two commanders, contrary to O'Conor's orders, joined together as they approached the Sierra del Sacramento from the south. By October 1, their combined force of some 440 Spaniards and Indian allies entered the mountains.[12]

That same day, as summarized by O'Conor, the forces under Bellido and Arrieta found indications of numerous Mescalero encampments. They pressed forward to the eastern portion of the mountain range, where they located a large concentration of Apaches. Captain Bellido attempted an ambush, but "it being necessary to attack them beneath a hill, our [forces] were heard, and they gave the Enemy time to flee with their families into the thickness of the forest to which on one side or the other they sought shelter."[13]

Belllido had his men pursue the Mescaleros, but knowing the lay of the land, the Indians fought an effective delaying action. "They made war thusly," it was later noted, "for the brokenness of the terrain and the manner of the formation in which they arranged their rancherías, they saw our [men] closing in on one side or the other, this being so much an advantage for the Enemies, who could only be seen when they came out to shoot from within the forest; and when our men chased them from one side they fled out the other." Despite the Mescaleros skilled forest fighting techniques, the Spaniards still "succeeded in killing forty, wounding many others, and taking all the spoils . . . among which were eight *piezas* [a euphemism for prisoners] . . . and three hundred animals, horses and mules." The Spaniards did not suffer a single casualty.[14]

Soon after receiving Captain Bellido's report, Hugo O'Conor formally concluded the general campaign and returned to his base of operations at the Presidio of Carrizal southeast of El Paso. By December 1, 1775, he compiled a report summarizing the entire campaign and showing that over the length of the frontier, the Spanish had killed 132 Apache warriors, captured 104 men, women, and children, and seized almost two thousand horses and mules. The Apaches' single greatest loss had been that inflicted on the Mescaleros within the Sacramentos.[15]

Although the majority of his officers hailed these results, O'Conor was dissatisfied. The Spanish offensive had not stopped Apache raiding and indeed may have caused an escalation. Despite deteriorating health, O'Conor pressed ahead and organized a second general campaign for the fall of 1776. Once again, three converging Spanish columns attempted to envelope and destroy the Apaches in the area between the headwaters of the Gila River and the Big Bend of the Rio Grande. By December, the Spanish had killed sixty-seven and captured sixty-four Apaches of all ages and both sexes and taken many horses and pillage.

But the hardest blow inflicted on the Apaches came at the hands of other Indians, and again it would be the Mescaleros that suffered the most. Large numbers of their rancherías fled before the Spanish columns and were driven to the northeast. Somewhere near the upper reaches of the Pecos River, on the edges of the Llano Estacado, they were discovered by a large Comanche war party. Exulting in this unexpected prey, the Comanches fell upon the Apaches with a vengeance, reportedly slaughtering three hundred families, numbering perhaps one thousand individuals. A single Spanish captive and another Apache survived and soon thereafter led a Spanish scouting party to the scene. Amid the dead Mescaleros, the Comanches had contemptuously left large piles of recently harvested buffalo meat to rot along with the bodies of their victims. Even the Spaniards were appalled by the carnage.

Despite such victories, the Spanish still had not solved the problem of Apache raiding along the frontier. Further large-scale offensives might have brought results, but they were not to be. Commandant Inspector O'Conor's health was broken by his years on the frontier, and he was granted a promotion and transfer to less stressful duties. At the same time, the Interior Provinces experienced a monumental change in governance. Both events combined to stall the war against the Apaches.[16]

At the conclusion of O'Conor's second general campaign, the governance of the Interior Provinces underwent another series of changes that saw the Spanish increase the centralization and reorganization of their military forces along the northern frontier. Late in 1776, O'Conor was replaced by Teodoro de Croix, known as the Caballero de Croix. Holding the title commandant general of the Interior Provinces, Croix was invested with much greater authority than O'Conor, holding a variety of military, political, and economic powers that made him virtually independent of the viceroy in Mexico City.

Assuming command in October 1777, over the next year Croix concentrated on the internal arrangement of his forces, focusing his efforts on improving the arms, equipment, pay, and conditions of the soldiers' service. He also made adjustments to the presidial line and established a defense in depth by deploying provincial militiamen in strategic towns behind the cordon.[17]

Yet, in the midst of these reorganizations, Croix was continuously confronted by the seemingly never-ending hostilities with the Apaches. During the first years of his command, Apache raids had increased dramatically. Eastern Apaches, especially the Lipans and Mescaleros, had suffered another series of devastating blows at the hands of the Comanches, and were pressed southward into Spanish territory. Groups farther to the west, such as the Gileños and Mimbreños, had also escalated their attacks, possibly in response to the lack of pressure by Spanish offensives into their homelands. Whatever the reasons, the Spanish losses mounted across the entire frontier. The Caballero de Croix was determined to complete his internal reforms first; nevertheless, he also began plans for conducting a large-scale offensive. But international complications soon intervened. In July 1779 war with Great Britain was imminent, and the king ordered Croix to remain on the defensive until the conflict ended. In the interim, the Caballero was directed to seek peace with the Apaches and other hostile tribes through offers of alliance and the distribution of gifts. Leaders hoped this policy would bring the Indians into increasing dependency on the Spaniards for guns, alcohol, and other items they desired. Force was to be used only as a last resort. These new orders reset the entire Spanish policy regarding the frontier. The days of the mailed fist were now to give way to those of the velvet glove. Under Croix, the search for peaceful accommodation would replace the unrelenting warfare begun under O'Conor. Though all of the Apache peoples along the frontier would be affected by these changes, the Mescalero would be among the first.[18]

As early as February 1778, Croix had been amenable to granting peace to those Apaches that requested it, but he was extremely dubious given their past history. Over many decades, time and time again they had approached Spanish presidios and requested peace. Most often they did so only after suffering a military onslaught, either from the Spaniards themselves or from other Indians such as the Comanche, or if they were suffering from lack of resources such as during periods of drought. Usually the Apaches would stay at peace only long enough to recover from their want or until the danger from their enemies receded, at which point they would flee and begin a new cycle of raiding. This practice was so common that the Regulations of 1772 explicitly forbade any presidial commander to offer peace to the Apaches.

However, the Caballero de Croix decided early on that he would allow peace with any Apache group that requested it, provided they agreed to certain stipulations. First and foremost among these was that the Apaches would settle in permanent villages located immediately adjacent to Spanish towns or presidios. Second, they must support themselves by growing and tending their own farms. Finally, they must agree to serve the Spaniards as scouts and auxiliaries against other Apaches that remained hostile, even against their own kin. As inducements, Croix offered laborers to build the Apache houses, farmers to help them plant their first crops, and food, weapons, and horses to help equip them for battle. Taken altogether, Croix was willing to spend a considerable amount of time and money to entice the Apaches toward peace.[19]

It would be the eastern Apaches, especially the Lipans and Mescaleros, who would be the first groups to undergo these new tests. The Lipans were the Apache people most exposed to the onslaught of the Comanches and the Nations of the North; consequently, they had repeatedly sought temporary shelter under the protection of Spanish presidios. As a result, Croix and other Spanish officials regarded the Lipans as inconstant and treacherous and were dubious of any agreements with them. Then in 1778 the Lipans suffered egregiously from Comanche attacks and fled across the Rio Grande in large numbers, especially into the Province of Coahuila. Violence again intensified as the invaders now routinely raided Spanish settlements. However, several bands of Lipan approached the governor of Coahuila, Colonel Juan de Ugalde, with entreaties for peace. After Ugalde informed Croix of this development, the latter noted that the Lipans were so desperate that "exhibiting their natural perfidy they offered . . . the delivery of two rancherías of their relatives the Mescaleros who were close to the presidio of Aguaverde."[20]

Although Croix indicated his disgust at this treachery, he nevertheless did nothing to stop it. That the Lipans should offer to help attack their close kinsmen the Mescalero fitted perfectly within Croix's hopes that the Apaches might be induced to destroy one another. However, the Lipans soon reneged on their agreement and allowed most of the targeted Mescaleros to escape. Ugalde regarded this as an act of basest treachery and fulminated violently against the Lipans. His sentiments were soon echoed by the Caballero de Croix, who determined that incessant war should be waged against the Lipan. To this end, Croix now ordered Ugalde to switch tactics and solicit the aid of the Mescalero against the Lipan. If they were destroyed by Spanish, Comanche, or Mescalero attacks, so much the better.

In early 1779 near the San Sabá River in Texas, the Comanche set upon a large encampment of Lipans and reportedly killed three hundred men, women, and children. Then that spring, Ugalde contracted an alliance with several Mescalero headmen and with their aid launched more attacks against the Lipans. These were generally successful and pushed the Lipans out of Coahuila and north of the Rio Grande. Caught between Ugalde to the south and the Comanche to the north, soon thereafter many Lipans were again entreating the Spaniards for peace and protection.[21]

Concurrently with this new onslaught of violence, a serious drought seems to have struck the region, causing further distress to all the Native peoples. In desperate need of sustenance and succor, in July 1779 a group of Mescalero leaders approached the Caballero de Croix at his headquarters in Chihuahua with a request for peace. Recalling their recent services in attacking the Lipans, they intimated that they were now willing to settle down near the Presidio del Norte, located at the Junta de los Ríos on the Rio Grande. Croix was reluctant to trust the Mescaleros, whom he characterized as "more perfidious, cruel, and barbarous than the Lipans." But he soon overcame his wariness and agreed to another experiment in peacemaking. In January 1780 Croix ordered Lieutenant Colonel Manuel Muñoz to oversee the construction of a small village just northeast of Presidio del Norte for several rancherías of Mescaleros. In expectation of good results, he named the new Apache village Nuestra Señora de la Buena Esperanza, Our Lady of Good Hope.[22]

Eventually, four Mescalero capitancillos, whom the Spaniards identified as Patule El Grande, Alonso, Juan Tuerto, and Domingo Alegre, settled nearby with their rancherías. In exchange for the promise of receiving food rations and other supplies for one year and for Spanish protection from their enemies, they agreed to the terms laid down by Croix and even signed a formal document recognizing the peace. For some months the experiment seemed to promise good results despite the Apaches disinterest in farming the fields the Spaniards had planted for them, or working to maintain the village. Nevertheless, Mescalero warriors from Buena Esperanza accompanied the Spaniards on several of their military forays against the Gileño Apaches to the west and even assassinated one of their own, capitancillo Juan Tuerto, who had surreptitiously returned to raiding.

Then in August 1780 a smallpox epidemic swept through the settlement, and soon thereafter, flooding of the Río Conchos and Rio Grande destroyed Mescalero farmlands. Although many were forced to leave Buena Esperanza, the Mescaleros remained at peace in the nearby mountains and continued to solicit rations from the presidio. Nevertheless, some of them were reportedly still involved in raiding. Dissatisfied that the Apaches would not live continuously in the village, in July 1781 the Caballero de Croix ordered Muñoz at Presidio del Norte not to supply any more food or to offer support to any Mescalero that did not actually register and reside at Buena Esperanza. By September some capitancillos and their rancherías agreed to return, and the settlement's population increased. Once again these warriors were required to help the Spaniards in their campaigns.[23]

Many targeted in these attacks were other Mescaleros who had refused the Spanish demands to cease raiding. For example, in late 1781, Patule El Grande broke the peace when he led his ranchería into the Bolsón de Mapimí, where they joined other Mescaleros in launching attacks into Coahuila. Governor

Ugalde counterattacked, and with the help of some Mescaleros who were still at peace after many months, eventually drove Patule and his people out of Coahuila and back into Nueva Vizcaya, where they once again sued for peace, but this time at the Presidio of San Carlos. But in January 1783 the commander of the post, with Croix's approval, seized Patule and his people and shipped them off as prisoners of war bound for Mexico City. Several days into their deportation, Patule and a large group of his people broke free and fled their captors. Eventually, the guards of the escort caught up and killed Patule, along with another nineteen escapees, but forty-seven Mescalero men, women, and children managed to make their way back to the frontier.

The fate of Patule El Grande and his people highlighted the fratricidal nature of the warfare the Mescaleros at Buena Esperanza had agreed to. Having to fight their own close kinsmen may have worn on the residents at the reservation, because a few months after the escape and the killing of Patule, many of them silently slipped away. One small ranchería remained for a little longer, but by March 1783 they too had departed, and the Mescalero village of Nuestra Señora de la Buena Esperanza came to an end.[24]

Soon thereafter the efforts of the Caballero de Croix to master the Apaches also drew to a close, when in February 1783 he was appointed by the king to be the new viceroy of Peru. During his tenure in the Interior Provinces, Croix's policies had resulted in a significant increase in Spanish power across the frontier. His deft reorganization of forces resulted in an increase of troop strength from 1,908 to 2,840 soldiers, backed up by three thousand citizen militia and Indian auxiliaries located mainly in Nueva Vizcaya. He had also significantly strengthened the frontier by erecting a secondary line of defense behind the presidial cordon. Finally, he had overseen the creation of alliances with Indian groups hostile to the Apaches. In September 1783, the war with England was over, and the king once again ordered that offensive war be waged against the Apaches. But by this time Croix had left for his new assignment in Peru, and it would fall to others to conduct the campaigns for which the Caballero had laid the groundwork.[25]

In the spring of 1783, Croix was succeeded as commandant general by Brigadier Felipe de Neve. Neve had served as the governor of California for the previous seven years and had a long and distinguished military career. Almost immediately he availed himself of the crown's permission to wage offensive war, using the increased troop numbers the Caballero de Croix had put in place. In 1784 he launched another general campaign against the Apaches, but it achieved only moderate success. Neve contemplated further campaigns, but then in June 1784 he died suddenly while traveling to Chihuahua City. With his death, control of the Interior Provinces again became problematic and paved the way for a radical shift in military governance on the northern frontier.[26]

Changes at the highest levels soon began. In early 1785 the king appointed Bernardo de Gálvez as viceroy of New Spain. Bernardo was the nephew of one of the most powerful members of the Spanish court, José de Gálvez, the minister of the Indies, who was determined to advance his family. Yet despite the clear nepotism of his uncle, Bernardo had impeccable qualifications. As a young officer he had served as military commandant of Nueva Vizcaya, where he had personally fought against the Apaches. He had then been made governor of Louisiana, where he had led the highly successful Spanish campaign that conquered British-held west Florida during the American Revolutionary War. Promoted to captain general of Cuba, in early 1784 Bernardo succeeded his father Matías de Gálvez as viceroy of New Spain after Matías's unexpected death that November. Wishing to invest his nephew with as much power as possible, minister of the Indies José de Gálvez convinced the king to once again place the Interior Provinces under the direct control of the viceroy, as they had been in the years before 1776 and the tenure of the Caballero de Croix.[27]

Although the Provincias Internas constituted only a part of the vast realm he was to govern, after assuming office as viceroy in May 1785, Bernardo, now given the title of Conde de Gálvez, recognized the importance of the area as a buffer against rival imperial powers, especially Great Britain and the newly independent United States. Thus, he determined to exact as much military and economic efficiency from the region as possible. With the Regulations of 1772 as his starting point, Gálvez formulated a series of policies that in 1786 were codified under his name as the *Instructions for the Governing of the Interior Provinces of New Spain*. These instructions called for several major innovations regarding Spanish relations with the Indians throughout the frontier.[28]

During his time as governor of Louisiana, Gálvez witnessed first-hand the methods used by the French and British in their relations with Native peoples. He came to believe that trade was the most crucial component in dealing with the Indians. If Spain controlled and regulated the trading networks with the Indians within or bordering her territories, they would grow increasingly dependent upon the Spaniards, just as the French and British had done with many of the Indians in their spheres of influence. Controlling

Bernardo de Gálvez, Viceroy of New Spain, 1785–1786.
From Manuel Rivera Cambas, Los Gobernantes de México,
Vol. 1 *(Mexico, 1872), between pp. 454 and 455.*

the Indians' access to European goods, especially firearms and ammunition, would increase reliance by the Indians on the Spaniards and allow them to be more easily manipulated. Although many Indian nations might continue to raid and plunder, they inexorably would be pushed toward quiescence to gain the goods they needed to sustain themselves.

In the long term, Gálvez argued, fostering dependency among the Native peoples would be more effective than continuous conflict. "A bad peace with all the [Indian] nations who may ask for it will be more beneficial to us than the efforts of a good war." And while Gálvez's Instructions were to be applied to many different Indian peoples, he reserved a special ire toward the Apaches, writing, "I am very much in favor of the special ruination of the Apaches, and in endeavoring to interest other tribes and even other Apache bands in it, because these Indians are our real enemies in the Interior Provinces."[29]

Although often cited by historians as a turning point, the Instructions were in reality nothing new. Most of the policies called for had in fact been attempted on the northern frontier since 1779, when the king had ordered the Caballero de Croix to cease offensive operations. What was unique about Gálvez's Instructions was that they synthesized the most effective programs of past administrations into a coherent and calculated strategy. In sum, the Instructions of 1786 were, as historian Max Moorhead characterized them, a "highly sophisticated, brutal and deceptive policy of divide and conquer, of peace by purchase, of studied debilitation of those who accepted it and of extermination of those who rejected it."[30]

At the same time Gálvez was drawing up his Indian policy, he also implemented a change in governance that was to trigger a great deal of confusion and overlapping authority. In August 1786, he divided the Interior Provinces into three administrative commands. Brigadier General Jacobo Ugarte y Loyola was appointed commandant general and would be the senior officer in the Interior Provinces. Ugarte had a long and distinguished career and was well familiar with the frontier, having served as the governor of Coahuila and Sonora. He was to have direct control over the western interior provinces of Alta and Baja California and Sonora. Gálvez then named José Antonio Rengel as commandant inspector in charge of the central provinces of New Mexico and Nueva Vizcaya, the same position he had held during the administration of both the Caballero de Croix and Felipe de Neve. Finally, the eastern provinces of Coahuila, Texas, Nuevo León, and Nuevo Santander were entrusted to Colonel Juan de Ugalde, a gruff veteran with more than forty years of service, including a previous stint as governor of Coahuila, where he dealt with the Mescaleros that had sued for peace a few years before.

Each of these officers was to be responsible for his own area so that he could rapidly react to any local threat or emergency. However, they were all enjoined to cooperate in any large-scale campaigns approved by Viceroy Gálvez himself. With the viceroy's sure guidance, the military policies of the Interior Provinces would enjoy a uniformity of purpose that would surely lead to success. But despite his confidence in his plans and in himself, subsequent events would prove Bernardo de Gálvez's hopes much easier to conceive than to execute.[31]

4

BETWEEN TWO FIRES

JURISDICTION OF THE REAL DE MAZAPIL, ZACATECAS, JULY 11, 1786—The reports were that the Indian attackers numbered at least forty. They had begun their assaults on the small ranch of Sabana Grande, an outlier of the much larger Hacienda de la Gruñidora. Inside the ranch buildings, they had killed six men and four women and had not even spared a nursing infant. All had been put to a most cruel death, the victims' bodies repeatedly pierced with arrows and darts. The attackers stole anything of value or that struck their fancy. But demonstrating their contempt for the faith of their victims, the raiders smashed and desecrated the images of Christ and the saints that had adorned the walls. They spared three young boys they seized as captives, along with a large number of horses and mules, and then rode on in search of more targets.

The next afternoon the Indian attackers descended without warning on the small village of San Antonio. Again, they killed and looted with impunity. Here, the raiders came upon a large number of sheep, and after slaying the shepherds, seemingly for sport, put arrows through all the lambs and ewes. Riding on, they quickly found more shepherds and flocks at the small estancia of Copas and the village of Santa Rosa. Yet again, they slaughtered both men and animals, leaving a large number of rotting carcasses in their wake.

Two days more saw the raiders ambush a large drove of pack mules and their *arrieros* (mule drovers) at a campsite known as El Pozo. The mules bore supplies for the nearby Hacienda de Bonanza, the property of the Marqués de San Miguel de Aguayo, scion of one of the most influential families in New Spain. But the raiders were oblivious to the powerful connections of the marqués as they killed his drovers, looted his property, and stole his mules.

Now fully aware of the danger their people faced, the local authorities feverishly organized a detachment of some twenty-five armed vaqueros to pursue the raiders. But these hastily recruited horsemen were too few and too far behind their quarry to accomplish much more than follow the trails of destruction. Moving in the wake of the raiders, the vaqueros found and buried sixty-three men, women, and children, but they probably failed to locate other victims. Within days the raiders disappeared back into the nearby mountains.

On July 19, a senior civil servant in the region, Joseph Cavallero y Basve, wrote to Viceroy Bernardo de Gálvez describing the carnage. Cavallero y Basve was the administrator of the royal sales tax, or *alcabalas,* for the Real de Mazapil in the Province of Zacatecas. Mazapil encompassed an area containing both silver mines and large haciendas owned by some of the wealthiest and most powerful of Mexico's *criollo* elite, and they would want answers about why their property had suffered such losses. Though Mazapil had experienced raids before, they had not been of such wanton ferocity. Cavallero believed that the reason these recent attacks were so different owed to the perpetrators' nature. Residents of the Mazapil region cast blame squarely on "the barbarous cruelty of the Indios Apaches."

Viceroy Gálvez knew that his superiors would place at his feet responsibility for allowing the attack. In early August, communications among Spanish military authorities in the Interior Provinces proffered explanations. The Real de Mazapil lay several hundred miles south of the northern frontier and far removed from the Apaches' normal raiding range. The Province of Coahuila, to the northeast, was nearest to the frontier, as the crow flies. The governor, Colonel Pedro de Tueros, ventured his opinion that the attack on Mazapil had been carried out by Mescalero and Lipan Apaches in league with rebel Indians and other malcontents from the region. However, Tueros's views were contested by Jacobo de Ugarte y Loyola, the official in charge of military operations for Nueva Vizcaya. Ugarte maintained that the attack was most likely the work of rebellious Tarahumara Indians, along with renegade mulattos and other "infected castes." Ugarte noted that such groups had been a problem throughout Nueva Vizcaya for many years, and they were more likely to have staged the raid. Regardless, the official conclusion stated that there were at least some Apaches among the raiders, most likely Mescaleros and Lipans. As such officials resolved that they were to be attacked and crushed, so that they could never again enter the region.¹

For Bernardo de Gálvez the problem of crushing and containing the Mescalero and other Apaches was something he had been dealing with for some time. He was in the midst of issuing his *Instructions for the Governing of the Interior Provinces of New Spain,* which he believed would ultimately either control or exterminate the Apache. Gálvez hoped that the consistent application of his policies would, over time, achieve this end. Unfortunately, time was running out.

Less than five months after the raid on Mazapil, on November 30, 1786, Bernardo de Gálvez died suddenly in Mexico City after a brief illness. His death threatened to leave the implementation of his Instructions stillborn. Although the ideas within the Instructions remained official Spanish policy, the power vacuum following Gálvez's death left no guarantee that either the intent or the spirit of that policy would apply. Indeed, the idea of seeking out the Apaches and destroying them, or seeking accommodation with them, now depended on the attitudes of individual Spanish military officers. The clearest indication of this was the differing actions and attitudes of Jacobo Ugarte y Loyola and Juan de Ugalde.

When news of Galvez's death reached the frontier, Commandant General Ugarte as senior officer had assumed, on an interim basis, direct control over all the Interior Provinces. But Colonel Ugalde in the east was reluctant to relinquish his authority. A power struggle developed between the two officers that would not be settled until the appointment of new viceroy, Manuel Antonio Flores, in March 1787. Then in December, the situation further deteriorated when the king divided the Interior Provinces in half, with Ugalde promoted to commandant general of the eastern provinces while Ugarte remained commandant general of the western provinces. Both commandant generals reported to the viceroy but, significantly, they were independent of each other.

Although this new arrangement was ostensibly designed to allow for greater initiative and flexibility for the Spanish military in the Interior Provinces, the result was exactly the opposite. The separate commands led to a confusion of aims and tactics employed by the Spaniards, especially against the Apaches. In the west, Ugarte advocated the more pragmatic policies outlined in the Instructions of 1786, alternating military campaigns while holding out the prospect of peace at new reservations. Ugalde in the east favored a renewal of large-scale campaigns into the Apache homelands designed to force them to either make peace or face extermination. The result of these different policies would see a marked increase in violence throughout the frontier as Apaches struggled to accommodate between the two. Managing the rivalry between Ugarte and Ugalde would finally force the Mescaleros to make peace—but not before the shedding of much more blood.²

The winter of 1786 saw many Mescalero rancherías on the brink of destruction. They, along with other eastern Apache groups, had suffered considerably from the unrelenting Comanche attacks in the vast plains of the Llano Estacado. To make matters worse, Spanish forces from New Mexico, Sonora, Nueva Vizcaya, and Coahuila had also continued to strike against them along the entire frontier. Over the course of the year, scores, if not hundreds, of Mescaleros had been killed, and many others taken captive. Their horse herds had been seriously depleted and their ability to hunt buffalo drastically curtailed. Assaulted by both native enemies and the Spaniards, the Mescaleros were truly caught between two fires. Finally, and perhaps most importantly, nature herself seemed to have turned against them. Prolonged frosts in the early months of 1786 damaged many of their seasonal crops, and then later in the year a severe drought followed, which further depleted their food sources. Famine stalked the people, and for many Mescalero capitancillos, the only option that seemed to remain was to seek terms from the Spaniards.

In late January 1787, a Spanish scouting party stumbled upon a band of Mescalero hunters in the region north of Presidio del Norte. After a series of tense discussions, these Apaches made it known that they wanted to come into the presidio and talk peace. The sides held tentative discussions for two months, but eventually in March the followers of at least eight Mescalero leaders, an estimated three thousand people, appeared across the Rio Grande opposite Presidio del Norte. Astounded by their numbers, the post commander, Captain Domingo Díaz, urgently communicated with his superior, Commandant General Ugarte, about how he should handle the situation. Díaz reported that the Mescaleros had arrived "in total misery." The drought that had affected the region had left them with very few horses, and in turn they had been unable "to harvest the fruits that for part of the year sustains them." He felt compelled "to feed the great number of women and little children that daily come down to this Presidio," for if he did not feed them, they "would be obliged to commit robberies for supplies in this vicinity."³

Assuming that he was still bound by the Instructions of 1786, Ugarte favored maintaining the policy of offering Apaches peace if they agreed to settle near presidios subject to Spanish control. He therefore instructed Captain Díaz to treat with the Indians as long as they agreed to Spanish terms. These were largely the same as they had been when the Mescaleros had sought peace in 1779 at Buena Esperanza, namely that they must establish settled communities outside the presidio, that they must support themselves by growing their own crops, and that they aid the Spaniards in military attacks against those Apaches that refused to make peace. However, realizing the delicate nature of the situation, Ugarte allowed Díaz to adjust these terms if so required.

Such flexibility would prove crucial to the success of the negotiations. A few of the Mescalero leaders who approached Captain Díaz were the same ones that had negotiated peace back in 1779. These included Domingo Alegre and Volante, and as a demonstration of their clear intent to make peace, they presented Díaz a copy of the treaty they had signed eight years earlier. Nevertheless, these leaders were resolved that they would agree to peace only if certain of their own demands were met. First, they refused to agree to settle in established towns or to raise their own crops. When they had done this at Buena Esperanza in 1779, smallpox had decimated their people and flooding destroyed their plantings. They then demanded the return all of their kinfolk who had been captured by the Spaniards. They also declined to recognize a principal chief who would speak for all the Mescaleros, maintaining instead the independence of all the eight leaders present. Finally, they insisted that Díaz issue them rations, as they were suffering greatly from famine.

Utilizing the freedom of action he had been given by Commandant General Ugarte, Captain Díaz hammered out a compromise that was acceptable to both sides. The Mescaleros would not have to settle in established towns or grow crops as long as they remained in clearly defined areas on the other side of the Rio Grande where the Spaniards could monitor them. There would be a mutual exchange of prisoners by both sides, and the Mescaleros would agree to cease all raiding and to ally with the Spaniards in waging war against all other Apaches, including their kin who refused to make peace. For their part, the Spaniards agreed to provide an escort for these Indians on their annual buffalo hunts to the southern plains in order to protect them from the Comanches. With all sides generally satisfied, they drew up written documents to conclude the pact.

Yet even as these peace celebrations were underway, they had been already undermined by the actions of Colonel Juan de Ugalde, farther to the east.[4]

Ugalde had assumed command of the eastern Interior Provinces on October 11, 1786, taking up his headquarters in the Province of Coahuila. Having previously served as governor of the province between 1779 and 1783, he was determined to pick things up from where he had left them three years earlier—namely by attacking those eastern Apache groups that continued to plague his command, especially the Mescaleros. If he needed any further justification, Ugalde cited the devastation wreaked on the Real de Mazapil in July as the most recent example of atrocities attributed to the Mescaleros. With this raid in mind and declaring that he was following the admonitions of Viceroy Gálvez, who Ugalde characterized as "his guiding light," he would seek out and punish the Mescaleros. In January 1787 he set out on a general campaign with more than four hundred soldiers and militiamen, hundreds of horses and mules, and enough supplies to last him for seven months.[5]

Entering into the Bolsón de Mapimí for almost three months, Ugalde and his men searched fruitlessly for Apache raiders. He then decided to move into the mountains of the Big Bend country of the Rio Grande. Finally, in April he attacked several large gatherings of Mescaleros. However, these unfortunates were part of the same group that had just concluded peace with Captain Díaz at Presidio del Norte a month previous. When officers from that presidio tried to stop Ugalde, he became enraged at their efforts. He pointed out that the Mescaleros had often raided into Coahuila, after which they would flee back into Nueva Vizcaya and take refuge under the protection of Spanish officers at del Norte. Infuriated at what he regarded as a sham peace, Ugalde let it be known that he would attack the Mescaleros at every opportunity. With that he led his troops north across the Rio Grande determined to hunt for more Apaches.

Ugalde's actions left chaos in his wake. Four of the eight Mescalero capitancillos gathered around Presidio del Norte immediately led their people away from the presidio and back into the hinterland. Four other capitancillos chose to remain, but they were vocally resentful and filled with mistrust. Many members of their own bands decided to leave as well, clearly diminishing the leaders' authority.[6]

Such mistrust seemed to permeate the frontier. At almost the same time that Ugalde had attacked the Mescaleros near Presidio del Norte, a large-scale defection of "peaceful Apaches" had also occurred farther west. For several months almost eight hundred Chiricahuas had settled outside the Presidio of San Buenaventura in Nueva Vizcaya. In May, the majority of them rose up and fled, killing several Spaniards and three other Apache auxiliaries who attempted to stop them. Although most likely coincidental, the timing of this uprising occurred so close to the partial breakdown of peace with the Mescaleros at Presidio del Norte that it confirmed many Spaniards' mistrust of the Apaches to live in peace.[7]

War now raged across the Interior Provinces. In the east Colonel Ugalde was still hunting Mescaleros north of the Rio Grande. Despite his zeal Ugalde's efforts had proven largely ineffectual, so he determined to try his hand at peace. During the campaign Ugalde had encountered a powerful Apache chief named Picax-andé. Ugalde labeled him a leader of the Lipiyan group of Llanero Apaches. However, Picax-andé was known as El Calvo, or "the Bald One," by the Spaniards of Nueva Vizcaya, who believed he was one of the Mescalero leaders that had sought peace at Presidio del Norte. Whether Ugalde was aware of this distinction or not, in July 1787 he negotiated a treaty with Picax-andé.

Following up on what he regarded a great achievement, Ugalde then demanded that all Mescaleros seeking peace must relocate outside the Presidio of Santa Rosa in northwestern Coahuila. All Mescaleros that did not move, especially those outside Presidio del Norte in Nueva Vizcaya, would be considered hostile. By October 1787, some 150 Mescalero men, women, and children, led by eight chiefs whom Ugalde claimed "spoke for the entire nation," arrived along the Río de Sabinas close by Presidio Santa Rosa.[8]

However, when Commandant General Ugarte in the west heard of Ugalde's actions, he was incredulous. Ugarte realized that the Mescaleros outside Santa Rosa represented only a fraction of the tribe and did not contain any of the most important leaders. In addition, Ugarte understood the impossibility of forcing the Mescaleros to move several hundred miles beyond their traditional homelands. Ugarte wrote to Ugalde and called for him to recognize the fragile peace negotiated at Presidio del Norte and not require the Mescaleros there to relocate.

The situation remained at an impasse for several months during the fall of 1787. Then on November 21 the newly installed Viceroy Manuel Antonio Flores ordered Ugarte to have all the Mescaleros living around Presidio del Norte relocated to the Río de Sabinas under the conditions that Ugalde demanded.

If they would not move, the Spanish would deem the Mescaleros hostile and immediately attack. Ugarte protested, to no avail, that this policy appeared dangerously counterproductive.

In the meantime Ugalde, now promoted to brigadier general, busily pursued his own agenda. In late February 1788 he concluded a peace treaty with the Apache leader Picax-andé at Presidio Santa Rosa in Coahuila. Satisfied that he had secured a lasting peace, Ugalde then set out to inspect the Province of Texas. But on April 8, the Mescaleros gathered near the Río de Sabinas rose up, killed seven soldiers, and raided several settlements in Coahuila before fleeing into the mountains. Then only a few weeks later, Commandant General Ugarte finally bowed to vice regal authority and issued orders for the remaining Mescaleros gathered at Presidio del Norte to relocate to the Río de Sabinas. As he had warned, most did leave but headed back into their homelands and soon resumed raiding into Nueva Vizcaya and Coahuila.

Incensed by what he labeled the "treachery" of the Mescaleros, Viceroy Flores commanded both Ugarte and Ugalde to escalate offensive operations. Convinced that the Apaches could not be trusted for very long, Flores also ordered that both frontier commanders were not to concede peace unless it was under the most restrictive terms. By July 1788 warfare had intensified along the northern frontier. Throughout the remainder of the year, both commandant generals complied and launched large-scale attacks in their jurisdictions.

Then in early 1789 Ugalde committed an act that sent shockwaves throughout the region. After a group of Mescalero leaders approached him again requesting peace, Ugalde fumed that these same Indians had broken the peace treaty of the previous year, "which on our part we committed the error of conceding." Incensed at what he viewed as duplicity, Ugalde determined to employ "perfidy against perfidy, deceit against deceit, cunning against cunning." For several weeks he parlayed with the Mescaleros and enticed a number of them treat with him at the Presidio of Santa Rosa. On March 24, Ugalde suddenly ordered his men to seize the Apaches, and they captured seventy-eight of them, including three chieftains, twenty-three warriors, six boys, twenty-nine women, seven girls, and six infants. Two of the warriors fought to the death rather than submit, while the remainder were imprisoned in Santa Rosa and eventually deported from the frontier.[9]

As news spread of Ugalde's actions, many Spanish officers were appalled at what they viewed as treachery, but Viceroy Flores lauded the outcome. Hoping to maintain the pressure on the Apaches, the following month Flores directed that several Mescalero bands that had once again requested peace at Presidio del Norte be turned away.

In exasperation, these same Mescaleros moved eastward, launching raids as they went and even enlisting many Lipan groups. For many months thereafter the level of violence throughout the eastern Interior Provinces increased dramatically. In Coahuila, on June 24 and 25, 1789, Mescaleros and Lipans reportedly "killed in the ranches near to the Villa de Saltillo 34 persons of both sexes, carrying off 4 captives and burning 16 cadavers . . . feeding their cruelty as far as [killing] the domestic animals dogs, cats and chickens." They also ran off three thousand head of cattle in the same region.[10]

In Texas, between August 1789 and May 1790, Governor Manuel Muñoz reported that Mescaleros and Lipans had "killed 29 persons, destroyed more than nine thousand head of small cattle . . . and he was unable to say the number of horses and sheep that they stole and slaughtered in the ranchos near San Antonio de Bejar, [as they were] abandoned by their owners in order to save their lives."[11]

The Province of Nuevo Santander south of Texas also suffered heavily. Between March 17 and July 22, 1789, reports noted that in the three settlements of Laredo, Revilla, and Mier alone "the barbarians killed another 25 . . . and carried off 7 persons captive." In addition, the Indians had stolen "2,414 horses, mules, and large cattle and 3,756 head of goats," the loss of which the governor calculated totaled "more than twenty-three thousand pesos have been lost by the poor vecinos." Finally, in Nuevo León the story was much the same but with a greater loss of life. There, during the four months between March and June, Lipans and Mescaleros killed a total of forty-three persons, "carrying off two captives and despoiling the province of the moveable goods."[12]

The rising tide of conflict reached the point that Juan de Ugalde himself even asked permission to attack his one-time ally Picax-andé, who reportedly aided the Mescaleros. Determined to decisively crush the Apaches, in August 1789 Ugalde set out on a massive campaign against the Mescaleros and Lipans. With an unprecedented force of 522 troopers, including officers, he headed out into the vast expanse of the Llano Estacado in an often fruitless pursuit of the enemy.[13]

Yet, at the same time that Juan de Ugalde was engaged in his large-scale campaign in the east, his rival to the west, Jacobo Ugarte y Loyola, was sending out his own forces on expeditions into the Mescalero heartlands that were to yield much more favorable and long-lasting results. As Commandant Pedro Nava would do in a few years, Ugarte turned to then-Captain Antonio Cordero y Bustamante to lead one such expedition. Cordero was already one of the most experienced and knowledgeable Spanish officers in the Interior Provinces. Not only was he an aggressive and successful field officer, but Cordero was also somewhat of a diplomat who had negotiated with many Apache groups. For example, in 1787, Cordero had served as *agente de paces,* or peace agent, to several bands of Chiricahua Apaches, whom the Spaniards labeled Mimbreños and Gileños. As a result, he had developed a familiarity with their lifeways that far surpassed most of other Spanish officers along the frontier.[14]

In 1789 Cordero was serving both as captain of the Presidio of Janos and as the commander of the "first division" of the presidial forces in the central province of Nueva Vizcaya with authority not only over his own presidio but of several other posts as well. Thus it was that in September 1789, he received orders from Commandant General Jacobo Ugarte de Loyola to organize his forces for a campaign to penetrate the Sacramento Mountains and attack the homelands of the Mescalero Apaches.[15]

On September 13, Cordero and his men crossed the Rio Grande about eighty miles north of El Paso and headed east toward the Sacramentos via the Sierra de las Petacas, as he called the modern San Andres Mountains. Reaching the latter range, "half-way along our route," that same night Cordero reported that his men "found a great number of fresh tracks, which I pursued with tenacity and which led to three rancherías in the same mountains." Cordero divided his men into three groups and attacked all the Apache camps simultaneously. After a sharp fight, the Spaniards killed three Apache men and one woman and captured another twenty-nine persons, while they suffered one man killed. However, "due to the impossibility of the horse herd to continue as many had died along the march of forty five leagues in thirty hours," Cordero decided to return to his original encampment along the Rio Grande.[16]

After allowing his horse herd to recuperate, Cordero once again set out on September 15 toward his ultimate target, the Sacramento Mountains. However, as he approached his destination, on September 19 he came across signs that a large number of Apaches had eluded him and doubled back toward the Rio Grande, crossing to the river's west bank. Tenaciously, Cordero followed them. Despite his determination, Captain Cordero soon began to feel somewhat out of his depth as he was entering "into lands totally unknown to our troops and our allies." The Spaniards were in the neighborhood of the Rio Salado, north of present-day Magdalena, New Mexico. This region was well known to the Spaniards of New Mexico, but to Cordero's men out of Nueva Vizcaya, they were in virgin territory.[17]

Despite being unfamiliar with the terrain, the Spaniards soon found an Apache ranchería in the surrounding mountains. Cordero noted that "on the twenty first of the current month at four thirty in the afternoon they attacked many Apaches who were encamped on its most rugged and entangled [areas]." Although surprised, the Apache warriors "sustained the first impetus of our troops as was seen in order to give space for the flight of their families." Cordero reported that the Apaches fought effectively, but were eventually overcome, writing: "They succeeded in wounding four men and some horses, but many of them were wounded and our troops coming up to finish them, they fled precipitously, leaving dead a man, a woman, and a boy. We followed and pursued with vigor but as the terrain was rough and as the night began to close in we only succeeded in taking twenty-three prisoners and twenty animals with all the rest of the goods of the ranchería." Deciding that his men had accomplished all they could and running short of supplies, Cordero elected to return to El Paso without completing his expedition into the Sierra del Sacramento.[18]

Although Commandant General Ugarte was pleased with the results that Cordero and his men had achieved "in castigating the enemy," nevertheless, in a letter of October 3, he reminded the captain that "the principal object of these maneuvers" was to enter and reconnoiter the Sacramento Mountains and discover all the hiding places of the Mescaleros "as this is one of their principle sanctuaries and there are many more that live in that site confident in the advantages of its dense forests, canyons and rugged terrain in order to evade the blows of the troops." Therefore, Ugarte ordered Cordero to rest and refit and return to the Sacramentos to complete his reconnaissance.[19]

Having been given his orders in no uncertain terms, by October 31 Captain Cordero was ready to set out again from his base of operations in El Paso into the Sierra del Sacramento. His force consisted of 275 men, including presidial soldiers, citizen militia, Indian auxiliaries from El Paso, and perhaps most significantly, twenty-three Chiricahua Apache allies.

Seeking to cloak his movements, Cordero moved up the Rio Grande far to the north before heading east and entering into the "*malpaises* denominated de la Calera," around the present-day Valley of Fires. Coming out of this wasteland, Cordero entered into the Sacramento Mountains from the northwest, which caught the Mescaleros by surprise. The Spaniards engaged the Apaches at several points, including one large fight at an undetermined location they called la Laguna de la Victoria, possibly a large pond or marsh near the modern-day Rio Bonito or Rio Ruidoso. Altogether, the Spaniards delivered a brutal blow. Captain Cordero himself gave a brief summary of the fighting in the Sacramentos in a report prepared for Commandant General Ugarte dated November 18, 1789:

> We had on the 10th, 11th, 12th and 13th of the current month five engagements with the *Apachería Faraóna* that inhabit them, leaving in all of them these enemies totally destroyed, with the success that none of those living in the rancherías attacked escaped, neither little nor big, so that all that did not surrender were put under the knife, notwithstanding the vigor with which they defended themselves, and the courage with which they solicited to have their liberty. They left dead on the field twenty-two gandules and seven women, whose ears I send to Your Lordship, and of prisoners, sixty-nine persons including in this number two Gandules, and for us their horse herd, dogs and all they possessed.

Exulting in his victory, Cordero concluded his report by praising the valor of his troops in delivering "this bloody chastisement to these Barbarians."[20]

When Commandant General Ugarte received news of the success of Cordero's expedition into the Sacramento Mountains, he hailed it as a "glorious action" and promised to recommend Cordero and his men to the viceroy and ask him in turn to report this to the king. However, for the Mescaleros, the attack was more than just another page in a seemingly endless and ruthless war. If the Spaniards could thrust so deeply into the Mescalero homelands, then there truly was no place where they could be safe. Yet again, making peace was their only option. The only question that remained was, would the Spaniards agree.[21]

5

FORGING A BAD PEACE

EL PASO DEL NORTE, JUNE 1790—At some point word reached him that two Mescaleros had appeared at the edge of town. In broad daylight they had swum across the Rio Grande and openly approached the settlement. In what must have been a tense encounter, the two Apaches soon made it clear that they had come to parley and that they had a message from their chief, Nzazen. Whether he went out to meet them, or whether he had the two envoys brought before him, the Spanish leader was soon given the import of their message: Nzazen and his people wished to discuss terms for making peace.

For Francisco Xavier de Uranga, lieutenant governor of the Province of New Mexico, the arrival of these two Mescalero envoys represented both an opportunity and a puzzle. He had recently overseen the deportation of a substantial number of Mescalero prisoners of war, captured by Spanish forces led by the redoubtable Antonio Cordero in another highly successful wintertime campaign into the Apache heartlands. Now, the envoys of Nzazen clearly hoped to recover their kinsmen, or at the very least reach some accommodation with the white men that would end the recent hostilities. This offered Uranga the possibility of having Nzazen and his people gather outside El Paso and, perhaps, settle down in peace.

Yet only four months before, another large group of Mescaleros had also approached El Paso, requesting to parley. They were led by three capitancillos that the Spaniards called Alegre, Volante, and Bigotes el Bermejo (The Red Mustached One). These leaders had journeyed far from the east in search of succor in the face of continuous Comanche and Spanish attacks against their homelands in that region; clearly, they hoped to obtain terms from Lieutenant Governor Uranga, terms that the Spanish leaders in the east refused to concede them. After a series of tense negotiations, the rancherías of Domingo, Patule, and Bigotes agreed to settle near El Paso in peace, much to Uranga's satisfaction. But shortly thereafter they had seemingly reneged and rode back toward the east into the Llano Estacado and home.

The departure of these three eastern Mescalero leaders merely confirmed to Uranga that they were innately untrustworthy and incapable of sustaining peaceful relations. Yet if he had cared to see things from the Mescaleros' perspective, he might have recognized that it was the inconsistency of Spanish policies that contributed to their vacillations. Differing tactics by different commanders in the western and eastern Interior Provinces hamstrung Spanish efforts to control the Apaches. This inevitably led to confusion about how the white men should marshal their forces and exert their power, a confusion the Apaches, especially the Mescalero, would repeatedly exploit for their own ends.[1]

The meeting with the messengers was merely the latest in a long series of encounters Francisco de Uranga had with the Mescaleros over the previous twenty years, in both war and peace. A native of the villa of Chihuahua, purportedly of noble lineage, Uranga had served as an officer in the local militia, raised in the 1770s to help stem the continuous Apache raiding in the region. In 1779 he obtained a commission in the regular army, appointed alférez of the Presidio del Norte. Here, he commanded several pursuits against the Apaches, riding out against them and successfully recovering large numbers of stolen stock. However, his most extensive interactions with the Mescaleros revolved around the village established for them at Buena Esperanza that same year just outside the presidio.

In October 1779, Uranga had been commissioned by the Caballero de Croix "for the distribution of aid destined for the Apache Indians of the Mescalero Nation, and for the building of their new pueblo." During the next two years that the Buena Esperanza reservation functioned, Uranga oversaw the construction of a substantial number of adobe houses, an extensive irrigation canal, and the clearing and planting of fields for corn and other crops. Throughout all of this, he interacted continuously with the Mescaleros and witnessed their lifeways first hand. Despite the ultimate failure at Buena Esperanza, Uranga fulfilled his duties with such efficiency that in 1782 superiors promoted him to lieutenant at Presidio del Norte.

Having clearly manifested a talent for administration and organization, Uranga then assumed the task of overseeing the construction of new military quarters for two companies of troopers in Nueva Vizcaya. Again, his abilities earned notice, and in the spring of 1788 he received a particularly important appointment as the lieutenant governor of the Province of New Mexico. With his wife and family, Uranga took up his new post at El Paso del Norte, officially assuming office on April 20.[2]

Over the next year and a half, Lieutenant Governor Uranga became intensely involved in the escalation of warfare between the Spaniards and Apaches. In the fall of 1788 his capital of El Paso served as the staging area for a series of campaigns launched against the Mimbreño and Gileño Apaches to the west by Lieutenant Colonel Antonio Cordero and other Spanish commanders. Uranga again assisted Cordero in September 1789 when Cordero led another incursion that scoured the traditional Sacramento Mountain homelands of the Mescaleros. Throughout, the lieutenant governor dealt continuously with supplying the field operations men, horses, and supplies, and in the aftermath of these successful campaigns, he organized the concentration and deportation from the frontier of the several hundred prisoners.

By the early months of 1790 the Spaniards' military efforts appeared to bear fruit. Uranga in February received word that the three Mescalero capitancillos, Alegre, Volante, and Bigotes el Bermejo, had put out peace feelers. The latter two were among those capitancillos who had attempted to make peace at Presidio del Norte in 1787. Bigotes sent his son to negotiate, and Uranga received him cordially, presenting him with several gifts. It appears that there was some sort of general understanding that the Mescaleros would be allowed to settle in peace outside del Norte as they had three years earlier. Regardless, for unknown reasons the Mescaleros soon broke off their negotiations, packed up, and left El Paso.

Four months later, in June, the Spaniards had better fortune in their negotiations with capitancillo Nzazen, whose envoys swam to the river to speak with Uranga, concluding a much more concrete agreement. Nzazen was the leader of a substantial ranchería living in the Sacramento Mountains. After being harried by the invading troopers under Cordero the previous winter, Nzazen, whom the Spaniards came to call Barrio, decided to send emissaries to El Paso to seek an accommodation. These talks continued for several weeks. Finally, in July Nzazen himself arrived on the scene. With twelve of his warriors, along with five women, he and another capitancillo called Arco crossed the Rio Grande into El Paso and negotiated face to face with the Spaniards, while another sixty of their people encamped on the other side of the river.

As the discussion unfolded, Nzazen and Arco declared that they wished to settle outside El Paso in peace. Clearly wishing to capitalize on the offer, Lieutenant Governor Uranga sent dispatches to Commandant General Ugarte informing him of these latest developments. Ugarte directed that Nzazen and his compatriot Arco should be awarded some gifts and be escorted to Chihuahua City to complete the terms. Nzazen agreed to most of the conditions, including providing warriors to assist the Spaniards in their military campaigns, but on one point, he stubbornly refused. He would not agree to settle his people farther downstream outside the Presidio of San Elizario, insisting that they remain across the river from El Paso. Uranga was exasperated by this intransigence but reluctantly agreed. Indeed, this concession seemed rather insignificant at the time.³

But soon the number of Mescaleros coming in to request peace with the Spaniards throughout the Interior Provinces began to increase dramatically. At the same time that Uranga was negotiating with the Mescaleros gathered outside El Paso, an even greater number had collected outside Presidio del Norte, almost two hundred miles downstream on the Rio Grande. In June capitancillos Alegre and Volante (the same men that had attempted negotiations at El Paso in February), along with another leader, Joseph, approached the presidio and initiated peace talks with post commander Captain Domingo Díaz. Díaz contacted Commandant General Ugarte requesting instructions, and in July Ugarte ordered that the Mescaleros be admitted to peace under the conditions that they settle near the post, return all their captives and stolen property, and agree to fight alongside the Spaniards as auxiliaries. Unlike their abortive negotiations at El Paso, the three chieftains agreed to the terms and quickly established their rancherías outside Presidio del Norte. Almost immediately they demonstrated their good intentions when in August eight Mescalero warriors enlisted to help Captain Díaz in a campaign against a raiding party of Gileño Apaches.⁴

Soon thereafter even more Mescaleros from the hinterland came into Presidio del Norte. By September 1790 a total of eight Mescalero leaders and their followers had gathered on both sides of the river and were clamoring for peace and supplies. Captain Díaz and his officers struggled to make a count of the various groups, but fortunately one of their soldados spoke Apache and was able to act as an interpreter. Francisco Perez was a native of the Province of Coahuila and had served as a soldier of del Norte for thirteen years. How he came to speak Apache is unclear, but he was able to clarify the identities of the Mescaleros that now gathered at his post. Perez reported that these were "the Rancherías of Volante, named among their own Cheguindilé, that of Alegre or Daban Chu, that of Bigotes el Bermejo or Chialitsó, that of Esquin-yoé, that of Joseph or Josnatesdey, Montera Blanca or Chal-coay, and Cuerno Verde named by them Pases-flá, which number of gandules or men at arms appears to pass one hundred."[5]

While Perez could identify the leaders, Captain Díaz estimated that the number of warriors was much greater, between 200 and 250. Modern historians have reckoned that this would have resulted in somewhere between eight hundred and nine hundred Mescalero men, women, and children outside Presidio del Norte. Clearly the Spaniards had serious problems in comprehending the mass of people that had decamped on their front steps.[6]

If the Spaniards were confounded by the identity and numbers of the Apaches outside del Norte, they had a much clearer picture of those who had settled outside El Paso. By the end of July at least five Mescalero headmen and their rancherías were ensconced across the Rio Grande from the town. Soldado Juan Pedro Rivera, who spoke Apache, identified the principal capitancillos as "Nzazen or Barrio whose *gandulada* [warrior band] is a hundred men more or less, Maselchindé with twenty five more or less, Tucon chujaté or Mayá with some thirty gandules, and Chimeslán," with an undetermined number of warriors. Another resident of El Paso, Diego Antonio Candelario, also listed "Francisco or Tlayelel with the number more or less of a hundred gandules." Though other citizens of El Paso gave varying numbers of warriors, there appeared to be approximately two hundred, which would indicate that there were more than five hundred Apaches settled outside the town.[7]

When asked why these Mescaleros had come to request peace at this particular juncture, the most likely answer put forward by the El Paso residents was that they had been forced to by necessity. Captain of Militia Francisco Xavier Bernal stated flatly, "peace began to take place after the return of the troops having made a campaign in the Sierra del Sacramento," meaning the campaign carried out by Lieutenant Colonel Cordero in the winter of 1789–1790. With somewhat less specificity, interpreter Soldado Rivera declared "that the friendship that the Indians proffer us derives solely from the fear they have our arms so they will not be destroyed . . . and with the object of relieving their necessities." Although these opinions may have been self-serving to Spanish pride, they were nevertheless essentially correct.[8]

During the winter of 1789 and 1790, the Mescaleros and other Apaches along the length of the Interior Provinces suffered a series of prolonged and violent assaults by the Spaniards. At the same time, a pronounced drought struck the vast Llano Estacado beginning in the winter and stretching into the spring and summer. With forage scarce, the Comanches escalated their never-ending warfare against the Apaches to find new pastures to graze their vast herds of horses and to follow the buffalo. Attacked by enemies at every turn and assailed by the ever-widening drought, many Mescaleros found themselves with no other option than to approach the Spaniards to seek peace and beg for sustenance.[9]

In October 1789 the bellicose Viceroy Manuel Antonio Flores handed the office over to his successor, the second Conde de Revillagigedo, who soon showed himself of a temperament quite different from his predecessor. Revillagigedo believed firmly that the maxim of a bad peace being better than a good war was the most cost-effective method of dealing with the Apaches. Yet while he favored encouraging the Apaches to make peace, he was also not above enforcing harsh policies against those that still defied the Spanish.

Nevertheless, at the same time that Revillagigedo was encouraging a peace with the Apaches that would lead to mutual accommodation, for many frontier officers the concept seemed impossible. The personal experiences of several Spanish commanders, combined with the constant raiding of various bands of Mescaleros and Lipans, appeared to preclude any possibility of a negotiated settlement. Either these Spanish leaders would have to change their beliefs or be removed from power, or the Apaches would have to change their ways. If recent events were any indication, neither prospect seemed likely.[10]

Throughout the last half 1789, the commandant general of the Eastern Interior Provinces, Juan de Ugalde, had marshaled a strikingly large number of men for a protracted campaign designed to scour the Mescalero and Lipan

Juan Vicente de Güemes Pacheco y Padilla,
second Conde de Revillagigedo, Viceroy of New Spain, 1789–1794.
From Manuel Rivera Cambas, Los Gobernantes de México,
Vol. 1 (Mexico, 1872), between pp. 472 and 473.

Apache heartlands. In central Texas on January 9, 1790, Ugalde and his men, aided by a force of one hundred Comanches, surprised an encampment of more than three hundred Lipan, Lipiyan, and Mescalero Apaches at the Arroyo de la Soledad, near the present-day Sabinal River Canyon. Ugalde's forces killed fifty-seven Apache men and women, captured another thirty, and seized eight hundred horses. The victory was so overwhelming that the Spanish named the battlefield the Cañón de Ugalde, from which over time the city and county of Uvalde, Texas, derived their names.

Buoyed by this success, Ugalde continued his search-and-destroy operations until August 1790, but achieved only limited results. By the time he returned to his headquarters in Coahuila, his forces over the course of the almost year-long campaign had "killed and captured 215 Indians of both sexes, including three captives they had in their power, and recovered 1,143 horses, with the only losses on our part of three soldiers killed and 6 wounded."[11]

For eastern Apaches like the Mescalero and Lipan, the warfare waged by Ugalde and other Spanish forces throughout the first half of 1790 would prove only the beginning of their tribulations. The rains of March and April failed to appear, and as the weeks passed and summer began, drought scorched the region, stunting grass and crops. As the grass died, so too the buffalo died or moved farther north. With the buffalo gone and with the Comanches barring their hunting farther afield, the eastern Apaches stared starvation full in the face.

The immediate solution, born of desperation, was for the Apaches to increase their raiding activities into Spanish territories. In the spring of 1790 the governor of Coahuila, Lieutenant Colonel Miguel de Emparan, reported a dramatic spike in the number of attacks by the eastern Apaches and decried "their innate inhumanity." The raiders had struck almost simultaneously at several vulnerable areas in Coahuila, and Emparan believed that the Apaches succeeded because "the Lipans and Mescaleros have full knowledge of the entire Province," including the locations and conditions of the military garrisons. "To this bloody scourge," Emparan noted, was added "the dreadful famine that resulted from the drought" that had lasted for a year.[12]

To make matters even worse, the campaign waged by Commandant General Ugalde had so denuded the military garrisons in Coahuila that the remaining troopers were far too few to deal with the Apaches raiders. Emparan implored the viceroy to order Ugalde to return. "I leave it for the consideration of Your Excellency my situation and that of this miserable Province without the help needed to contain the irruptions of these Barbarians and without the forces to prevent its ultimate desolation."[13]

As if to prove that his importunities were not mere hyperbole, Emparan reported that in March the Apaches had killed thirty-four men, three women, and two children, and stolen 716 horses and slaughtered another 96, along with 580 sheep and goats. With almost poetic desperation, the governor wrote, "My pen is too weak to paint that which my spirit endures." But if the soldiers out on campaign with Commandant General Ugalde returned, Emparan believed the situation could be turned around. "This is, most Excellent Señor, the comfort that sustains me and that offers to me the hope that in a short time the help of the Troops for which I have been begging." Unfortunately, for Governor Emparan, his hope would prove vain. Several times over the spring and summer Viceroy Revillagigedo sent out dispatches ordering Ugalde to cease his operations, but the dispatch riders could not locate Ugalde to deliver the viceroy's directives.[14]

Finally, in June, the violence reached a crescendo. Over the course of two days, June 24 and 25, Apaches launched twelve separate attacks throughout the jurisdiction of the villa of Saltillo, the region's largest city. They killed thirty-eight people and carried off or destroyed large numbers of cattle. The single greatest loss of life occurred at the Rancho de los Sartuchis, where Governor Emparan reported "sixteen persons killed with all of the domestic animals, fowls, dogs, and cats, and not being satisfied, they burned the sixteen persons."[15]

Yet at almost the same time, other Apaches were requesting peace. In late June the commandant of the Presidio of Aguaverde reported to Governor Emparan that six Lipan capitancillos were seeking terms. Unable to communicate with his superior Ugalde, Emparan sought advice from Commandant General Ugarte, commander of the west, who recommended that "if the Lipans arrived requesting peace it should be conceded under just terms." Reluctantly, Emparan offered terms, or *capitulaciones*, as the Spaniards termed them. Though the negotiations offered hope, Emparan remained wary, noting that "I will admit these and greater indulgences until to see if with the capitulations they can puff up their perfidies."[16]

The advice of Ugarte to offer peace reflected the general pattern along the frontier. In July 1790, the Mescalero leader Nzazen had negotiated terms outside El Paso, and during the same period several hundred more Mescaleros had assembled outside Presidio del Norte. Now, like their Mescalero kinsmen, the Lipans around Aguaverde had also decided to make peace. These Apaches had suffered through months of drought, famine, and want, and another bloody round of strikes and counterstrikes with the Spaniards. Seemingly, their only hope lay in negotiation.

Still, the constant pattern of one group of Apaches treating for peace, while others continued to raid, exasperated the Spaniards. Governor Emparan in Coahuila decried the "unfaithful friendship" of the Lipans, whose failure to come to terms was proof "of their innate, incorrigible perfidy." For Emparan and other Spanish officers, the continuing hostilities called into question the wisdom of granting peace to any Apaches, a sentiment that may have doomed the prospects of Mescaleros outside El Paso and del Norte. However, in the midst of these considerations, a power shift in the Interior Provinces led to the arrival of a Spanish leader whose determination to implement a peaceful system would throw the Apaches a lifeline.[17]

The frustrations visited upon Viceroy Revillagigedo by Commandant General Juan de Ugalde had finally reached a crescendo. Ever since assuming office in the fall of 1789, Revillagigedo had determined to make changes to the command structure of the Interior Provinces, and he had hoped to do so with as little disruption as possible; but the intransigence and stubbornness of Juan de Ugalde dashed the viceroy's hopes. Throughout 1789 and 1790, when Ugalde had been out on his massive search-and-destroy campaign, Revillagigedo repeatedly issued orders recalling him to defend the provinces under his command. But Ugalde refused to heed the viceroy's directives and his actions clearly bordered on insubordination. When Ugalde finally did return, he boasted that his forces had killed 215 Apaches and recovered 1,143 horses and mules. But Revillagigedo countered that over the same period, the Apaches had killed 151 people and stolen or destroyed 5,614 horses, mules, and cattle along with 12,756 head of sheep and goats. With his patience exhausted, the viceroy dismissed Ugalde, removing him from command.[18]

Wishing to make a fresh start throughout the frontier, a few months later Revillagigedo also oversaw the replacement of the western commandant general, Jacobo de Ugarte y Loyola. Although he supported the ideas of Viceroy Revillagigedo, Ugarte complained about the strains of age and had requested a transfer to a less-demanding posting. With the approval of the court in Madrid, Revillagigedo orchestrated the promotion of Ugarte to a prestigious administrative position, as head of the Audiencia of Guadalajara.

With these changes completed, Revillagigedo now found himself dependent on King Charles IV and his ministers in Spain for the selection of two new commandant generals. Fortunately, the first choice was a man destined to at long last implement consistent and effective policies across the frontier.

Like many other Spanish officers of his generation, Pedro de Nava y Porlier had enjoyed a long and distinguished career but curiously had engaged in very little actual fighting. Born about 1741 to minor nobility in the Canary Islands, Nava was commissioned as an officer cadet at age twelve in the prestigious Regiment of Spanish Guards. After a brief three years and at the tender age of fifteen, he returned home to the Canary Islands and was appointed colonel of militia. By the time he turned twenty, Nava rejoined the regular army, securing a commission as captain in the Infantry Regiment of León. He participated briefly and seemingly unspectacularly in the Spanish invasion of Portugal in 1762 during the Seven Years' War. In 1773 Nava rose to captain of Grenadiers with a brevet of lieutenant colonel. At this rank he served with his regiment as part of the garrison of Puerto Rico for two years before returning to Spain. Four years later, he worked as an instructor at the Royal Military Academy in Avila. Finally, in 1781, superiors sent him to the Americas a second time, appointing him commandant of the Fixed Battalion of Caracas, Venezuela, in 1781, with a promotion to colonel. Nava's performance at this strategic post earned him recognition as a talented and effective administrator. In 1789 these traits led to his promotion to brigadier, and in March 1790, he rose to commandant general of the Western Interior Provinces of New Spain.[19]

In August 1790, Nava arrived in Mexico City and immediately began to prepare himself for his new duties. However, after a few days, Viceroy Revillagigedo informed him that the newly appointed eastern commander, Colonel Ramón de Castro, had been delayed in assuming his duties. Because Nava would be able to reach the northern frontier much sooner than Castro, the viceroy ordered Nava to conduct an inspection of both the eastern and western commands as his first major duty. Revillagigedo enjoined Nava to treat the Indians of the frontier, whether they were at war or peace, according to "the prudent dispositions of the late Condé de Gálvez." Foremost among these dispositions was the policy of making peace with the Apaches. Revillagigedo concluded that these policies were the best methods to force the Apaches "to lessen their hostility."[20]

As he began his tour, in October 1790, Nava noted that the Lipan Apaches were in a state of constant warfare. He knew that much of this animosity stemmed from Juan de Ugalde's determination not to grant them any quarter, declaring that the Apaches could not be trusted to keep their word and that they had broken numerous treaties before. While realizing that there was much truth in Ugalde's beliefs, Nava could not help but contrast the greatly different situation prevailing in the western Interior Provinces. There, under Nava's predecessor, Ugarte, the peace policy had been pursued longer and with greater consistency, with an overall reduction in Apache raiding throughout the area. For example, numerous groups of Chiricahuas lived outside several presidios in Nueva Vizcaya and Sonora. More recently, large numbers of Mescalero Apaches had settled outside Presidio del Norte, while others had congregated around the town of El Paso. Nava hoped that their example might be an inducement for their Lipan kinsmen in the east.

In February 1791, after several weeks of negotiations, Nava convinced a group of Lipans who had gathered outside the Villa de San Fernando in Coahuila to sign a peace treaty. Under the capitulaciones that Nava drew up, the Lipans agreed to surrender all of their captives, to remain in specified areas near Spanish presidios, and to aid the Spaniards in warfare. In exchange, Nava promised to provide them with goods, allow them to trade horses and mules with Spanish settlers, and most significantly to offer them protection from the dreaded Comanches. Nava also proclaimed one leader, José Antonio, as *caudillo principal,* or principal chief of the nation, who presided over a formal investiture.[21]

Despite this grandiloquent theater, Nava was trying to establish a precedent with the Lipans that many other Apache groups had already accepted. If even some Lipans could be brought under Spanish influence, they might prove invaluable, either in attracting others of their people to settle down, or failing that, assisting the Spaniards in tracking down and castigating the recalcitrant. This was the cynical but pragmatic course called for in the Instructions of 1786, which both Nava and Viceroy Revillagigedo adhered to, and which at the very least satisfied the legalistic strain of Spanish officialdom promoting an attempt at peace before declaring open war.

For proof that such an agreement might prove lasting, Nava had only to look to similar ones with the Mescaleros, who had recently congregated outside El Paso and Presidio del Norte. The reports of Lieutenant Governor Francisco de Uranga at El Paso and his superiors can provide insight into how the system actually functioned. After the arrival of the Mescaleros in July and August 1790, relations appeared quiescent. Then in early September, Apaches raided the Piro Indian settlement of Senecú, downriver from El Paso. When Uranga reported this to his superiors, they advised him to tell capitancillo Nzazen (who seems to have played a prominent role in these relationships both for good and ill) that he was expected to warn the Spaniards if he knew of such plans, not just remain neutral. Perhaps in response, soon thereafter several Mescaleros reportedly volunteered to seek out and attack the raiders in the hinterland.

Though such promises may have mollified Uranga, his trust in the Mescaleros was almost immediately put to the test. That same month, most or all of the Apaches left the area, much to the Spaniards' alarm. However, over the following weeks they gradually returned and it appears many had departed to hunt buffalo and gather mescal in their seasonal subsistence patterns, despite having received a substantial amount of rations from the Spaniards. This became a pattern that they would continue to follow and that the Spaniards grudgingly tolerated.[22]

Several months later, in February 1791, came Nzazen's turn to complain. He protested that two other Mescalero capitancillos, Francisco and Quencla, had been acting aggressively. Nzazen felt they were impinging on his authority and were plotting to murder him. Lieutenant Colonel Antonio Cordero, serving *ad interim* as Spanish commander in the area during Pedro de Nava's absence, replied that as both Francisco and Quencla were settled in peace and as they had not directly violated any of the regulations, there was nothing he could do. He feebly recommended that Nzazen settle the matter himself as best he could.

Also in February, reports claimed that Faraón Apaches, a branch of the Mescaleros living in the Robledo Mountains northwest of El Paso, had raided the region, kidnapping a young boy and stealing livestock. Cordero directed that the Mescalero de paz should inform the Indians in the Robledos that if they did not return the boy, Spanish soldiers and Apaches de paz would attack them. Cordero, true to his word, ordered Lieutenant Juan Francisco Granados of the Second Volante to prepare for a campaign against the Indians in the Robledos, declaring that they had disturbed Mescaleros from the Sacramento and Organ Mountains at the peace establishments. Whether Granados actually launched his expedition is unclear, but the military preparations seem to have had an effect. By March Cordero noted that the Faraónes around El Paso were quiescent.[23]

Such close proximity of the Mescaleros de paz with their kinsmen who remained outside the peace establishments proved an insurmountable problem. Independent Mescaleros were constantly mixing with the Mescalero de paz in hopes of obtaining supplies, while those at peace were also regularly moving into and out of their designated areas, sometimes with permission, sometimes not. Thus, the close interaction between Mescaleros at the peace establishments with those outside and the Spanish inability to control movements between them led to ever-increasing tension.

For example, in April 1791 Lieutenant Colonel Cordero received reports that the Mescalero capitancillo Mayá was responsible for a series of livestock thefts around El Paso. When Cordero ordered Lieutenant Governor Uranga to apprehend Mayá, Uranga responded that the capitancillo was actually away from the establishments and probably not responsible. The confusion may have stemmed from the inability of the Spaniards to distinguish the identity of individual Apaches and their tendency to give the same names to multiple persons. To prevent such occurrences, Cordero ordered that all Apaches should be identified by their proper names in their own language, not those bestowed by the Spaniards.

Tensions rose again in May when a vecino of El Paso killed a Mescalero de paz who was in the act of pilfering the man's horse. Capitancillo Iticha, who the Spaniards called Arrieta, and his ranchería were incensed at the killing, and rumors spread that they were instigating a revolt. However, tensions eased and the danger faded. Later that same month, another incident occurred when two more Apache leaders, identified as Squielnocten and Bucanneti, were accused of leading their people on a series of livestock raids. Cordero ordered a detachment of troops and several Mescalero de paz to pursue the culprits, but the results are unknown.[24]

Despite all these tensions, the overall behavior of the Mescaleros de paz near El Paso seems to have been generally acceptable in the Spaniards' view. Indeed, in the early summer of 1791, Uranga sent in a report that painted an almost idyllic portrait, writing: "The Apaches have not given us any trouble in this jurisdiction in all of the month of June. The Apaches at peace come and go happily to eat, returning to their rancherías on the other side of the river."

In the late fall, many of the Mescaleros dispersed in preparation for their buffalo hunt and to gather seasonal crops, but unlike the previous year, this time the Spaniards were able to track their movements. In September 1791, Uranga noted that capitancillo Francisco was in El Paso with twenty-five warriors, thirty women, and sixty children. However, in October Francisco declared he was going deer hunting in the Ojito de Samalayuca, but left many of his people behind. Whether or not this was an excuse to engage in some covert raiding, Francisco clearly took the precaution of preparing a plausible excuse for his absence. In similar fashion in September, the capitancillos Nzazen, Maselchindé, and Chimeslán relocated to the Sacramento Mountains northeast of El Paso, while reports placed Mayá in the Jornada del Muerto region, to the northwest. By October, the first three leaders remained in the Sacramentos, but no one knew the whereabouts of Mayá.[25]

Despite the fluctuations and inconsistencies that Lieutenant Governor Uranga reported from the Mescalero peace establishment at El Paso, Commandant General Pedro de Nava increasingly came to believe that the policy of concentrating Apaches in these settlements was the most effective method for curtailing their proclivities for raiding. In April 1791, after completing his inspection of the eastern provinces, Nava assumed personal command of the western provinces with his headquarters in Chihuahua. For several months, he carefully scrutinized the workings of the peace establishments. He had no doubt that many of the Apaches came into the establishments only when it suited them and that their acceptance of Spanish control was only for temporary expediencies. Nevertheless, the establishments had gone a long way in curbing the seemingly never-ending cycle of raid and counter-raid between Spaniards and Apaches.[26]

But if Nava was convinced he had reached an acceptable accommodation with the Apaches de paz in the west, his counterpart in the east would never achieve the same results. On April 14, 1791, Colonel Ramón de Castro arrived in Coahuila to assume command over the eastern interior provinces. Soon thereafter he met with Nava for a series of strategic talks concerning how to deal with the Apaches. Though Castro expressed reservations about their trustworthiness, he agreed with Nava that peace should be negotiated with any Apaches who requested it. Yet, if Castro was initially reluctant to treat with the Apaches, subsequent events soon drove him to regard the idea of peace with absolute and total disdain.

Later that month, at the Valle de Santa Rosa in Coahuila, Castro agreed to a parley with several Lipan leaders. However, on May 1, after only one capitancillo and a small retinue of followers arrived for the meeting, Castro ordered the headman and thirteen of his warriors seized as hostages until the remaining Lipan leaders came in to Santa Rosa. But that night the capitancillo and two warriors escaped from house arrest, and when an outraged Castro confronted the remaining Indians, they suddenly attacked. Eventually all the Apaches were slain, but not before they had killed two soldiers and wounded eight more, including Castro. Although his wounds were not serious, Castro emerged from this encounter furious, convinced more than ever that the Lipans were incapable of making peace and that they should be utterly exterminated.[27]

But as violence escalated, on August 17 Castro wrote to Viceroy Revilagigedo and pleaded for a reinforcement of four hundred men, stating that his forces were simply stretched too thin to handle all of the duties required. Revillagigedo dutifully summoned a *junta superior* (superior assembly) of the

Royal Treasury to examine Castro's request for more troopers, but it was a foregone conclusion that they would not agree to the enormous financial cost of the reinforcements.[28]

Though the recommendations of the junta clearly left Ramón de Castro unsatisfied, this latest round of complaints had a lasting impact on Viceroy Revillagigedo. Perhaps unjustly, the viceroy came to believe that the talents of Pedro de Nava were clearly more effective in dealing with the Apaches than those of Ramón de Castro. As such, Revillagigedo would now consistently advocate that Nava's policies, especially in regard to the peace establishments, be applied throughout the frontier.

With the viceroy's backing, Nava soon became convinced that he could forge a system at the peace establishments that would reduce the level of violence and induce the Apaches into a more regulated existence. What Nava failed to realize was that the Apaches themselves would seek other alternatives and attempt to manipulate the system to their own needs. In reality, both the Spaniards and the Apaches were performing an interrelated balancing act at the peace establishments, treading the fine line between a bad peace and a good war. Should unforeseen circumstances affect either of them, the whole system might collapse.

6

THREATS TO FRAGILE PEACE

PARIS, FRANCE, JANUARY 21, 1793—When the condemned man stepped from the carriage, the silence seemed profound despite the enormous number of people. The carriage had been escorted by 1,200 horsemen, and the route to the place of execution was filled with soldiers and armed citizens. More than thirty cannons had been placed around the perimeter of the city square, leaving a large opening for the elevated scaffold. Drummers had been stationed around the edge of the scaffold to drown out shouts or cries that might break out in support of the condemned. Three guards surrounded the prisoner while he removed his coat and neck stock and arranged his shirt collar. With a priest beside him, he then walked away from the carriage and slowly went up the steps of the scaffold. He protested when they first attempted to bind his hands, but then grudgingly acquiesced.

As the man approached the place of execution, he spoke out. Some say he forgave his executioners and prayed that his death would not be used against his country. Others maintained that he proclaimed his innocence. A mounted officer ordered the drums to beat, drowning out the man's words. A moment later the executioners strapped him to a plank and placed his head underneath the guillotine blade. The blade fell and in an instant severed the head completely. The priest who accompanied him later recalled: "The youngest of the guards, who seemed about eighteen, immediately seized the head, and showed it to the people as he walked round the scaffold; he accompanied this monstrous ceremony with the most atrocious and indecent gestures. At first an awful silence prevailed; at length some cries of 'Vive la République!' were heard. By degrees the voices multiplied and in less than ten minutes this cry, a thousand times repeated became the universal shout of the multitude, and every hat was in the air."

So it was that Louis XVI, King of France, was executed at 10:22 in the morning by his own people. This act marked another milestone in the French Revolution, one that would serve to plunge the nation ever deeper into war with almost every major European power. Among those would be Spain, whose king, Charles IV, was a cousin of Louis XVI. Charles had endeavored to save his doomed relative. For making that attempt, the revolution's zealots would declare war on Spain and set loose a chain of events that would inevitably lead to the Spanish empire's destruction. Along this tortuous path, the outbreak of this war would determine a policy shift half a world away. Pressed for funds in the wake of war, the Spanish government would be forced to make draconian budget adjustments that would cause disruptions among the peace establishments set up to help contain the Mescaleros and other Apaches. Combined with increased military activity and recurring drought, these adjustments would cause profound stress among the peace establishments, stretching resources to the breaking point.¹

The Mescaleros de paz along the northern frontier of New Spain were oblivious to the deaths of kings and the struggles of republics in faraway Europe. To them the new order they had accepted at the peace establishments outside El Paso and Presidio del Norte was destined to last for the foreseeable future. Indeed, for the first few years the stability of the establishments looked so promising that Spanish officers concluded that a general peace had descended along much of the Interior Provinces. Despite scattered irruptions of low-level violence and thievery, the peace policy adopted by Pedro de Nava appeared to have been successful.

However, in the eastern Interior Provinces, Commandant General Ramón de Castro struggled to control the Lipan Apaches. Between November 1791 and March 1792, Spanish officials in the provinces of Coahuila, Texas, Nuevo León, and Nuevo Santander detailed a total of thirty-five separate Apache attacks with eighteen people murdered, six wounded, and numerous horses, mules, and cattle stolen or destroyed. As if these losses were not bad enough,

Castro's officers reported that the Lipans were receiving muskets, powder, and ammunition from the Mescaleros de paz settled outside El Paso and del Norte, and that many Mescaleros were riding with the Lipans on their raids. After Castro complained to Viceroy Revillagigedo about these reports, the viceroy ordered Pedro de Nava to determine the truth.[2]

Nava again called on Lieutenant Colonel Antonio Cordero to utilize his unique knowledge and skills to investigate the allegations. On June 23, 1792, Cordero arrived at Presidio del Norte to conduct his inquiry. He had designated Lieutenant Blas de Aramburu from the Presidio del Príncipe as his secretary. Together, they drew up a series of questions that they would put to the soldiers and civilians at the post, all of which revolved around the Mescalero de paz and their actions.

Cordero and Aramburu first asked about the particulars of the Indians at the peace establishments, including the names of their capitancillos, how many members were in each ranchería, if anyone knew if they had ever attacked the eastern provinces, "and if they returned with animals, clothing or other goods of unknown origin, or with animals with unknown brands and if they had traded or sold any of these to the inhabitants of the area." Next, they asked if the Mescaleros de paz "had been given in this Presidio firearms, lead, and balls in exchange for animals, or other goods that they had robbed from the Provinces in the East." Additionally, Cordero and Aramburu would determine if there was actually "a Tailor or other vecinos who had been the intermediary with the Apaches."[3]

Finally, the two asked about the identity the rancherías of other Mescaleros outside the peace establishments "in the vast terrain on this Frontier and those of the adjacent Provinces," and whether or not the natives would request peace or remain hostile. Cordero and Aramburu wanted to know if any Lipan Apaches had come in to request peace or to trade goods, and they were particularly interested in whether or not "the Lipillan Captain known on the eastern frontier as Picax-andé-Ynstinclé de Ugalde, and commonly called El Calvo in this Province had come any or several times to solicit peace."[4]

Over the course of the next eight days, the two officers interviewed a total of eleven witnesses, including two commissioned officers, two sergeants, two cavos, two soldados of the garrison, and three vecinos living at the presidio. Whether the witnesses uniformly told the truth or whether they had been allowed to consult with each other about the questions, the men had clearly gotten their stories straight because their testimony was remarkably similar.[5]

The majority of witnesses maintained that it had been almost two years since the Mescaleros had come into the peace establishments. They also listed the rancherías of Volante, Alegre, Joseph, Bigotes el Bermejo, Montera Blanca, Dayél, and Esquin-yoé as those that were resident, estimating their numbers at about two hundred warriors with their families. Most noted that there was one capitancillo named Cuerno Verde who had initially come into the establishment, but since then had been gone on many occasions. Some suspected he had raided the eastern provinces. Lieutenant Joaquin Peru, who was on detached duty from the Presidio of Janos, reported that evidence of Cuerno Verde's raiding in the east "was proven by some mules from Mapimí that the Lieutenant Dn Ventura Moreno took from the expressed capitan." However, Peru noted that other Mescalero de paz had helped recover the stolen stock, testifying "it had not been much time since with troops from this Presidio and twelve Mescalero auxiliaries went out and got them in view of said robbery."[6]

As to the Mescaleros being given arms and munitions, all the witnesses were adamant that this had occurred only under a single circumstance, namely when the Indians were going out on campaign in support of Spanish operations. Alférez Nicolás Villaroel served as the quartermaster for Presidio del Norte and "had under his care the Arms and Munitions of the Reserve." Villaroel swore that he knew "that only when the Apache friends are employed in union with our troops, are they supplied with firearms and munitions, which are recovered after they are concluded with an individual account and voucher, and that at no time lacked anything." Sergeant Felix Colomo backed up this view, saying "at no time have the Indians been given firearms, powder or balls in this Presidio over which point there have been given very strict orders and they have been observed inviolably." Cavo Saturnino Rodriguez agreed, saying that it had been made clear that there would be "severe punishment to the soldados or vecinos if they gave as much as one cartridge" to the Mescaleros.[7]

Regarding rumors that "a tailor" at Presidio del Norte had been involved in supplying guns and other illegal trade items, the witnesses offered an explanation. A carpenter named Manuel Marquez readily admitted that he had traded with the Mescaleros for "about fifty mules . . . for which he gave the Indians clothes from his own possession, effects, and horses of the same." All of the mules Marquez acquired had been branded but none of the brands were recognized by the presidio residents. Though it was illegal to trade in branded stock, Spaniards in other areas may have bartered the mules to the Mescaleros surreptitiously, or they may have been stolen, or they may have been branded by the Mescaleros themselves. But as no one could say exactly where the mules came from, Marquez felt free to acquire them. Marquez then had taken the drove of fifty mules, along with another thirty that other vecinos at Presidio del Norte had acquired, and sold all eighty head in Chihuahua. In addition, Lieutenant Alberto Maynez of the presidio had also traded for another thirty-four mules. However, far from being remorseful, Marquez firmly maintained that the trade in mules was permitted, because it had occurred at the very beginning of the peace with the Mescaleros in 1790. That Marquez was correct was obvious to all, as even Lieutenant Colonel Cordero's original questions stated that prohibited trading with the Indians "was not to include the animals they [the Mescaleros] had when the peace was first conceded by Field Marshal Jacobo Ugarte y Loyola by order of 8 June 1790 until the 19 of August of '91 when the order ... by Señor Brigadier Dn Pedro de Nava ... permitting only the exchange of animals that were ownerless or without brands."[8]

When authorities asked the witnesses whether the Lipan or other Apaches had approached the establishments, especially the chieftain Picax-andé, a general sense of uncertainty prevailed. All agreed that some Lipans under a capitancillo named Pino Blanco had visited once or twice and that Picax-andé was with them. Alférez Villaroel provided the most specificity, reporting that "last April the Lipan Captain Pino Blanco came with eleven of his to request peace, and three of these went to Chihuahua to treat with the Commandant General and that they left their rancherías on the Rio Colorado where they moved many of them to the Peña Blanca distant thirty leagues northeast of this Presidio." As for Picax-andé, the alférez recalled, "He has seen the Lipillan Captain known as El Calvo no more than two days in company with Pino Blanco."[9]

Having concluded his interrogations at Presidio del Norte, Cordero rode upriver to El Paso, where he continued his second round of investigations, beginning on July 12, 1792. As he had done at del Norte, he and Lieutenant Aramburu summoned nine witnesses, including three militia officers, one soldado interpreter, three civilian officials, an official from the Piro Indian pueblo of Senecú, and one of the oldest living vecinos of El Paso.[10]

As the questioning began, the witnesses confirmed the identities of the Mescaleros established at peace in the region. There were five principal rancherías under the capitancillos Nzazen, Maselchindé, Mayá, Chimeslán, and Francisco. These leaders together commanded between one hundred and two hundred warriors and had been living in the region for two years. None of those interviewed ever reported having seen Picax-andé, known to them as El Calvo, or any other Lipans at the establishments.

Regarding whether or not the Mescaleros had surreptitiously obtained weapons, the militia captain, Francisco Xavier Bernal, declared "there has never been given to the Apaches de Paz in these Pueblos, not by gift, nor by exchange, firearms, powder, or ball." Bernal's assertions were backed up by Francisco del Barrio, who served as the *Administrador de la Renta de Tabacos, Naipes, y Polvora* (Administrator for the Tax on Tobacco, Playing Cards and Gunpowder) at El Paso. In this position, Barrio oversaw those items on which the Spanish Crown exercised a commercial monopoly. He stated categorically, "There has never been given nor exchanged with the Indians that treated for peace in these Pueblos not even a grain of powder nor any munitions of war." Barrio was absolutely certain of this, because he personally oversaw the distribution of gunpowder for all purposes. Furthermore, he declared that in the two years he had served in his position, "there had not arrived for distribution more than one arroba [twenty-five pounds] . . . for the population of this district."[11]

The witnesses were next asked about other types of illicit commerce, especially horses and mules stolen from the eastern provinces. Militia captain Bernal replied, "They never traded for animals from this or other provinces, with the exception of when they [the Mescaleros] first came under the peace, that they sold some branded animals, but that this ceased immediately after the order from the Commandant General arrived." Joseph Manuel Telles, one of the oldest vecinos in El Paso, corroborated this, testifying that the citizenry did trade some mules for horses, blankets, and oxen at the beginning of the peace but stopped thereafter.[12]

When asked whether or not the Mescaleros de paz had engaged in raiding, witnesses generally conceded that some had at a low level, but that they were often restrained by their leaders. Captain of Militia Bernal stated, "The Apaches' *capitanes* or *principales* and in general all of the Apaches in these lands are known as friends and proceed in good faith; nevertheless some one or another of them are of a bad inclination and have committed some small robberies." However, when this occurred, the rest of the Mescaleros de paz forced the culprit "to escape and flee in order to evade from the good ones their punishments and they take back the theft, as has happened many times." Vecino Joseph Manuel Telles agreed, saying that there had been some robberies of animals, but he felt it was "by those who do not recognize a Captain; but in general the peace was good and was always much more if the Apaches supplied Troops for the detachments." Perhaps the relationship between the Spaniards and Mescaleros was best summed up by Francisco Balizan, the *alcalde de aguas* (water or irrigation judge) of the villa and one of the oldest vecinos of El Paso, when he testified, "There have been some bad among them just as there likewise have been among us the same."[13]

Having completed his interviews, Cordero felt compelled to prove that the Mescaleros de paz were not serving as a conduit for illegally traded weapons. On July 17 he issued an order to Lieutenant Governor Franciso de Uranga to report on all the firearms and munitions present. The following day, Uranga presented a scrupulously detailed account of all the weapons, gunpowder, and ammunition received and distributed throughout the jurisdiction of El Paso for the previous four years.[14]

Two days later, Cordero officially concluded his investigations. In his written report to Commandant General Pedro de Nava, Cordero first addressed the allegations that there had been illegal arms trafficking with the Mescaleros. He stated flatly, "There is no necessity to apply any remedy to suspend the abuse of the supposed supplying of arms and munitions to the Indians as there have not been any." He went on to say that there had indeed been an exchange of animals and goods, but that it had only occurred when the Mescaleros had first entered into negotiations at the peace establishments in mid-1790. After August 19, 1791, when Nava himself had ordered the trading to cease, the Indians had complied, "with the only exception being the animals that the Indians had and wanted to sell that had no earmarks or brands."

In assessing the peace establishments, Cordero wrote with an almost sappy idealism: "The Mescalero Indians that have been brought to peace in el Norte . . . look with respect to that Presidio and show love and gratefulness to its Inhabitants, and they manage in that Post with the greatest harmony and in general, they observe scrupulously good faith with the rest of the Spaniards." Still, Cordero realized that there were tensions, which he ascribed to the natural inconstancy and inherent violence among the Apaches. "The insubordination that reigns among this class of People," he wrote, "that when the occasion is put into their hands, by reason of the vast and deserted terrain . . . there are some that separate themselves from the rest under the pretext of hunting or some other similar [reasons], they enter in to commit robberies and attacks, not only in the interior of the Province of [Nueva] Vizcaya but also some in the interior of those in the East; but this goes on infrequently and it is hidden from the Spaniards of Presidio del Norte."[15]

Whether Cordero's assessment that the Mescalero peace establishments were essentially stable was accurate or not, Spanish officials feared to upset the balance and were determined to avoid any disturbances from the outside. For many officials, just such a threat seemed to come from the Apache leader Picax-andé. The actual tribal affiliation of this leader was the cause of great confusion. He had been identified by various officials as being a Lipiyan, Llanero, Lipan, and Mescalero. However, some modern historians claim that the Lipiyan or Llanero were in fact an amalgam of dislocated Lipan, Mescalero, and Natagé families that had coalesced around a single strong leader in the face of unrelenting Comanche pressure. Whatever his true nature, the Spaniards had come to regarded Picax-andé with suspicion.[16]

Soon after Antonio Cordero completed his investigations of the Mescalero peace establishments, Spanish misgivings about Picax-andé (still called El Calvo in the west) and his influence over the Lipans came to the fore. In July 1792, a large group of Lipans again approached Presidio del Norte requesting peace. The Spaniards recorded that they were led by "capitancillo Chu-ul-y-cué known among us by the names of Pino Blanco and Moreno, bringing in his company many Indians." When Commandant General Nava received this information, he informed the Lipans that because their homelands were farther east from Presidio del Norte, they would have to settle down at presidios in that region. As such, he would pass on the Lipans' request to the eastern commander, Ramón de Castro. But Castro remained adamant that the Lipans could not be trusted and was against making peace. While the Spanish commanders wrangled, the Lipans impatiently waited several months for an answer. Finally, in late September, with no resolution in sight, they departed Presidio del Norte in anger and disgust. As Nava later reported, "As they retired they treacherously killed two men and one woman of the Mescaleros, who had given us constant proof that, although barbarous, that they preferred our friendship to that of those Indians, their relatives."[17]

Spanish officials blamed the murders of the Mescalero de paz and the continued hostilities of the Lipans on Picax-andé. In October 1792 Captain Domingo Díaz, the commander at Presidio del Norte, wrote privately to Commandant General Nava conveying his concerns: "Increasing in me every day are the misgivings about the close union of these three Nations, Mescalero, Lipan and Llanero, which compose a considerable number of Indians in arms, and all obedient to the pernicious influences of the Llanero Capitancilllo El Calvo; and considering that . . . we should expect dire results over the frontiers." Specifically, Díaz warned, "If there arrived to settle in peace at this Post the Lipans . . . [because of] El Calvo and his evil spirits . . . the Lipans would not remain quiet, due to the influence of this Caudillo." Díaz feared that if this happened, the Mescaleros de paz would in turn join the Lipans and rebel.[18]

On October 9, Captain Díaz called together the Mescalero leaders Volante, Alegre, and Joseph. They had just returned from their seasonal buffalo hunt, in which they had been joined by Picax-andé and a considerable number of Lipans. Díaz communicated to the Mescalero leaders his fears about the influence of Picax-andé over the Lipans, and that some Mescaleros de paz might succumb as well. The captain reported, "These and other words they listened to in silence, and then at the end they rose up and took their leave, telling me that they would repair it in the same manner as I would find to my liking." However, Díaz claimed he was unprepared for what happened next. "The next day," he wrote, "they put to death in view of the people of this Post, two Lipans and their families that were from the ranchería of capitancillo Pino Blanco, and that had stayed a few days in that of José." Díaz claimed complete ignorance of the act and stated that "once I became aware of it, I reprehended them quite severely with respect to their having killed those Indians in cold blood." But the Mescaleros had a ready excuse for Díaz: "They answered me that as they were sorcerers, and as . . . they would bewitch us, they were put to death." The Mescaleros then asserted that the same supernatural force was present in Picax-andé, and assured Díaz that they would kill him too if he returned to the area.[19]

Despite his protestations of innocence, it seems improbable that Captain Díaz did not expect some reaction among the Mescaleros de paz after he had harangued them about the influence of Picax-andé. From the available evidence, it is difficult to determine if this incident was a piece of calculated treachery on the part of the Mescaleros to curry favor with the Spaniards and as vengeance for their three tribal members murdered by those Lipans seeking peace several weeks earlier, or if the Spaniards themselves had tacitly encouraged these actions and then sought to justify them. Regardless, with the murders of these Lipans, whether orchestrated by the Spaniards or initiated by the Mescaleros, the result was the same. A breach had opened between the two Apache peoples, and the Spaniards realized they could use that breach to their advantage. Soon thereafter, the Mescaleros de paz began to serve regularly with Spanish search-and-destroy expeditions launched against the Lipans.

While the Spaniards sought to control outsider influence on the Mescaleros in the peace establishments, directives from Europe once again influenced events on the northern frontier. In November 1792, King Charles IV of Spain ordered that the Interior Provinces should again become independent of the viceroy and placed under a single commandant general. These changes were ordered as a result of the Spanish crown making preparations for war with revolutionary France. In April 1792, France had declared war on Austria and Prussia after these two powers threatened to intervene to restore the absolutist rights of King Louis XVI. In August, an insurrection broke out in Paris that resulted in the arrest of Louis and his family, abolished the monarchy, and declared France a republic. Warfare escalated dramatically, and the new French government pledged its determination to eliminate all vestiges of monarchy throughout Europe.[20]

Correctly sensing that war was inevitable, the Spanish government began to gather its resources and realign its military forces. In the Viceroyalty of New Spain, officials considered the coastal regions particularly vulnerable to foreign attack. As a result, the Californias in the west and Nuevo Santander (and neighboring Nuevo León) in the east came under direct control of the viceroy, whom Spain felt had the military resources to respond more decisively and rapidly than the commandant general of the Interior Provinces. The latter officer would now deal with any foreign threat that might arise via the former French colonies of Louisiana and Canada directed against Texas, New Mexico, or other areas of the northern frontier. Despite this diminution of his authority, Viceroy Revillagigedo gave genuine if reluctant support to this rearrangement, and concurred with the appointment of Pedro de Nava as the sole Commandant General of the Interior Provinces.[21]

By April 1793, Nava had reorganized the newly independent Interior Provinces under his sole authority. Yet despite the specter of European wars and foreign threats, he continued to focus most of his efforts on dealing with the Apaches. One of the first measures he initiated was an attempt to extend the peace establishments that he believed so successful into the eastern provinces, according to the same dictates he had employed in the west. That same month, a substantial group of Lipans approached the villa of San Fernando in Coahuila asking for peace under the same terms given to the Mescaleros outside Presidio del Norte. Nava agreed to this proposal in the belief that a peace treaty with the Lipans pointed to a gradual acceptance by the Apaches of a new order throughout the frontier.[22]

Yet despite the increased numbers of Apaches de paz associated with the peace establishments during the years 1793 and 1794, many of these Indians grew increasingly dissatisfied with their new regulated lifestyles, especially when the Spaniards began to unilaterally alter the conditions. For example, on February 1, 1793, Commandant General Pedro de Nava issued an order that from this point on, rations were to be dispensed to the Mescaleros de paz of the El Paso and San Elizario jurisdictions only at the latter presidio. While ostensibly designed to increase efficiency and reduce costs, the new directive placed an added burden on many of the Mescaleros, forcing them to travel a considerable distance to obtain their sustenance.[23]

Similar constrictions apparently occurred among other Apaches de paz. In October 1793, Governor of New Mexico Fernando de la Concha resigned his office, owing to a recurrent illness. Since 1791 Concha had shepherded the development of a peace establishment for several hundred Gileño and Mimbreño Apaches at Sabinal, a site located between the Spanish villas of Albuquerque and El Paso near present-day Belen, New Mexico. Despite considerable effort and cost and the apparent success of the establishment, Concha's accomplishments were undermined after his departure. His successor, Fernando de Chacón, regarded the establishment at Sabinal as too costly, and throughout 1794 apparently began to restrict support, especially rations at the establishment, to the point that most of the Apaches left the reservation by the end of the year.[24]

Whether because of a real or perceived diminution of food and gifts, vacillations and mistakes in Spanish policies, or simply the restraints now placed on their cultural inclinations, Apache dissatisfaction with the general operation of the peace establishments during this period began to increase noticeably, and this in turn led to larger and larger Spanish retaliatory expeditions. All of these circumstances undoubtedly contributed to a rise in suspicion and mistrust between the Spaniards and the Apaches.[25]

For the Mescaleros de paz living outside El Paso, Presidio San Elizario, and Presidio del Norte, the changing nature of their conditions reflected these increasing tensions. Perhaps as a result of Nava's 1793 order that all rations

Organ Mountains, New Mexico, by John Russell Bartlett, 1852.
Courtesy of the John Carter Brown Library at Brown University, John Russell Bartlett Collection.

were to be distributed only at San Elizario, many of the Mescaleros de paz had shifted their encampments, and by early 1794 were ensconced in mountains beyond the frontier. Some rancherías were living in the Organ Mountains, some forty miles north of El Paso, while others were located to the northeast in the Sacramento, the Guadalupe, and the Hueco Mountains. The capitancillos Joseph, Volante, and Alegre, associated with Presidio del Norte, were also living north of the Rio Grande, often in close proximity to their compatriots out of San Elizario. Unfortunately, because of these relocations, these Mescaleros de paz often found themselves caught up in Spanish campaigns ostensibly directed against hostile Apaches living in the same regions.

    A prime example occurred in January and February 1794. Lieutenant Dionisio Valles from the Presidio of Janos set out with 170 men, including twenty-four Chiricahua Apache auxiliaries, "to batter the lands of the Enemy." These most likely were the mountain ranges between the Mimbres River and the Rio Grande to the northwest of El Paso, in what is now southwestern New Mexico. Over the course of six weeks, Valles's men "succeeded in killing 12 Indians of both sexes and making 58 Prisoners of War." Whether any of these unfortunates were Mescaleros or not, Valles's campaign clearly rattled all of the Apaches in the region.²⁶ Commandant General Pedro de Nava recorded that as a result of this action, "there approached to the Presidio of San Eleazario to solicit peace a large number of Indians from the Sierras Blanca, Oscuro, Sacramento, Organos and others from that direction." The commander at San Elizario, Manuel Vidal de Lorca, opened peace talks with these Mescaleros and laid out "the just conditions that would be conceded." Foremost among these was determining the areas where they were to locate their rancherías. Reflecting Commandant General Nava's previous order that rations were only to be issued at Presidio San Elizario, Spaniards directed the Mescaleros to camp only in specifically designated locations, so that the Spanish could distinguish them as "peaceful."²⁷

However, before completing these negotiations, a number of these Mescaleros "returned to their country furtively, showing by this the little sincerity with which they went under peace." Captain Vidal de Lorca responded by launching a pursuit against those who had left. On February 26, he located some of them in the Cerro del Aire (in the modern Cornuda Mountains northeast of El Paso), where he "succeeded in killing two Gandules, capturing three women and a muchacho and taking [back] a captive and 28 beasts."²⁸

Stung by this attack, the capitancillos Nzazen, Mayá, and Maselchindé, who were considered Mescaleros de paz, withdrew from across the Rio Grande at El Paso northwest into the Organ Mountains. At about this same time, rustlers stole some twenty animals from the pueblo of Ysleta near El Paso, and the recently departed Mescaleros were suspected. Hoping to retrieve the stolen stock, Captain Vidal de Lorca set out with a hundred men and headed into the Organs. On March 15, 1794, the captain decided to personally lead an advanced guard into the mountains on a reconnaissance. But the Mescaleros had been watching closely and ambushed him. Commandant General Pedro de Nava succinctly summed up the result of Vidal de Lorca's last campaign: "He was beaten by the Enemy on account of their numbers and the advantageous terrain, and they killed that officer, a sergeant, another nine troopers, and four vecinos; they wounded and carried off the Alférez Dn Antonio Arce, whose exchange the same Indians proposed and this is already verified, and in addition there also came out as well ten men wounded including one of the Apache auxiliaries."²⁹

Alférez Antonio Arce was Vidal de Lorca's second in command in this campaign, and with his capture, the Spaniards ignominiously retreated to

San Elizario. As they left the mountains, they came across a small group of Mescaleros, and venting their anger and frustration, "the sergeant commandant of the train killed two Indians and three women that he encountered on his return, and imprisoned another one." Whether or not these unfortunates had anything to do with the Spanish defeat was not recorded. Within a few days, the Mescaleros returned Alférez Arce and agreed to cease hostilities and resume peaceful relations. Nevertheless, the incident indicated that at least some of the Mescaleros, even those nominally at peace, believed that the stark brutality of open war was increasingly coming to the fore.[30]

Feeling that Spanish policy demanded a retribution for this insult, in early June 1794, Commandant General Nava sent out a punitive expedition under the command of Captain Joseph Manuel Carrasco of the Presidio of Carrizal and Captain Manuel Rengel of the Presidio of Janos, "in order to punish the Indians that beat the party commanded by Don Manuel Vidal in the Sierra de los Organos." However, Carrasco and Rengel seem to have launched their expedition over a much wider area, crossing the Rio Grande near San Elizario and sweeping northeast into the Sierra de Guadalupes and beyond toward the Pecos River. By the end of the month, in two separate attacks their forces "killed three Indians and a woman and made seventy-nine prisoners of both sexes including six gandules and men at arms; secondly they killed one and made prisoner twelve persons. " However, after passing an area of *arenales* (sand pits) and mountains, they discovered that "the Comanches from the area of New Mexico had attacked the Apache Llaneros and other tribes that inhabited them and against whom . . . they made considerable destruction in their Rancherías, according to the cadavers they found, and carried off many captives according to the prisoners."[31]

Despite this success, Commandant General Nava felt that the expedition had not punished its initial target. He, therefore, ordered Captain Rengel "to continue to operate against the Apaches that beat the party of Captain Dn Manuel Vidal and killed that officer to the end that, after they had been punished, they would solicit peace with greater disposition and conserve that which had been conceded to them and which they broke." As so often had happened in the past, fear of the Comanches soon compelled the Apaches to seek succor with the Spaniards. After several more weeks campaigning in the regions around the Organ Mountains, Captain Rengel reported that he had succeeded in "putting under peace . . . the Capitancillos Barrios [Nzazen] and Mayá with their numerous Rancherías." For his part Nava still did not trust these Mescalero capitancillos, and he instructed Rengel to determine if the Mescaleros "really want to live in peace without causing damages." If they did not give assurances of "a permanent peace," then Nava threatened that "they may return to their nations, where I shall persecute them continuously until they surrender or I finish them all."[32]

The continuous strikes and counterstrikes that both Spaniards and Mescaleros endured during the first half of 1794 continued to play out for the remainder of the year. In July and August Captain Rengel led another attack into the Guadalupe Mountains, killing two Mescalero men and one woman and seizing seventeen prisoners. A smaller Spanish force out of Presidio del Norte "attacked the Mescalero capitancillo Cuernoverde who had made attacks with his band; they succeeded in taking prisoner two women and a *muchacho* [boy], and restoring a Spanish captive that they had carried off from the Presidio del Príncipe." Seemingly undeterred, on August 21 Mescaleros stole eighteen cattle near the same presidio and then fled northward with their booty across the Rio Grande. However, as Nava recorded, they "were followed by the Captain Dn Joseph Tovar with a party of Troops who succeeded in recovering fifteen [horses] in the cordillera of the Sierra de Guadalupe, and taking prisoner six women and muchachos, having put to precipitous flight the gandules as they saw the Party from a long distance." In yet another incident, "a detachment from the Presidio del Norte under the orders of Lieutenant Dn Blas de Aramburu made prisoner on the 1st and 3rd of September a Mescalero Apache, two women and a muchacho who had gone about causing harm."[33]

Taking these and other incidents together, a clear pattern emerged wherein the Spaniards were responding to relatively low-intensity Apache raids with what one could view as disproportionate force. For example, in June a Spanish force of more than three hundred troopers, militia, and Pueblo Indian allies from Santa Fe, swept down from the north into the Sierra Blanca and Sacramento Mountains. Although they failed to engage the Mescaleros, their reconnaissance was clearly intimidating. In September a one-hundred-man detachment under Alférez Dn Cayetano Limón moved north of the Rio Grande into the same region, where they put to flight a large ranchería, although one of the troopers was slain. Then, in November, another Spanish expedition of eighty-six men from Presidios del Norte and Príncipe headed eastward, where they killed four more Apache men and one woman and captured fifty-four horses. Finally, two more expeditions out of Santa Fe during November and December launched attacks into the mountains east of the Rio Grande near the Jornada del Muerto, where they "succeeded in killing twelve, making two prisoner, and taking six horses and various other spoils."[34]

The overwhelming use of force by the Spaniards against the Apaches during this period was demonstrated not only by the number and size of the search and destroy expeditions sent out against those not registered at the peace establishments, but also by the policy of deporting captured Apaches to central Mexico and Cuba. The Spaniards utilized this practice as a means of applied terror, designed to compel the Apaches to accept Spanish control, especially regarding those Apaches de paz who joined the peace establishments. As a result, practically all of the Mescaleros captured during the many fights between 1793 and 1795 were immediately deported in *colleras*, to Veracruz and Havana, Cuba.[35]

For the Mescaleros, the seemingly disproportionate use of force and their inability to redeem any of their captured tribal members may have made it seem there was little difference between being at peace or war with the Spaniards. But even for those hoping that the peace establishments still offered them some benefits, that hope soon diminished even more as a result of events that unfolded half a world away.

On March 7, 1793, less than three months after the execution of King Louis XVI, the French Republic declared war on Spain. The Spanish king, Charles IV, had pressured his government ministers to try and save his cousin Louis and the French monarchy, despite the opposition of many of Charles's advisors to remain neutral. But the increasing radicalism of the French government soon made these disagreements moot, as the French zealously declared war on almost all the major European powers.

Faced with the inevitable, the Spaniards girded for war with a nation that had been their major ally for almost a century. In what came to be called the War of the Pyrenees, the Spaniards enjoyed some initial success and occupied portions of southeastern France. But the French eventually counterattacked in overwhelming numbers and launched their own invasion of northern Spain. In the midst of these seesaw campaigns, the Spanish government found its finances woefully inadequate and desperately sought to increase revenues. One of its primary resources was the remittances of silver from Mexico, and as the war progressed, the demand for silver rose dramatically. Viceroy Revillagigedo responded by increasing the amount of silver coins he dispatched to protect

Spain's empire. For the year 1793, Revillagigedo found the ingenuity to send more than ten million silver pesos of remittances directly to Spain, along with another five million to support the Spanish military establishments in Cuba, Puerto Rico, and other strategic Caribbean posts. The total exceeding fifteen million pesos sent out from Mexico almost doubled the amount from the previous year. But to meet this demand, Revillagigedo found it necessary to dramatically increase taxes, take out loans, and transfer funds from other governmental agencies into the central treasury. Many bureaucratic agencies were forced to cut costs wherever possible and to drastically reduce their overall budgets.[36]

In the Interior Provinces, cost cutting as a result of the war effort also became increasingly urgent. Although technically independent of Viceroy Revillagigedo, Commandant General Nava was in reality quite dependent on the viceroy in several key financial areas. Thus, the fiscal restraints emanating from Mexico City had a substantial ripple effect in the Interior Provinces. Among these it seems that the peace establishments for the Mescalero de paz and other Apaches were identified as a ready source of revenue.

As a result, in October 1794 Nava issued directives that sought to restrict the monthly food rations previously distributed to the Apaches. To accomplish this, Nava now required that the Apaches would no longer be permitted to live near Spanish presidios but instead relocate into designated areas approximately thirty leagues beyond the presidios, where they could live off the land. Only those Apaches with special permits from the presidial commanders would be allowed to collect rations or trade for goods on a weekly basis. The Spaniards would consider hostile those Apaches found without permits or who established their rancherías within the thirty-league limit.

Though these new limitations may have been useful in easing the burden on the imperial treasury, they would prove increasingly onerous to the Apaches. Indeed, for the Mescaleros de paz settled outside El Paso, San Elizario, and Presidio del Norte, the very notion of remaining at peace with the Spaniards appeared foolish. Some, perhaps many, began to call for a return to the old ways of taking what they needed if they could no longer trust the white man to give it.[37]

7

SPARKING THE FIRE

Santa Cruz de Tarahumaras, July 25, 1795—The Mescalero raiders would have been able to see the town's mission church even from a great distance. Set on a high bluff, the impressive structure of Mission Santa Cruz de Tarahumaras marked out the surrounding settlements along the Rio de Balleza's banks. Meandering north for several miles, the river irrigated an impressive number of cultivated fields and pastures dotted with farms and ranches, before emptying into the larger Río Conchos. The raiders had covered more than 250 miles from the time they had crossed the Rio Grande from their homelands and headed south. Whether they stuck to the mountains of the Sierra Madre or ventured farther east along the course of the Río Conchos is unknown, but all the while they had moved stealthily, avoiding contact with any inhabitants. When they finally reached the environs of the town, they located what they had come for. The Rancho Santa Cruz was but a short distance from its namesake mission; the small pueblo of San Nicolás de la Hoya lay several miles downstream. From both settlements, the Mescaleros were able to drive off a total of twenty horses.[1]

At first it appeared that the raiders had not drawn too much attention to themselves, and they cleared the immediate area heading back the way they had come. That they should have been able to move their stolen stock unmolested was not unusual. For decades, this area had been a hub for the raising of livestock by both the native Tarahumara Indians and the ever-increasing number of Spaniards, mestizos, and other mixed-race populations. Indeed, the nature of the terrain had proven so favorable that it had supported a vast interconnected web of cattle thieves and rustlers, who moved stolen stock along the various streams and rivers that flowed out of the Sierra Madre Mountains.

These *abigeos,* or rustlers, were often a mixed lot. Some were disaffected or rebellious Tarahumara Indians seeking to break out of the political, social, and cultural restraints imposed by the Spanish authorities. Others were Spaniards and mestizos from the surrounding areas who controlled an illegal subterranean economy that seasonally drove large numbers of animals between regional markets, where they were sold to willing accomplices. Others were simply outlaws.

Regardless of their origins, the abigeos all had some things in common, not the least of which was their willingness to use and be used by the Apaches. From about 1750 the network of rustlers had plied their trade throughout the province of Nueva Vizcaya. Sometimes they had formed covert alliances with Apache raiders—Chiricahuas, Mescaleros, and Lipans—in stealing and moving their stolen herds. At other times they would conveniently cast blame for their own thefts on these same Apaches, diverting the authorities' attention. For their own part, the Apaches were just as content to manipulate the abigeos, trading horses and cattle for other goods. Over time the Apaches came to regard the area as a prime location for raiding.[2]

Whether these Mescalero raiders had any assistance from the clandestine network of rustlers is unknown, but they appear not to have been pursued by any of the locals. Nevertheless, at some point they split into two smaller groups, one of four and one of six men, in hopes of increasing their chances of escape. For some period of time the tactic worked, but as they moved north, two large groups of Spanish troopers from the Villa de Chihuahua and from Presidio San Carlos set out to hunt down the Apaches. Now fully aware they were being pursued, the one group of four raiders headed farther west and succeeded in eluding their pursuers at the Paraje de Bachíniva, about ninety miles west of Chihuahua, while the other group appears to have moved farther to the east. At some point one or both parties turned loose eleven of the stolen horses in hopes the trailing soldiers would be satisfied to take the animals back and give up the chase. But the soldiers were persistent and continued the pursuit. Nevertheless, both groups of Mescaleros doggedly maintained a general course to the north, heading for the Rio Grande, and home. Once arrived, they would show that they had achieved some success in the raid, and perhaps convince others to follow their example. But many had already been convinced.[3]

By the early months of 1795 a growing number of the Mescaleos de paz outside Presidio del Norte, San Elizario, and El Paso had reached the end of their tethers. The combination of repeated Spanish military attacks, their inability to rescue captured relatives, and their lack of access to regular food supplies, or even to trade for goods, made continued association with the peace establishments seem increasingly futile. Among their councils, the calls for a large-scale raid into Spanish territories for both revenge and for sustenance were undoubtedly increasing. By the summer of 1795 many of those at peace, augmented by their independent kinsmen beyond the frontier, had chosen this path and began to plan for such an incursion.

Judging by later Spanish reports, it appears that a clear split had taken place among the Mescaleros de paz. Of those leaders affiliated with Presidio del Norte, the capitancillos Joseph, Alegre, and Volante had been consistently regarded as the most "loyal" as far as the Spaniards were concerned. However, it appears that Joseph and his ranchería, including his brother Chiyal-toé, joined in preparations for the raid, while the rancherías of Alegre and Volante did not. The ranchería of Bigotes el Bermejo, including his son Gaslán, who was known as a magician, also chose to participate, as did those of capitancillos Montera Blanca and Esquin-yoé.

Among the Mescaleros associated with El Paso and San Elizario, a similar division appeared. The capitancillo Mayá clearly joined the movement, while Francisco and his people remained staunchly "loyal." We may never know the true intentions of capitancillos Nzazen and Maselchindé, but it is likely that at least some members of their rancherías prepared to participate. The atomized nature of Mescalero society and the limited authority of their leaders allowed many rancherías to have it both ways, with some members raiding and supplying food and horses, while others could honestly tell the Spaniards that they and their people were not involved.

As plans progressed, other Mescaleros beyond Spanish control also joined in the planning. A capitancillo named Yusipeyé, whose ranchería lived in the Tinajas Hondas Mountains northeast of El Paso, threw in his lot with the raiders, as did Cambalza and Viguis, whose people dwelled in the Sacramento Mountains. A later rumor claimed that the dreaded Picax-andé and his Llanero Apaches, with their Lipan connections, were also included in the planning, but this is uncertain. But Bigotes el Bermejo had very close ties with the Lipans, and it seems likely that some Lipans either as individuals or under their own capitancillos enlisted as well.[4]

By July 1795, the Mescaleros were ready. A considerable number of rancherías, containing perhaps five hundred individuals, including women and children, began to converge into the mountain ranges north of the Rio Grande in the hundred-mile stretch of country between San Elizario and Presidio del Norte. Eventually, they all came together in the Sierra de los Ojos Calientes, the present-day Quitman Mountains of southwest Texas. The hot springs that gave the mountains their name were considered an important site with spiritual significance for the Mescaleros, indicating that the choice of this location may have had ceremonial as well as practical implications. Additionally, they could easily ford the Rio Grande there.

Once they were safely established in the Sierra de los Ojos Calientes, the Mescaleros began the process of planning for a large-scale raid into Spanish territory. According to Apache customs, it would first be necessary to name an overall leader to organize and control the expedition. The Spaniards were impressed by the method in which the Apaches traditionally selected a commander for their raids. Viceroy Bernardo de Gálvez noted that "they choose among themselves one to lead them, the most intrepid, wisest, and most distinguished. . . . This leader they obey upon the pain of death [but] only on campaign." Lieutenant Colonel Antonio Cordero wrote that the ideas of a leader once selected were "always preponderant, especially as far as the disposition of the camp is concerned, the method of defense in case of being attacked, or undertaking any hostile maneuver."[5]

With representatives from many different rancherías and several prominent capitancillos, the choice for an overall leader may have proven difficult. Nevertheless, the group undoubtedly reached a consensus to command the expedition. Eventually the unnamed leader gathered around him a force containing approximately 150 warriors that would go out on the raid. Following traditional customs, a number of young boys would have accompanied the more veteran fighters. The presence of the boys was a standard practice among the Apaches; they were novices, learning the arts of war from their elders.

The actual destination of the raiding party was most likely one of the first major issues the newly designated leader would have to address. For decades, the Mescalero and other Apache groups had utilized two major regions from which they could operate in their raids on the Spaniards. The first was the vast expanse of the Sierra Madre Mountains, which lay to the southwest of the Mescalero lands, and the second was the Bolsón de Mapími to the southeast. Both held certain benefits but also risks.

The Sierra Madres offered easier access to food, water, and forage. Movement through the rugged mountain chains would also increase the raiders' chances of reaching their targets undetected and offer a ready refuge should they be forced to retreat. But these mountains contained a greater population of both Spaniards and Native groups, and many of the latter, like the Ópata, were inveterate enemies of the Apaches. In addition, this route was farther away, and the Mescaleros would have to initially penetrate through a barrier of several presidios and other military forces before the Apaches could actually enter into the mountains.

As for the route through the Bolsón de Mapimí, the harsh and arid landscape would prove difficult to traverse for such a large number of people and horses. Yet this route was closer at hand and once established inside this generally uninhabited region, the Mescaleros would be virtually undetectable to the Spaniards. The raiders would then have the ability to launch attacks in multiple directions south and west into Nueva Vizcaya and east into Coahuila and perhaps Nuevo León. Many of the settlements bordering the bolsón were rich in cattle and horses but also lacking in any substantial Spanish military forces.

Whether the leader had decided on the expedition's route, a clear demonstration of the fluid nature of Apache leadership emerged. Sometime in mid-July, a small party of about ten Mescalero warriors crossed the river ahead of the main group. Whether this small party represented a freelance operation or whether they planned to coordinate with the larger party is unknown, but they quickly headed south, undetected and unchallenged, deep into Spanish territory.

Meanwhile, the plans of the main raiding party coalesced. The Mescalero leaders ensured that their warriors gathered sufficient weaponry, including lances, bows and arrows, and most importantly, a considerable number of muskets with an ample supply of ammunition and gunpowder. A large quantity of uncooked venison and other food supplies were also distributed to supply the warriors. If they followed the usual tactics, every man selected a single horse, with a light, stripped-down saddle and minimal trappings to decrease the weight carried by the horse and help increase their speed. As these practical preparations concluded, the Mescaleros also looked toward their spiritual and cultural necessities. They would have staged a communal war dance coordinated by the designated leaders, and the group performed other ceremonials designed to foster good fortune and achieve success in the coming incursion.[6]

Around the first day of August, the Mescalero raiding party finally set out, crossing the Rio Grande at the ford below the Sierra de los Ojo Calientes. They most likely moved at night to avoid their dust being seen. Twenty-four hours later found them in the flatlands near a watering hole known as the Agua del Cuervo. Here they kindled thirty-three fires, in which they cooked the raw venison they carried as rations and made their final dispositions. A few miles beyond Agua del Cuervo lay a pass between the Sierra del Lágrimas and the Sierra del Carrizo. The Mescaleros headed for the pass, but were cautious as their route took them close by the town of Coyamé, where the Spanish stationed a garrison of soldiers at Presidio del Principe.

Soon after entering the Sierra del Carrizo, Mescaleros riding in from the south joined the main party. These men were among the small group that had set out independently in mid-June and raided the Spanish settlements at Rancho Santa Cruz and San Nicolás de la Hoya in Tarahumara country. Whether by happenstance or foresight, these six men brought news that they had been tracked by a large Spanish force for many days, but had apparently eluded them. However, their route had taken them dangerously close, only some thirty miles, to the Spanish garrison town of Coyamé. But they were few and had moved carefully, and with luck their tracks would not be discovered.

Despite their caution, by the early hours of August 3, dust rising from the southeast told all the Mescaleros encamped in the Sierra del Carrizo that luck had turned against them. A Spanish force of fifty troopers from Coyamé, led by Alférez Josef Urías, was fast approaching. Whether the Mescaleros felt they had been discovered or whether they hoped the Spaniards would pass them by soon became a moot point. If they fled they would be seen and pursued, and as they had no special passports even if they attempted to parley, the Spaniards would regard them as hostile. A fight became inevitable. Fortunately for the Mescaleros, they were well armed and had come to raid anyway. They carefully set their ambush along the sides of a canyon and the Spaniards soon entered into it.

In a little over an hour, it was all over. The Mescaleros virtually annihilated the detachment of soldados that rode into the canyon, and then pursued the few survivors out of the trap down to where other soldiers were guarding their remount and supply animals. After another brief fight, the remaining Spaniards were put to flight and the Mescaleros were left alone. They now turned to enjoy the fruits of victory. While some stripped the dead soldiers of their weapons and uniforms, others rounded up the dead men's mounts. Among the horses and mules, the Mescaleros were delighted to find the pack animals of the soldiers' supply train, loaded with rations, cigars, tools, gunpowder, and ammunition.

Altogether in this single battle they found themselves with more booty than they could have hoped to garner over many months of raiding. Whether after careful consultation or on the spur of the moment, the Mescaleros decided to abandon their original plan. They all turned back the way they had come and headed home.

A few days' travel found them back across the Rio Grande and back into the Sierra de los Ojos Calientes where they had first started. Here they joined with the families and those who had remained behind in the encampments near the hot springs. Once reunited, the raiders undoubtedly brandished their captured weapons and looted goods before the camp. However, within a short time any frivolity vanished when four more Mescaleros unexpectedly rode into camp. These were the second group of freelancers who had rustled horses around Santa Cruz de Tarahumaras far to the south during the past weeks. Unfortunately, they had not been able to shake off the Spanish soldiers that had pursued them. Word spread quickly throughout the encampment that more soldiers were fast approaching.

Whether flush with confidence inspired by the recent victory or out of perceived necessity, the Mescalero encampment chose to fight. On the late afternoon of August 6, 1795, as the Spanish detachment under Alférez Cayetano Limón approached the Sierra de los Ojos Calientes, after fording the Rio Grande, the Apaches sprang another ambush. This time the Spaniards fought tenaciously and it took several hours for the Apaches to finish them off. But the outcome was inevitable, and by evening the corpses of another thirty-three troopers were being stripped by the victorious Mescaleros. Only eleven Spaniards escaped in the gathering darkness, and the Apaches were content to take what booty they had.

By morning, the members of the encampment decided to break up into their individual rancherías and return to their traditional homelands. Although almost twenty Mescalero warriors had been slain, and others gravely wounded, the amount of plunder the combined encampment had accumulated was impressive. Despite this, surely some of their leaders must have been aware that the Spaniards would soon seek revenge for their losses. But it had always been so, and they had become inured to the cycle. However, whether or not any of the Mescaleros dreamed how much suffering their people would have to endure in the future, it evaporated in the fleeting delight of food, cigars, horses, and weapons seized by their victorious warriors.[7]

8

BLOOD AND SUFFERING

EL PASO DEL NORTE, AUGUST 27, 1795—The vecinos of the town had only occasionally seen such a large assembly of men and beasts. Moving through the streets and plaza were more than 250 riders, along with almost a thousand horses and mules. Showing a degree of uniformity, many of the horsemen wore short blue coats, trimmed with small red collars and cuffs, and black flat-crowned, broad-brimmed sombreros. These were the soldados from the presidios and the compañias volantes of Nueva Vizcaya, armed with lances, muskets, and pistols, and distinguished by their *cueras,* jackets of seven layers of tanned deer or antelope hides, worn as armor and virtually arrow-proof. As they passed through the town, the majority of soldados probably carried their cueras slung from their saddles, as the heat of the day would have made wearing them unbearable.

Similarly clad, the forty-three Ópata soldiers from the Sonoran presidio of Bavispe could be readily distinguished from the other troopers, riding mules and carrying bows and arrows as well as firearms and lances. Renowned for their ability to fight on foot in mountain terrain, these Indian soldados disdained the use of the cuera, as it was an encumbrance for their method of warfare. The Ópatas had proved in numerous engagements to stand among the assembly's most skilled warriors —and the most feared by the Apaches.

There were other contingents of Indians as well. These were the Piros, Mansos, and Tiwas from the nearby mission communities of Ysleta, Senecú,

Church at El Paso del Norte, by John Russell Bartlett, 1850.
Courtesy of the John Carter Brown Library at Brown University, John Russell Bartlett Collection.

and Socorro. Their ancestors, remaining loyal to the Spaniards after the Pueblo Revolt of 1680, had moved south to live near the white men at El Paso. For over a hundred years, they had continued to provide military support, serving as scouts and auxiliaries in the seemingly never-ending war against the Apaches.

Undoubtedly, the most closely observed riders among the throng were the substantial number of Apaches themselves. There were twenty-four Chiricahua Gileños who had come from their rancherías near the Presidio of Janos, located slightly more than a hundred miles to the southwest. For the vecinos of El Paso, the Gileño Apaches had for decades been viewed only as fierce enemies, who stole cattle, kidnapped women and children, and killed travelers along the roadways. But for the last ten years these Gileños had agreed to become Apaches de paz, and now these once-dreaded foes were allies of the Spaniards.

Aside from the Gileños, another group of four Apaches from the Presidio of San Elizario appeared. As Apaches de paz living outside that presidio for more than five years, they may have been recognized by at least some of the people of El Paso. Yet for these four Apaches the mustering of such a large-scale military force embodied more than just the fulfillment of the terms of an alliance; instead, it was an intensely personal endeavor, for they were Mescaleros and they were riding out to hunt down and kill their own people.[1]

For Lieutenant Colonel Antonio Cordero, the passage through El Paso of his troopers was merely the continuation of an already hard campaign. For the past two weeks he had been in pursuit of the Mescaleros that had ambushed and destroyed the two detachments of Spanish soldiers led by Alférez Urías and Alférez Limón. At this point neither Cordero nor his superior, Commandant General Pedro de Nava, had been able to ascertain if these attacks were a localized occurrence or heralded a general uprising along the entire frontier. As such, Cordero had scrupulously sought to gather as much information as he possibly could.

When he had first received word of the destruction of Urías's and Limón's commands, Nava had ordered Cordero to proceed to Presidio del Príncipe to organize a pursuit of the Mescaleros. Cordero quickly organized a force of about 125 men, and on Sunday, August 16, 1795, they set out. That day they covered nineteen leagues, more than forty-five miles, "course to the North until the site of the first combat of the Party destroyed under Alférez Dn Joseph de Urías." The field of battle in the Sierra del Carrizo had been disturbed by previous efforts to recover the dead men's bodies. Nevertheless, Cordero and his troopers quickly reconnoitered the area. They noted the remains of two slain Apaches that had lain putrefying in the summer sun for a full two weeks, but left them untouched before the Spaniards headed out again, continuing north and making for the Rio Grande.

By August 18 they had reached a watering hole at Agua del Cuervo. Here Cordero found substantial signs of the Apaches that gave him much information, noting all in his field journal: "By the trails of the Enemy on their entry and egress and 33 fires they had made at a time that they had established themselves in the Agua del Cuervo in order to cook venison that they brought, I recognized that the number of Gandules that attacked Urías exceeded 150." Wary of the large number of Apaches, Cordero divided his force into two, "and in the afternoon I moved with a party of one hundred men to the rolling and broken terrain near the River."

Moving upstream, the Spaniards searched both banks of the Rio Grande for signs of the Apaches, but found nothing until they came to the location of the second battlefield. At the site of the destruction of Alférez Limón and his men, Cordero deduced that "the force that destroyed Urías . . . had already reunited with an equal or greater body that was there with part of their families in the small Sierra de los Ojos Calientes, in which the action was." Whether to assuage Spanish pride or to record soon-forgotten valor, Cordero eulogized Limón and his men, writing, "It was a very glorious defense that these made against the very numerous Indians . . . in whose field there were the bodies of three Apaches and the vestiges that unequivocally showed the great destruction that they [the Apaches] suffered despite their excessive force."

Leaving the field of battle, on August 21 Cordero and his men continued moving northwest following the Rio Grande. He sent out several scouts, who brought word that they found tracks leading into nearby mountain ranges, "in which are situated the several Indians that are called pacified from San Eleceario." Later that same day, Lieutenant Antonio Vargas, the commander of Presidio San Elizario, rode into camp. Cordero questioned Vargas about whether the Mescaleros de paz established near that presidio had been involved, "from whose reports I ended up ascertaining who were the accomplices in the hostilities from the nearby rancherías that lived under safe conduct." Over the next several days, as the Spanish commander made his way toward the Presidio of San Elizario, his scouts brought in reports on Mescalero movements in the surrounding countryside.

Meanwhile, new detachments of troops continued to arrive and join forces, so that by August 25 Cordero had some 445 men at his disposal. Nevertheless, the most important developments occurred when Cordero learned that Mescaleros de paz from the ranchería of the headman Francisco, living near San Elizario, had detained some members of their own nation who were implicated in the recent attacks. Cordero recorded in his field diary, "I secured immediately the capitancillo Yusipeyé with another two Gandules and two women who were there and who were from the rancherías in the Tinajas Hondas. . . . Another two who were in the ranchería of Francisco had fled despite the diligence of these and their own to apprehend them all for being involved in the hostilities."[2]

Marshalling his forces at the nearby town of El Paso, Cordero interrogated his prisoners and compiled their testimony, together with all the other information he had gathered thus far. On August 27, he sent his report to Commandant General Pedro de Nava in Chihuahua: "From the news that has been reported to me from the prisoners I have secured, and available from the dispatches . . . there died in the actions eighteen Apaches, among these a brother of Joseph named Chiyal-toé; that among the large number of wounded there was accounted the death of Gaslán, the magician, a son of Bigotes, and several other Indians. That there were four hundred Gandules [including] Faraónes, Mescaleros and Llaneros that united to approach our Frontiers not having even yet assembled El Calvo [Picax-andé] who hopes with another considerable band to make a general irruption."

In addition to identifying some of the Mescaleros that took part in the attacks, Cordero was also able to report that other Apaches had actually aided the Spaniards. "The Indians of the Ranchería of Francisco proceeded with fidelity in uncovering for me the accomplices in the evil who had come from las Tinajas Hondas to the environs of Tiburcios; and with zeal and efficiency the Gileños of Janos who served me in securing the three Gandules and two women that were apprehended. . . . These first steps have clarified the behavior of the Indios de Paz of San Eleceario, in whose environs there necessarily remain those who have been good."[3]

On August 23, Cordero fortuitously received a substantial reinforcement when "there arrived the Troops of the west, comprising a party of 142 men." Immediately, Cordero drew up a plan to use these men to cross the Rio Grande and scour the major mountain ranges where the Mescalero traditionally lived. Moving in a broad, sweeping arc, this detachment was to move north and then west, before rejoining Cordero and his main force farther upstream along the Rio Grande, beyond El Paso where the river turned sharply north. He entrusted the detachment to the lieutenant of Presidio del Príncipe, Blas de Aramburu, who he ordered to "set out for twelve days to beat the Tinajas Hondas, Cerros Huecos, Cornudo, that of del Aire, and the Sierra de los Organos."

Pressing on upriver, Cordero reached the Presidio of San Elizario the following day, where he took custody of several Mescaleros who had been detained by their own kin "for being involved in the hostilities." On August 25, he again received reinforcements, noting in his field diary, "I was joined by 20 Ópatas of Bavispe and 35 men from San Buenaventura under command of Lieutenant Dn Nicolás de Almansa, 25 from Janos with a sergeant, and 25 from San Eleceario and the 2nd [Volante] with the Alférez Dn Joseph de Carrasco." The colonel now had a powerful force of 250 men, and the next day they all set out for the villa of El Paso.[4]

After a short day's march, Cordero billeted his men on the citizens of the town while he held council with Francisco Xavier de Uranga, the lieutenant governor of the province of New Mexico, whose official residence was the villa. In the midst of these discussions, Cordero received word of the arrival of twenty-four Gileño Apaches from those settled at peace outside the Presidio of Janos, along with four Mescaleros who had come up from San Elizario.

These Mescaleros confirmed for him the identity and mountain homes of Apaches involved in the attacks, telling him "that some from the Sacramentos and Robledos had concurred in the last campaign against us, and that they had taken flight after killing one of the faithful Apaches of the ranchería of Francisco; which incident they assured me, has left cut off from now on the relations between the true friends with the disloyal."

Finally, sometime during the day of August 27, Cordero found time to write a letter to Commandant General Pedro de Nava, detailing the events of the expedition thus far and further laying out his plans for continuing operations. "I will leave for now in this Pueblo," he wrote, "some part of the supplies so as not to over encumber the train, which are deposited under the charge of a trusted cabo and four working sick. And I will have the Troops carry munitions of war and food for 40 days which is the amount necessary for this first sally."[5]

Having marshaled his forces, Lieutenant Colonel Cordero marched out of El Paso the next day following the Rio Grande as it turned north into what is now New Mexico. On August 29 he divided his forces. He ordered Lieutenant Nicolás Almansa with seventy men and the baggage train to follow the river as far as the Paraje de San Diego, about eighty miles upstream from El Paso, and make camp there. The colonel in turn would take a force of ninety men into the Robledo Mountains northwest of present-day Las Cruces, New Mexico. In this area, his scouts had found "an old trail of Indians coming in from the hostile lands on the other bank" of the Rio Grande and heading into that range.[6]

For three days Cordero led his detachment in a fruitless quest for Apaches, searching "the Sierra Robledo and that of Mesilla of the same name." But the only signs the Spaniards found showed that these mountains "had already been abandoned by the Enemies," with indications that the inhabitants had fled westward toward the Mimbres River, the homelands of the Chiricahua Mimbreños. This discovery raised the suspicion among the Spaniards that perhaps some of the Chiricahuas may have joined the Mescaleros in the recent attacks. In spite of these fears, the colonel turned away from the Robledos and headed back to the Rio Grande. On September 1, he reached the Paraje de San Diego, where he rejoined Lieutenant Almansa and the baggage train.

That same day the Spaniards ranks increased when Lieutenant Blas de Aramburu and his 142 men rode into camp. During his sweep from Presidio

San Elizario, Aramburu and his men had searched several mountain ranges looking for the Mescaleros. As Cordero noted in his field diary: "On this day I incorporated Aramburu with his party who gave me two Gandules that they had taken prisoner in the Tinajas Hondas and three pairs of ears from three women who they had been forced to kill in the Sierra de los Organos because they would not surrender, and not foreseeing this result attempted to escape." Whether the Spaniards killed the women in cold blood or in a failed attempt to capture them, the result was the same.

While the two Apache prisoners and the severed ears of the three women may have given some credence to Aramburu's account, Cordero was more interested in the evidence Aramburu had discovered, showing the Mescaleros were fleeing the region. "He likewise gave me notice about the tracks of the ranchería of Mallá . . . that had been alarmed and aware of our movements in the vicinity." Mallá, or Mayá, was one of the capitancillos of the Mescaleros de paz living outside Presidio del Norte. The Spaniards believed he and his people had joined in the attack on Alférez Urías and Alférez Limón, and the fact that they were now fleeing was for Cordero and his men proof of their guilt.[7]

Having concentrated all his forces, the colonel counseled with his officers and evaluated his situation. He had become convinced that "the Indians of one and the other banks of this River agreed and cooperated in a general gathering to attack our Frontiers." In this he maintained that not only had the Mescaleros been involved in the rising, but Apaches from "the other bank" west of the Rio Grande, meaning either the Gileños or Mimbreños, had participated as well. What proof shaped Cordero's beliefs are not known, but whether they were conclusive or flimsy, he had "decided that they would be the first to experience our strikes, giving time to those of the east to let down their vigilance in order to surprise them." After interrogating the two Apache men captured by Aramburu's party, he resolved to continue his operation by heading north, "where I had news from the prisoners that there were many Indians of war."[8]

On September 2, Lieutenant Colonel Cordero began his foray by reviewing all his troops. After dispatching the prisoners with a guard of ten of his troopers back to El Paso, he singled out 314 men to continue the campaign. These included soldados from six of the eight presidios and all four of the flying companies of Nueva Vizcaya, along with forty-three Ópatas from the Presidio of Bavispe in Sonora, and thirty-four Indian auxiliaries from El Paso. Perhaps most significantly, he now had a substantial contingent of forty Apaches de paz, both Gileño and Mescalero, who would take the lead in scouting for their own people.

Wishing to search as broad an area as possible, the Spanish commander divided his force into three sections. Lieutenant Miguel Mesa from the Fourth Volante with 110 men was to cross to the Rio Grande's east bank and move away from the river, searching the Jornada del Muerto and surrounding mountains from south to north. He was to go as far as the Paraje de Fra Cristóbal, where the jornada reached the Rio Grande. Mesa would then recross the river and head west toward the Mimbres Mountains, where he would rejoin Cordero "in the cañada of the Mimbres named las Calabazas." The expedition's supply train was placed under the command of Lieutenant Phelipe Peru of Presidio San Buenaventura, with 80 men. They were ordered to head directly to Fra Cristóbal, where they were to encamp and serve as the base of operations. Cordero himself would lead a force of 124 men directly west into the Mimbres Mountains and then move north to eventually link up with Lieutenant Mesa and his men. This combined force would then return to join the supply train at Fra Cristóbal.⁹

With their plans set, the three Spanish detachments set out on September 3. The next day Cordero and his party entered the foothills of the Mimbres Mountains, where his men captured "a shepherd and a woman" who informed him that nearby there were "many Indians celebrating with dances the misfortune that befell our people, and in which they had taken part; and that they were awaiting my departure in a mountain crest from the news that they had been given by two Gandules recently arrived from El Paso." Fearing that he had been discovered, the colonel moved to attack. Guided by his prisoners, the Spaniards located the Apaches in "one of the highest elevations in the Sierra." Cordero observed that they were in several rancherías, "which occupied the most rocky, most broken, and mountainous [terrain] that rose from the depths of a funnel formed by three eminences of the Sierra and surrounded by a canyon whose flat could barely be descried from the cusp where I was."

Dismounting many of his men, the colonel left his horses and a small supply train of twenty-four men under command of Alférez José Ygnacio Carrasco of San Elizario. He then split his remaining force into three detachments: the first had fifty men on foot under Alférez Nicolás Madrid of Buenaventura; the second contained thirty mounted men under Lieutenant Aramburu; and the third consisted of thirty horsemen under Cordero himself. Heading single file down a narrow trail, the commander led his men to the attack. As the footmen climbed toward the Apache encampments scattered among the broken and rocky terrain, the two parties of cavalry swept around along the flats of the funnel and up the sides of the canyon below the rancherías to try and surround them. The alarm then sounded, so the Apache women and children immediately abandoned their dwellings while their menfolk tried to organize a defense.

Pressed by the Spaniards, the Apaches took refuge "in a dense *cachaniyal* [thicket]" halfway up the slope of the mountain. There, they formed a large ring and fought back. Cordero noted, "The force of Indians, favored by the rockiness, resisted our fire and fought desperately." The fight became protracted, and the colonel later reported that after "three hours of hard action we had very much reduced the ring made by the Enemy, and most would have perished, and left their families in our power if the day had not ended so briefly." Fortunately for the Apaches, as night came on the colonel recalled his men and the battle ended as abruptly as it had begun. He recorded in his field diary: "I cannot calculate the great destruction suffered by these Indians, and only know that between the much blood that stained the rocks where they went, there were already dead in the evening seven Gandules and one woman, and they left of these 5 living in our hands."

But the Spaniards had not come out of the battle unscathed. An Ópata soldado from the Presidio of Bavispe was killed and another two of his comrades wounded, along with two of the Apaches de paz. The Spaniards also missed a golden opportunity to cripple the mobility of their foes and lost some of their own horses in the process. At one point during the battle, three Apaches de paz, apparently without orders, "returned to the canyon to recover the horse herds of the Enemy but were attacked by another group that countered them and they were obliged to abandon it, losing as well the saddled animals on which they arrived." Cordero complained that this unauthorized action by his own Apache allies "squandered" the chance to capture the enemy's animals.

As darkness closed in, the colonel had his command make camp "on a plateau named el Corral de Cuellar" along the mountain crest. He ordered his men to remain under arms to thwart any counterattack by the Apaches and detailed Lieutenant Almansa "to repel some Indians who were intent on stampeding our animals." At ten o'clock that night, Alférez Carrasco brought up the twenty-four men of the supply train and rejoined the main body. Cordero recounted in his diary, "There was not heard anything more that night other than the crying and howls of the Enemies who were searching for their families in the thickets, and the working of others who were forming a stone trench on the summit of the mountain crest, which they finished by sunrise the next day."

With the morning light, the colonel withdrew his men from the battlefield back up the mountain they had climbed down to launch the previous day's attack. The Spaniards could now clearly make out that the Apaches had constructed rudimentary field entrenchments and were ensconced in a good defensive position from which it would be very difficult to dislodge them. Cordero allowed a few of the Apache de paz to go forward, noting that "some of our Indians parleyed with the Enemies that had remained in the trench to delay us, while the rest fled with their families." Realizing that the majority of the Apaches had made good their escape, the Spanish commander decided to move his camp to good water nearby and rested his men and horses for several hours before continuing the pursuit.

Setting out that same afternoon, it soon became clear to the Spaniards that the Apaches had scattered in all directions. The next day, September 6, scouts found the trail of five individuals heading into the Black Range, and Cordero ordered his men to give chase. After several hours his vanguard emerged from the mountains into a plain where, with a curious mixture of seeming indifference and nostalgia, the colonel noted, "They succeeded in killing one Gandul in the pleasant valley of the Sierra Negra."

Apparently enjoying this setting, the commander ordered his troopers to make camp and then sent out two Apaches de paz to see if they could make contact with Lieutenant Mesa and his party. They were successful, as the next day, September 8, the lieutenant and his 110 men rode in. After dismounting his troopers, he delivered his report to Cordero. The colonel, with obvious disappointment, concluded that Mesa had returned "without having achieved any advantage in the vast reconnaissance that he had undertaken because a Ranchería that he had located . . . fled before being attacked." In addition to failing to locate the enemy, the lieutenant also reported that an Apache de paz from Janos from his detachment had deserted two days earlier. Cordero and his officers "imputed this to the bad character of the said Indian." Anticipating that the deserter might cause trouble among the other Apaches settled at Janos, the colonel sent a warning letter to its post commander, carried by eight other Apaches de paz, "for allaying any uprising that the fugitive might intend among the peaceful of that establishment."

That same day, the women prisoners taken in the recent battle revealed that there was another "enemy ranchería in the same sierra two days travel course to the north." Perhaps giving him a chance to redeem himself, Cordero detailed Lieutenant Mesa with 150 men, along with Alfereces Carrasco and Madrid, on the best horses to set out deeper into the Black Range in pursuit of these Apaches. At the same time, the colonel with 80 men would continue to hunt for the ranchería that had fled before the lieutenant from the Jornada del Muerto and crossed to the west bank of the Rio Grande.

For four days Cordero and his men searched in vain for the fugitive Apache ranchería, all the while gradually making their way eastward, back toward the Rio Grande. On September 12 the detachment reached the Paraje de Fra Cristóbal, where they rejoined the supply train under Lieutenant Peru. Two days later Mesa and his detachment returned, and this time he had succeeded in coming to grips with some Apaches.

Mesa undoubtedly told Cordero about his scout, but the colonel required the lieutenant to prepare a written report as well. That evening, he composed a brief but concise account, with the formality common to Spanish officers:

> In compliance with the order of Your Honor, on the 8 of the current [month] in the pleasant Valley of the Sierra Negra I went with one hundred fifty men which composed my party, course to the North, by all the cordilleras that are from Zuni in search of the Enemy Ranchería which Your Honor had informed me, whose tracks I cut on the same afternoon. And following hard after them, succeeded on the tenth in killing a Gandul and three women and taking alive eight piezas of both sexes; and on the eleventh, in the morning, attacked the Ranchería wherein nine Gandules were killed, who made a great resistance, among whom was capitan Cladensdy; and likewise there died two women, and eleven piezas of all ages were taken. The officers and Troop behaved as they should, and we had only two soldados wounded and two horses killed; one that of the Cadet Don Facundo Melgares and the other that of Sergeant Fermin Urives; and an Apache Auxiliary missing. God Keep Your Honor many years.[10]

With these results, Lieutenant Colonel Antonio Cordero resolved to return to El Paso. He dispatched copies of his field operations to Commandant General Pedro de Nava via Indian messengers, and shortly thereafter led his command back down the Rio Grande. During this operation his forces had killed eighteen Apache men and ten women, and captured two other men and twenty-seven women and children. Given the areas he had swept, many of the casualties inflicted were upon the eastern Chiricahuas, both Gileños and

Mimbreños, and not the Mescaleros. Nevertheless, Cordero was convinced that at least some of the former had taken part in the uprising and that it was a strategic necessity to punish them first. Satisfied that he had done so, he now turned his attention to the east, where he planned to strike as hard as he could against the Mescalero.

Several days later the citizens of El Paso welcomed the return of the Spanish expedition. The undoubtedly exhausted troopers and their animals were once again billeted on the villa, while the twenty-seven Apache prisoners of war were consigned to the *carcel,* or the jail of the town. From there these unfortunates were destined to be dispatched to Chihuahua. Commandant General Pedro de Nava would then deport them in another collera to Mexico City and from there ship them overseas to Havana, Cuba.

Still outraged by the losses his men had suffered, Nava was resolved to inflict the terrors of deportation and worse on the Mescaleros who had risen in August. Armed with the information that Cordero had provided on the scope of the outbreak, Nava knew that it involved only the provinces of Nueva Vizcaya, New Mexico, and Coahuila, and had not spread farther west into Sonora or, apparently, farther east into Texas. As a result, the commandant general began to marshal more of his forces in a planned escalation of operations across the region of conflict.

Nava now sent word to Governor Miguel de Emparan of Coahuila and Governor Fernando de Chacón of New Mexico ordering them to put men into the field to attack the Mescalero homelands. The commandant general envisioned that the detachment from New Mexico would strike into the regions of the Sacramento Mountains and Sierra Blanca from the north, while troops from Coahuila would move into the same areas from the east. Finally, a third detachment from Nueva Vizcaya would push up from the south. For this last thrust, Nava called again on Antonio Cordero, ordering him to immediately set out as soon as he had resupplied his command.

With barely two weeks respite for himself and his men, Lieutenant Colonel Cordero mustered his forces around El Paso del Norte and once again began noting his progress in a detailed field diary. On October 13, 1795, Cordero was ready for the campaign with a force 250, including soldados, forty Indians from the El Paso area, and an undetermined number of Apaches de paz, all of them from the same force he had set out with in late August. As before, he ordered them to equip themselves with munitions, rations, and mounts for at least forty days. His subalterns included Lieutenants Phelipe Peru and Nicolás Almansa, and Alférez Nicolás Madrid from Presidio San Buenaventura, Lieutenants José Escageda and Miguel Mesa from the Fourth Volante, and Alférez José Ygnacio Carrasco from San Elizario.

The next day Cordero dispatched twenty men with the baggage train and horse herd downstream to Presidio San Elizario, which would serve as his base of operations and supply depot. The rest he led north, heading for the Sierra de los Organos, a favorite Mescalero camping area. On October 18, the Spaniards entered Soledad Canyon on the western slopes of the mountains. Cordero then ordered his spies to scout "the three parallel canyons that leave the Sierra as far as San Agustín." Moving cautiously through the mountains as far as San Agustín Springs, these spies found tracks leading across the Organs into the Tularosa Basin, heading east toward the Sacramento Mountains.[11]

The Spaniards followed these tracks into "the center of the Sierra de San Nicolás," (present-day San Andres Mountains) skirting to the west of the natural barrier of the White Sands. Here, Cordero noted in his field diary, "I kept hidden all day and at sunset undertook my march with the greatest speed in order to cross the large plain between, as far as the Sierra del Sacramento at which I arrived before sunrise and halted in the Cajon de Jesus Nazereno." The Spaniards were near the present-day city of Alamogordo, New Mexico, and from there they sent out scouts, who on October 21 "crowned the heights of Nuestra Señora de la Luz, at the front of the Sierra Blanca."[12]

The following day Cordero's men came across a trail, which they interpreted as a Mescalero ranchería fleeing before them, heading north into the Sierra Blanca. They gave chase but could not overtake the Apaches. With the coming of darkness, Cordero ordered a halt at the Cajon Sombrio, where he made camp. The next morning the Spaniards located the tracks of a second group of Apaches and, changing targets, pursued this new quarry. For two full days the chase continued, with the soldados gradually closing the distance. On October 24, the Apaches saw their pursuers as they reached the top of Cumbre del San Rafael and increased their speed. The Spaniards also picked up their pace, but were only able to catch up with the tail end of the fleeing Apaches. Cordero lamented, "I only succeeded in attacking the most exhausted of which they left a shepherd prisoner in our power, one woman dead, and several wounded Gandules who escaped. In this action we had a horse killed and they lightly wounded the Auxiliary Tagajla."[13]

Frustrated by not being able to catch the Mescaleros, Cordero interrogated his prisoner to find out how they knew of his approach. The latter recounted that "the tumult of the Indians of that Sierra was due to the arrival five days before of a wife of the Indian Vida Licay with the news that her husband had been captured by the Spaniards, and that of these, there came more than the seeds of grass to avenge their grievances." The Mescaleros had been forewarned of the Spanish campaign by the wife of an Apache de paz living near San Elizario who left to alert her kinsmen. "The result of this," Cordero continued, "was that the four rancherías that were left there determined to divide up, each seeking its own safety." The Spanish commander then had the prisoner serve as a guide, and the man eventually brought the Spaniards to another location that "cut the trail of another large ranchería over which we travelled until the Río de Sacramento."[14]

Coming up on the Mescalero ranchería in an unnamed canyon in the evening of October 25, Cordero dismounted part of his force and had them make a night march up the mountain slopes on either side, while the remaining mounted troopers waited at the canyon mouth. At daybreak the Spaniards sprung their ambush, "but they found nothing besides the fires they [the Mescaleros] had raised the night before." When the Spaniards gave chase, they found that the Apaches had escaped "to a cliff impassable for horses and very difficult for those on foot, through which they saved themselves and frustrated our efforts."

Stung by the Apaches' successful stratagem, Cordero and his men turned back toward the Río Sacramento. There, they luckily hit upon the trail of another group of Mescaleros, whom their prisoner identified as the ranchería of capitancillo Esquin-Yoé Viguis. Unfortunately for them, Cordero recorded, "these were less cautious than the others and I followed and reached them at sun set, taking prisoner eight persons of both sexes, killing four, and wounding several Gandules, having on our part in this number [i.e., wounded] a soldado of the Company of San Buenaventura." Undoubtedly pleased with this victory, the Spaniards also may have felt a sense of justified retribution as "in this ranchería as well as that attacked the previous day, there were found many fragmentary items of the soldados that died at the hands of the Barbarians this past August."

Believing that he had driven the Mescaleros before him out the east side of the Sacramentos, Cordero hoped to make contact with the other Spanish forces coming either from New Mexico or from Coahuila. To that end, "in the night I arranged to go down to the Río de Pecos two Apaches familiar with that terrain to search for them or their trains and to give them notice of me and my command with papers, that I had given them to this effect, and orders for them to look for me by afterwards going over my trail." At the same time, Cordero continued his own operation, heading northeast into the modern Capitan Mountains, "where I found no more than the vestiges of the numerous Apaches."

Realizing that he could do no more on his current course, and sensing that the Mescaleros may have slipped behind him, on October 26 the colonel ordered his men to turn south, where they would sweep several more mountain ranges as they made their way back to the Rio Grande and Presidio San Elizario. He detailed Lieutenant Escageda along with Lieutenant Almansa and Alférez Carrasco with 115 men to reconnoiter the Guadalupe and Diablo Mountains of west Texas and southeast New Mexico, while Cordero would examine the Cornuda, Hueco, and Del Aire Mountains in the same regions.

The following day, Cordero led the men to the Cornuda Mountains, where he declared, "It was impractical to go mounted in this small Sierra or rather an impregnable fortress, arranged by the author of nature." He personally led a reconnaissance on foot with eighty men, but they only found some old tracks indicating that some of the Mescaleros had indeed headed back south toward the Rio Grande. Other signs indicated to the Spaniards that it was in these mountains that "the Enemy had their families in the month of August past" at the beginning of the outbreak of hostilities.

Over the next five days, the colonel vainly searched the region for signs of the Mescaleros. By November 2 he had reached the Rio Grande downstream from Presidio San Elizario, where he reunited with Lieutenant Escageda. The subaltern had been just as unsuccessful as his commander in finding the enemy, and it appeared that the entire operation had concluded on a rather unspectacular note. Anticipating this, Cordero dispatched his nine prisoners to the presidio and then dismissed "the forty El Paso auxiliaries so that they would not destroy their animals as they had come fatigued." Cordero then moved his men to an encampment called Loma Alta, "amidst a commodious *bosque* [wood] that hid us," and sent out five spies down river "as far as the abandoned Presidio of Pilares," in what must have been a last-ditch attempt of locate the Mescalero.[15]

Whatever the feelings of the Spaniards as the campaign wound down, they suddenly changed on November 6, when their spies returned with the report "that they had just cut a very fresh trail in the vicinity of the canyon," meaning a location farther downstream. Having finally let himself relax after forty days of continuous exertions, Cordero had fallen ill. "Mortified by an indisposition in my health," he noted in his diary, "I granted the command of this raid to Lieutenant Mesa giving to him one hundred fifty men with the object to attack the ranchería whose tracks the spies had cut and followed." Should the Mescaleros elude this blow, Cordero ordered the lieutenant "that afterwards he was to search all the cordillera of the River advancing until the Sierra del Mobano [Mogano]."[16]

After sending off this detachment, Cordero sat down to give an account of the campaign results thus far to Commandant General Pedro de Nava at Chihuahua City. He began by noting that he had begun the campaign by searching the "Sierras and terrains most frequented by the Mescaleros and Llaneros." He then summarized the forays and battles his men had encountered throughout a large section of central New Mexico and west Texas. Despite having had some success in harassing the Apaches that he believed responsible for the outbreak, his tone was notably pessimistic. Cordero concluded that part of the reason for his lack of success was that the Mescalero had dispersed over a wide area after hurriedly finishing their fall buffalo hunt in September, "the month following their hostilities." He recounted that Mescaleros had scattered into northern New Mexico, the Llano Estacado of west Texas, and all along the Rio Grande frontier of Nueva Vizcaya, declaring that "a few rancherías had pulled to the vicinity of New Mexico, others to the Cañon de San Sabas, and others to the Frontiers of this Province."[17]

"I am sensible My General," he wrote, "that the progress of this sally until now have not corresponded to our toils and efforts, mostly when I observe that the officers and Troops that accompany me have the most honorable and ardent desires to batter the Enemies." Still, Cordero felt he and his men had done all they could and asked Nava to take this into account, so that "the penetration of Your Lordship will not be obscured in judging us that this did not depend on the scarcity of opportunities, and that these have been sought with the activity corresponding to the performance of your worthy orders."[18]

Still, Cordero held out hope that further success would come as he awaited word of the results of Lieutenant Mesa's expedition, telling Nava that "on the return of Mesa I will give to Your Lordship an account of the results of his *mariscada* [raid], sending you the diary in detail." Having concluded his report and the special pleading he had made to the commandant general, Cordero recorded in his field diary, "I dispatched two Apaches of Carrizal with a packet that included the report of what has happened to this date." All he could do now was to wait.[19]

After sending off his dispatches, Cordero slowly shepherded his command and his exhausted horse herd up river toward Presidio San Elizario, which they reached on November 9 after a three-day march. For the next week and a half the colonel waited impatiently for the results of Lieutenant Mesa's final attempt to punish the Mescalero. Finally, on November 20, the lieutenant returned with news that he had located and attacked a Mescalero encampment in the Sierra de la Cola de Aguila, the modern-day Eagle Mountains of far west Texas. His written report to Cordero described the battle:

> Immediately after I separated from Your Honor on the 6th of the current month with one hundred fifty men of the Troop that you had placed under my orders, I went to take the trail of the Enemies in the same place where the spies had left it, which I verified on the 8th. And I followed with the greatest perseverance and caution and succeeded to discover the Ranchería on the tenth before day break, and they were found in a deep canyon in the Sierra de la Cola de la Aguila. I arranged to attack in two parties, one on foot of fifty men, to crown the crests commanded by the Sergeant of Bavispe, León, and the other of fifty cavalry, which I led over the mountain side; which was effected at sun rise succeeding between both in surprising the said Ranchería which was that of the Mescalero Esquin-yoé, el grande, that they call Friega la Olla, which was immediately put to flight offering very little resistance; but despite the precipitous nature of their flight, two Gandules and four women were killed and seven piezas of both sexes taken prisoner; and they left in our power all of their goods among which were items and five horses of the fallen Soldados; and there escaped very badly wounded eight Gandules, among them the referred to capitancillo, the rest of the people sorely hurt.

After the battle, Mesa continued his scout of the region as far as the Sierra del Mogano, before deciding to return to San Elizario. There, he turned over to Lieutenant Colonel Cordero not only his report but also "the cited prisoners and four pairs of ears as we had not been able to recover the other two because of the difficult terrain in which they fell."[20]

Buoyed somewhat by the success of Lieutenant Mesa's operation, on November 21, 1795, Cordero sent another set of dispatches to Commandant General Nava in Chihuahua. In these he included not only his detailed field diary, but also a copy of Mesa's report. He informed Nava that he had sent his prisoners to a more secure location, writing, "The sixteen prisoners that have been made in the strikes that I had in the Sierra del Sacramento as well as these last that Mesa has provided are guarded in the Presidio de San Carlos until whatever Your Lordship determines for them." Like the previous group of prisoners that he had sent south after his first expedition, Cordero undoubtedly knew that these Apaches would also most likely be deported in another collera, destined for permanent exile in Cuba.[21]

In reviewing the campaign of the last three months, Cordero knew that he and his men had inflicted a substantial number of casualties on the Apaches. In their first sally between August 27 and September 14, they killed eighteen Apache men and ten women and captured another two men, eight women, and nineteen piezas, most likely indicating children not having yet reached puberty. On their second foray between October 13 and November 10, they killed two more men and five women and captured one man and fifteen piezas. Of these eighty Apache casualties, some if not all of those from the first foray were most likely Gileño or Mimbreños. Those suffered on the second were undoubtedly Mescaleros.

From the standpoint of showing the reach of Spanish power, Cordero had clearly succeeded, raiding deep into lands that the Apaches considered theirs and into which few white men had ever ventured. Yet, in regard to "punishing" those Apaches actually responsible for starting the hostilities, the results were clearly unsatisfactory. Spanish pride had not been restored nor was Spanish honor satisfied. More blood and more suffering would inevitably follow, and Lieutenant Colonel Antonio Cordero and his brother officers were determined that it would be the Mescaleros who would bleed and suffer the most.

9

THE CRUEL SEASON

Lower Pecos River, September 23, 1795—The desert heat seemed to exacerbate the sickness that ravaged his body. He was constantly subject to fits of intense coughing that produced a flow of blood into his mouth. A military doctor would later declare that this was caused by a "laceration of some vessels of the lung by a sharpness of their humors, which hemorrhage is known by the name of *hemoptisis*." Although his illness was declared "not dangerous," the doctors recommended that if he wanted to be cured, he would "need to live in a country of rigorous cold." Instead of choosing a restful retreat to recuperate, however, he chose to do his duty. He would lead his soldiers into the mountain ranges that were the homelands of the Mescalero Apaches. The cold air of the mountains might actually offer him some relief from his ailment while he and his men tried to bring the Apaches to battle.

Despite his ill health, Lieutenant Colonel Miguel José de Emparan had received orders from Commandant General Nava to seek out and destroy the Mescaleros, and he was determined to do so no matter what it took. His determination mirrored that of Nava, who planned to expand the war against the Mescaleros far and wide. Consequently, he would have his men launch multiple campaigns all along the frontier, and drive deep into the Mescalero homelands and crush all that refused to sue for peace.[1]

Emparan had been the governor of Coahuila for some five years before setting out on this latest campaign, and during that time his physical ailments had mirrored the seemingly constant problems the Apaches had caused him. Prior to coming to the Interior Provinces, he had enjoyed good health, in an environment diametrically opposite to the heat and aridity of the frontier, as he had been a sailor and the sea had been his home.

When he had enlisted at the age of fourteen as a marine guard in the Royal Armada, Miguel José de Emparan had set out with the blessings of a family renowned for its antiquity and nobility. His father, José Joaquin de Emparan, was the fourteenth lord of the House of Emparan, one of the most distinguished families in the Basque province of Guipuzcoa. Like two of his brothers before him, the young Miguel José was destined for sea service, and when he joined in 1770 his future seemed assured. After laboring steadily for more than eighteen years, he had risen to the rank of *teniente de navio*, or ship's lieutenant. During this period he had made five cruises into the Atlantic, including two voyages to the New World and back, and had been involved in several major military operations against the Algerians and other Muslim corsairs off the coast of North Africa.

Still, the rate of Miguel José's promotions was painfully slow, and in 1788 he decided to transfer to the army. Whether through purchase, family influence, or both, he obtained a commission as lieutenant colonel in the Dragoon Regiment of Mexico. The move worked, and from this point forward, his career accelerated. After only eighteen months in Mexico City, Emparan attracted the attention of the Viceroy the Conde de Revillagigedo, who appointed him governor of the province of Coahuila, in the Interior Provinces. In 1790, Miguel José took up his residence at the villa of Monclova, where he also served as the captain of the presidial company stationed there.[2]

For several months, Emparan assiduously carried out his duties and jealously guarded his authority. But in 1791 he became embroiled in a series of disputes with the new commandant general of the Eastern Interior Provinces, Colonel Ramón de Castro. Feeling that his duty was first and foremost to protect his province of Coahuila, on several occasions Emparan was slow to follow Castro's orders regarding operations against the Lipan and Mescalero Apaches. The commandant general even brought Emparan up on charges of insubordination. The dispute escalated until it reached the attention of the viceroy. For more than two years, the legal wrangling continued until late 1792, when Castro received a promotion and a convenient transfer. This development relieved the cloud of insubordination hanging over Emparan but did little to help with his ongoing trouble with the Apaches, or to alleviate his chronic illness.

Over the next three years, Emparan endured the vagaries inherent within the Apache peace policies, alternating between periods of relative quiet with brief flurries of violence. He had often dispatched detachments of troops to punish thefts and murders attributed to both the Lipans and Mescaleros, and just as often his men had returned with little to show for their effort. Most frustrating were the complaints directed against the Mescaleros de paz settled around Presidio del Norte, who were routinely blamed, with much justification, for the attacks.

In late August 1795, Emparan received word from Commandant General Pedro de Nava of the general outbreak of the Mescaleros, along with orders to organize his forces and strike back into the land beyond the Rio Grande. Nava explained that he was organizing a three-pronged attack against the Apaches, with forces attacking from Nueva Vizcaya, New Mexico, and Emparan's province of Coahuila. Despite his continuing poor health, Emparan insisted on leading the retaliatory expedition himself, so that he could personally ensure that "these very cunning Enemies had the punishment deserved by their treacheries." Gathering his troopers, the governor set out on the campaign carried on a litter, "because my debilitated condition did not permit me to use a horse." Crossing the northern frontier of Coahuila, he had his forces head northwest until they reached the Pecos River. From there they would follow the river north into a region that would allow them to strike either into the mountains to the west or into the Llano Estacado to the east. Despite his weakened physical condition, Governor Miguel José de Emparan was resolved to find and engage the Mescaleros no matter how long it took.[3]

Soon after the war had broken out, Commandant General Nava had found himself hard-pressed to explain the conflict. Having previously assured his superiors in Madrid that the frontier was in a quiet and stable condition, he was clearly embarrassed after his assurances were proven false. In addition, Nava found himself in a delicate position with the Viceroy the Marqués de Branciforte, who had replaced Viceroy Revillagigedo in the summer of 1794. Although the commandant general was independent of vice regal control, economic and military concerns required both officials to work together. When warfare erupted on the frontier, the Provinces of Nuevo León and Nuevo Santander under Branciforte's authority were threatened, and the viceroy subtly cast aspersions on Nava for not having given him sufficient warning.

On September 1, 1795, Nava wrote to the Spanish minister of war in Madrid, the Conde de Campo de Alange, seeking to explain what had occurred and assuring the minister that the situation was under control. He reported that immediately after the outbreak, he had dispatched a large detachment from Nueva Vizcaya "that already is persecuting" the Mescaleros. This force was joined with other Spanish detachments, one from Coahuila and another from New Mexico. Demonstrating that the Spaniards had Indian allies as well as foes, Nava noted that the New Mexico detachment was to have set out "with a portion of Comanches Amigos." All together, these expeditions would attack the mountain ranges "where these Enemies commonly harbor, to punish them as they deserve and with which I will continue taking many measures that are appropriate." Concluding with a more exculpatory tenor, Nava asked Campo de Alange to realize that the outbreak had been contained to the frontier and had not as yet reached the settlements farther south. "I hope that it will serve Your Excellency to present to His Majesty that so far that there has not [been] experienced any misfortune in the populations or the Haciendas of this Province."[4]

The key to Nava's letter was the claim that *so far* the settlements, haciendas, mines, and other economic centers of Nueva Vizcaya and the other provinces of the Interior Provinces had not been assaulted by the Mescalero. But the commandant general realized that the vagaries of war would not allow for the declaration of absolutes. His experience on the frontier had taught him at least one cruel and certain lesson. The Mescalero would inevitably seek revenge for any blow they suffered, and they would strike back wherever the Spaniards were most vulnerable and where they least expected it.

Given such a realization, Nava determined to employ the one tactic the Spaniards traditionally turned to in such times: preempt the Apache counterstrike by attacking them where they felt most secure and at a time of year when their food supply was at its most vulnerable, namely the late fall and early winter. Such a tactic had been proven successful ever since the days of Hugo O'Conor in the 1770s and throughout the subsequent decades. In the face of having very few options and with the promise of much to gain, the commandant general inevitably embraced the tried and true action of the

Spaniards—unleash upon the Mescalero *guerra de fuego y sangre*, or the war of fire and blood. This would be a total war to destroy not only their warriors, but even their ability to feed their women and children.

It had long been understood by the Spaniards that the Mescalero and other eastern Apache groups would make annual expeditions onto the Llano Estacado to hunt buffalo. Conducted in the fall, these expeditions were perhaps the single most important economic and cultural activity for the Mescaleros because they provided much, if not most, of the food and supplies they would depend upon for survival. In conjunction with these hunts, they would also take the opportunity to harvest mescal cacti, a major food supplement and from which activity the Spaniards had applied to them the name Mescalero. The season of the buffalo hunt was crucial for their survival.

Yet ever since the 1750s, the ever-growing power and aggression of the Comanches had seriously disrupted the ability of the Mescalero, Lipan, and other eastern Apaches to engage in the buffalo hunt. As early as 1774 the Spaniards, led by Commandant Hugo O'Conor, had exploited the growing inability of these Apaches to sustain themselves. The Irishman had conducted two general campaigns specifically during the fall and winter, designed in part to disrupt the seasonal buffalo hunt. In 1776 his actions succeeded brilliantly when a large number of Mescaleros, fleeing before O'Conor's forces onto the Llano Estacado in a desperate search for buffalo, were destroyed by the Comanche. In the wake of O'Conor's campaigns, throughout the next decade the Spaniards sporadically repeated the tactic of disrupting the buffalo hunt, with the Apaches suffering continuous losses. In desperation, they turned to the Spanish for support, and beginning in 1788 many groups sought Spanish escorts as protection against the Comanche before heading out into the plains for the hunt.[5]

When the Mescalero uprising broke out in 1795, Commandant General Nava realized that they had presented him with an opportunity to disrupt their annual hunting cycle. When he drew up plans for the forces he mobilized from Nueva Vizcaya, New Mexico, and Coahuila, Nava knew that the detachments would each be attacking the Mescaleros during the time of year when they engaged in the buffalo hunt. If his troopers pressed them long and hard enough, the Apaches would be unable to organize themselves in sufficiently large numbers. Without such numbers they could not repel the Comanche and thus could not venture out into the buffalo plains. With the onset of winter cold, the Mescaleros would either return and make peace with the Spaniards or starve. For Nava, it appeared inevitable that at least one of his detachments would strike the Mescaleros and disrupt their ability to maintain their food supplies. Hunger would harry them as much as the Spaniards.

As Governor Emparan discovered a newfound vigor in leading his troops in search of the Mescaleros, during the same period Lieutenant Colonel Antonio Cordero continued to demonstrate a remarkably tenacious spirit as he sought the same foe. He had not been content with the results of the campaigns he and his men had waged between August and November 1795. In conjunction with Commandant General Nava's latest orders, Cordero now planned to launch another expedition from El Paso into the Sacramento Mountains to seek out the Mescalero rancherías still ensconced there. Picking out some 150 of his best men, including the Ópata troopers from Sonora and a contingent of Indian auxiliaries, Cordero entrusted command of the expedition to Lieutenant Nicolás Almansa of the Presidio of San Buenaventura. The lieutenant and his troopers' orders were simple—ride until they located the Mescaleros and then destroy them.

Setting out on December 1, Almansa and his men traveled upriver from El Paso about fifty miles to the ford of Doña Ana. Here they crossed to the east bank of the Rio Grande and rode "until reaching the front of San Agustin," in the Organ Mountains, "where I arrived at day break on the second." Almansa then directed his course across the Organs, moving northeast until he reached a portion of the San Andres Mountains, which the Spaniards called las Petacas. At this place, they found "a trail of Apaches that not many days earlier had been carried up from there." Almansa recorded that he and his men "followed in these tracks along the entire cordillera with hopes that they [the tracks] promised me to overtake them."[6]

Three days of tracking led the Spaniards throughout the San Andres Mountains and into the beginnings of the Sierra Oscura range, near the northern end of the modern White Sands Missile Range of New Mexico. On the night of December 5, they came up unexpectedly on "the bulk of a ranchería commanded by the Indio Mayá with other capitancillos who were joined together in the Cerro Redondo." The Mescalero Mayá and his people were believed to have taken part in the outbreak's initial attacks, and they had already fled before the Spanish forces under Lieutenant Colonel Antonio Cordero in late August. Having relocated far to the north in the Sierra Oscura, they may have been lulled into a false sense of security, believing that the Spaniards would not return to the area so soon. If so, it would prove a disastrous conceit.[7]

During the night, Lieutenant Almansa arranged his forces in what he hoped would be a decisive maneuver. The Mescaleros were encamped at the foot of the steep Cerro Redondo, with a large canyon to their front. The lieutenant detailed the bulk of his force, ninety men including the Ópatas and Indian auxiliaries, to make a forced night march up the sides of the mountain and work their way behind the Mescalero encampment. At the same time, Almansa and a picked force of thirty horsemen would place themselves across the canyon mouth. By daybreak, the men on foot "should crown the summit of the mountain," at which point they would attack the encampment. If the Mescaleros attempted to flee up the mountain, the footmen would be positioned above them, and if they made for the canyon mouth, the cavalry would ride them down. It was an ambitious plan that called for rather precise coordination, but the lieutenant felt confident it would succeed.[8]

At dawn on December 6, Almansa and his troopers, fully mounted and with weapons loaded, rode toward the ranchería and opened fire. The lieutenant attacked with "the belief that the troops on foot were placed in the appointed place and would assail almost at the same time." However, his belief soon proved vain. The infantrymen on which his elaborate planned envelopment depended were nowhere to be seen. Unbeknownst to Almansa, this contingent had failed to reach their objective "because with the darkness of the night they had strayed from the path that should have led them." In addition, authorities later found out "they were lost in much snow at a summit far from that they should have occupied."[9]

With nature herself seemingly thwarting his plans, Lieutenant Almansa and his cavalry soon found themselves in dire straits. Seeing only the thirty horsemen to their front, the Mescaleros made their superior numbers tell and counterattacked. The lieutenant reported, "I just had to sustain with a very small force against the impetus of a numerous Apachería that not only made me front, but were determined to destroy us." As the Apaches moved forward, Almansa ordered his troopers to dismount and take up a defensive position "and shield themselves with oak trees and rocks and I contained the Enemy for the space of an hour without losing an inch of ground."[10]

Just as it appeared that he might be overwhelmed by the Mescaleros, the lost contingent of infantry made their appearance. The footmen were still far from their appointed positions when the combat commenced, but "after they heard the firing, they overcame many difficulties that were presented to them, particularly the transit of two very deep canyons that they had to go through." Heading toward the sound of the firing, after about an hour of frantic effort, the infantrymen reached the battlefield. Lieutenant Almansa with obvious relief recalled, "There appeared on the rock outcropping to my left the party on foot, assailing them [the Mescaleros] from the side." Surprised by this flank attack, it was the Mescaleros' turn to take defensive measures. Under pressure from the now united Spanish force, the Apaches "were compelled to abandon the ranchería and the terrain that they occupied, and they took control of another rocky height to which they had dispatched their families."[11]

The battle now began anew, with the Spaniards moving to attack the Mescaleros in their new position on an adjacent mountain peak. A protracted combat commenced with the Spanish forces slowly advancing up the sides of the mountain while the Mescalero warriors fought a delaying action to protect their families. Almansa later maintained that "the boldness of the troop [succeeded] with the greatest ardor in dislodging them from this second summit, and forcefully achieved this after five hours of fighting." During the battle, the superiority of the Spaniards' firearms, along with an ample supply of ammunition, proved crucial. "The troop continued a well-ordered fire for the expressed time," Almansa recorded, "wherein they spent one thousand two hundred and some cartridges and some hundreds of arrows." This firepower overwhelmed the Mescaleros, who simply did not have the ammunition to sustain the fight. The result was that Almansa claimed his men "made a great slaughter of the Enemy as manifested by the blood they saw and they were compelled to flee hastily having to carry with them their dead, wounded and families."[12]

With the retreat of the Mescaleros, the battle came to an end. Almansa had personally seen six Apaches killed, but his men were only able to slice the ears from one of the slain because of "the hindrance of so many Indians in the rocks." A large number of Mescaleros had also been wounded, among which was "capitancillo Mayá, who was pierced by an arrow so sorely that he abandoned his weapons." Given the violence of the contest, the Spaniards were lucky in having suffered "only slightly wounded three soldiers of San Buenaventura, Príncipe and Bavispe." After tending to his injured men and recovering two horses the Mescaleros had abandoned, Lieutenant Almansa gathered up "all the possessions of the ranchería which were divided up between the auxiliaries and Ópatas, burning what could not be carried out of this place." He then headed out of the Cerro Redondo and retraced his steps, heading south through the

San Andres and Organ Mountains until he reached the Rio Grande at a place called Paraje de la Artesa. From there he sent out Indian messengers with a copy of his report for Lieutenant Colonel Cordero and a request for further orders.[13]

On December 13, 1795, from his headquarters in El Paso, Antonio Cordero was ready to forward another set of dispatches to Commandant General Pedro de Nava. Having received an account of the battle waged by Lieutenant Almansa, Cordero remained frustrated that his forces had not been able to deliver a more decisive blow. His dispatch to Nava revealed his frustration. In describing the battle, Cordero lamented that "there was not extracted from this action the whole fruit that could have been obtained" as a result of the failure to coordinate the forces' movements. Still, Cordero could not blame the lack of success on his men noting, "I have no doubt that the officers and troop carried out their duties, and that the number of enemies was very excessive to ours."[14]

Nevertheless, Cordero was convinced that the wounding of capitancillo Mayá and the attack on his ranchería had helped to disrupt further Mescalero attacks. He reported that Mayá and his people were planning to join with other rancherías led by "Jusnates-dey or Joseph on the frontier of this province, and that [they] had begun to meet in the Capitán [Mountains] according to the news reported by the Indios Amigos." The battle that Lieutenant Almansa had with Mayá and his people thwarted this planned meeting. In response to this news, Cordero ordered Almansa to retire with his detachment as far as El Paso, "executing it without hiding," so that the Mescalero would know the Spaniards would soon return "in order to continue . . . with their persecution and punishment."[15]

In keeping with these objectives, Cordero planned to send out simultaneous scouting parties throughout the region to locate other concentrations of potential enemies. No doubt seeking to further justify his earlier foray west of the Rio Grande against the Mimbreño and Gileños, he reported that a large party of these Indians had gathered in the mountains south of the pueblo of Zuni in northwestern New Mexico. But the most valuable reports came "with the return of the scout of ten Apaches that I dispatched heading east." From these Apaches de paz, the lieutenant colonel "ascertained that in the Sierras Hueca, Cornudas, Guadalupe, and Mobano that were examined and all the frontier as far as the Pecos River, there are no enemies." The allied Apache scouts continued with their report stating that the hostile Mescaleros had moved further to the southeast, beyond the modern-day Davis Mountains, and from there down to the Rio Grande. "All this news make me believe," Cordero wrote, "that the Mescalero Rancherías of Joseph, Bigotes, and Montera Blanca [have] by now changed entirely their schemes and that they will undertake some hostility, be it against the province of Coahuila or against the interior lands of Nueva Vizcaya, entering through the Bolsón [de Mapími]."[16]

Reacting to these reports, Cordero had sent two detachments of troopers downriver from El Paso as a precaution, but the winter weather hampered their progress. "The season is cruel in the day," he wrote to Nava, "due to much snow that covers the fields and rigorous ices that petrify it with great prejudice to the horse herds." As a result, he planned to forgo any further large-scale campaigns for the time being. Instead, he would employ the talents of the Apaches de paz to spy out the watering holes and resting places frequented by those Mescaleros at war. This would also shelter and preserve his horse herd, "so that thus the beasts do not get crippled uselessly and we find them lacking when we need them most."[17]

The good services that Cordero had received from the Apaches de paz had proven instrumental in achieving whatever success his campaigns had enjoyed so far, and Cordero conscientiously called Nava's attention to this fact. "I cannot fail to convey to Your Lordship that the Indian Francisco and his ranchería located in San Eleceario [Elizario] have proceeded with the most constant fidelity in our alliance."[18]

Additionally, other Mescalero leaders were also seeking to avoid the calamities of the war by returning to the Spanish fold. For example, Cordero received a letter from Lieutenant Nicolás Villaroel at Presidio del Norte (who was serving as post commander as Captain Domingo Díaz was seriously ill), noting that on November 10 "there came in the three rancherías of Alegre, Volante, and El Natajé for the buffalo hunt, with a passport [previously issued] from Captain Don Domingo Díaz; and the Indians Miguel and Xavier that were of the same rancherías and who with their families are living within this Presidio." Clearly, these Mescaleros were seeking to manipulate the Spaniards into granting them a safe haven for their families while they resupplied their winter larder. Whether they or any of their people had been involved in the hostilities was uncertain, but Captain Díaz believed it was better to keep them at least under a semblance of control by giving them official papers that they could show to any other Spaniards they may encounter while on the plains hunting buffalo. As a sign of good faith, the two Mescaleros, Miguel and

Xavier, had even left their families at Presidio del Norte and had volunteered to escort Captain Díaz, whose illness had worsened, to Chihuahua, where Díaz hoped "to be cured at that villa."[19]

The reports from Lieutenant Villaroel at Presidio del Norte reflected the complex reality of waging war against some Mescaleros while seeking to foster peaceful accommodation with others. For Lieutenant Colonel Antonio Cordero, the campaigns he and his forces had undertaken over the last four months represented in many ways the traditional Spanish response of immediate and overwhelming force in the face of perceived Apache intransigence. But the actions of the Spaniards at Presidio del Norte showed that peace was possible even in the midst of conflict.

Still, although individual Spanish commanders were allowed to employ discretion "on the ground" in dealing with the Apaches, Commandant General Pedro de Nava still directed the conflict's overall tenor. Unbeknownst to Lieutenant Colonel Cordero at El Paso and Lieutenant Villaroel at Presidio del Norte, the commandant general had unleashed forces beyond their purview, forces that would ensure that attacks against the Mescaleros designed to disrupt their ability to feed themselves would continue with unabated ferocity.

The troopers out of Coahuila may well have wondered if their commander was incredibly determined or incredibly foolish. For more than three months, Lieutenant Colonel Miguel de Emparan and his men had scoured a huge amount of territory with very little to show for their fatigues. They had set out on September 23 from the Villa de San Fernando. Here, Emparan had assembled a force of 250 soldados from the five presidial and one flying companies that comprised his command. It is unclear if he had any Apaches de paz or other Indian auxiliaries, but judging by the duration of the expedition, it seems likely that there were few, if any, of these crucial allies on the expedition.

Moving northwest, the Spaniards had first traveled until they reached the junction of the Pecos River and the Rio Grande. They had then apparently followed the smaller stream as it moved gradually westward, all the while seeking signs of the Mescalero. At some point they forded the Pecos, possibly at what was later called the Horsehead Crossing, and continued over well-worn trails into the Sierra del Mogano, a favorite Mescalero camping site. But the Spaniards found nothing. Pressing onward, they rode to the northwest into the adjacent Sierra de Guadalupe. The commander had his men systematically move throughout this range as it curved back toward the northeast, but they still could not find their enemies.

After many weeks of fruitless searches, Emparan turned back eastward. The detachment's supplies were probably beginning to run low and their horses and mules becoming jaded. Still, the commander insisted on seeking out the Mescaleros. By mid-December his men were once again in the vicinity of the Pecos River, but rather than following the river south toward it junction with the Rio Grande and head back into Coahuila, he ordered them to move farther to the east. Within a few days, the Spaniards approached the headwaters of the Río San Pedro, which the Americans would later come to call the Devils River. Here, after almost three months of seemingly futile efforts, Emparan's luck changed—his scouts had finally located signs of the Mescaleros in what was described as the "Lomería de las Caveseras del Río de San Pedro," the hill country at the headwaters of the Río de San Pedro.[20]

During the night of December 24, Christmas Eve, or *Noche Buena* as the Spaniards termed it, Emparan's men located the combined rancherías of two Mescalero capitancillos at a watering hole, upon which Emparan bestowed the name *Ranchería de la Parage de noche buena*. Within the encampment, the Spaniards counted twenty-one "lodges of buffalo hide," all of which most likely contained about seventy people. These were the rancherías of two Mescalero leaders later identified as Desmolado (or Toothless) and Mulatto, who along with their people, were apparently caught totally unaware.[21]

In the resulting assault, the Spaniards achieved a complete victory, killing fifteen Mescalero warriors and two women and taking a boy prisoner, while suffering no losses themselves. The rest of the Apache people in the two rancherías managed to affect their escape, but they left behind their horse herd of 212 animals as well as almost all of their worldly possessions, including their yearly food supplies.[22]

Although Emparan did not provide a description of the attack on the rancherías, the type of casualties inflicted and the quantity of spoils seized allows for some conjecture on the course of events. Clearly, the Spaniards had achieved total surprise in their attack, which suggests that they struck either at sunset or dawn, a typical tactic they had employed on many other occasions. However, it appears probable that at least some of the fifteen Mescalero warriors reported as killed, and perhaps at least two of their women, managed to fight back and apparently sold their lives dearly. Given that the Spaniards did not capture any other women, children, or elderly, except for the single boy, suggests that some type of ad-hoc defense took place that allowed the remaining Mescaleros time to escape into the nearby mountains.

Nevertheless and just as assuredly, those Mescaleros that did manage to elude the Spaniards probably did so with only their lives and very little else. Furthermore, the goods left behind indicated that the two rancherías had within the last few months completed a buffalo hunt and a harvest of native and domesticated crops. A close examination of the spoils seized makes this quite clear.

First and foremost the Mescaleros had been stripped of many of their most necessary tools, most especially their weapons. Emparan's troopers recovered a significant number of firearms and ammunition, including eight "fusils and escopetas," along with seven pistols and "10 powder horns, four with powder . . . two cartridge boxes with 20 tubes and 18 cartridges," and finally "many bags of cut lead balls and flint." Whether these items were traded clandestinely with French or American traders from beyond the Mississippi or with Spaniards in the Interior Provinces, the dealing in illegal commerce represented by the firearms confirmed a disturbing reality for Spanish officials.

The Indians had also lost many of their more traditional weapons, including nine lances, ten quivers of arrows, fifteen knives, two swords, and three pieces of an iron ramrod from a musket that the Apaches had transformed into daggers. They also lost defensive gear, such as armor that included "4 white cueras of 12, 9, and 8 layers" and seven round leather shields known as *chimals*.

In addition, these Mescaleros were now deprived of a large amount of clothing. Many of their own handiwork were made from *gamuza*, tanned deer or antelope hide, which produced soft, pliable, and strong clothing. Also found in the camp were eighteen women's shirts and nineteen skirts, eighty men's shirts, and four pairs of men's breeches ("a lo Apache"), all made of gamuza, along with numerous hides of deer, antelope, and buffalo, many already tanned, that had not yet been turned into clothing, robes, or blankets.

As with the weaponry, much of the clothing was of Spanish manufacture. Items seized included one pair of red breeches and two others of cotton, along with three short woolen jackets, one of white cordage with red collar and cuffs that resembled the fatigue coats worn by presidial soldiers; another of red with blue collar and cuffs; and most ominously, one blue coat that also resembled those worn by Spanish troopers, found with "blood stains, old and new." The mixture of clothing proved that members of these two rancherías had either direct contact with the Spanish settlements or at the least with the Mescaleros de paz who acted as middlemen. No matter the origin of the clothing, the quantity of items left behind indicated that those people who escaped the attack did so in the middle of winter, with literally only the clothing on their backs.

Perhaps most crucially, the attack succeeded in stripping the Mescaleros in the two encampments of almost an entire season's worth of foodstuffs. Emparan's men recovered "many sacks and hides with cactus fruit," eighteen sacks filled with walnuts, some other sacks filled with wheat, and most importantly "165 *tercios* of buffalo meat and fat, covered in hides." Given that a tercio weighed approximately 160 pounds, the haul of buffalo meat totaled just over thirteen tons. This huge amount of food would have been enough to sustain about seventy-five people with meat for at least six months.

For the people within Desmolado's and Mulatto's ranchería, the attack by Lieutenant Colonel Emparan and his troopers was undoubtedly a disaster that defied imagination. Even if the survivors managed to reunite during the following days, their lot would have been desperate in the extreme. With their horse herd captured, they could neither travel quickly, nor easily engage in hunting. With their firearms and other weapons seized, they could not defend themselves if they were attacked by the Comanches or other enemies. With their lodges, hides, clothing, and tools gone, they would be prey to the elements. And with the loss of their food supply in the middle of a harsh winter, they would be at the point of starvation within weeks, if not days. For these survivors, the quick death suffered by their fallen compatriots might have been preferable to the ordeal they would inevitably now have to endure.[23]

By early January, Emparan and his men had returned to their starting point of the Villa de San Fernando in Coahuila. On the eleventh of that month, the lieutenant colonel sent in his report of the expedition and the destruction of the two Mescalero rancherías to Commandant General Nava in Chihuahua. Nava must have been pleased to receive Emparan's report, especially as he had also received news from the New Mexico detachment of its success. The governor of that province, Fernando Chacón, had set out to attack the Mescaleros in early October 1795. On the twenty-second of that month the New Mexicans located and attacked a ranchería somewhere north of the Sacramento Mountains. They succeeded in "killing seven Indians and four women and making seven prisoners, and they took twenty-six horses. In the action one soldado was killed." After this assault, Chacón and his men returned to Santa Fe, where they concluded their rather brief foray on November 13.[24]

Nava compiled all these notes, and on February 2, 1796, he sent his own reports to his superiors in Madrid. He recounted the operations of the expeditions from Nueva Vizcaya, New Mexico, and Coahuila. Taken together, the detachments led by Cordero, Emparan, and Chacón had killed seventy-seven Apaches of all ages and both sexes, taken sixty-nine prisoners, recovered 245 horses and mules, and destroyed a huge amount of vital buffalo meat and other food supplies. Nevertheless, the commandant general remained vexed by a variety of petty thefts that continued to plague the region:

> From the jurisdiction of El Paso del Norte Indians carried off in November six horses and four head of cattle.
> On the 25th of December six Indians carried off six beasts and eight head of cattle from the Rancho de San Juan near the Presidio del Norte. . . .
> Three Apaches robbed nineteen beasts from the Hacienda de Dolores on the 30th of the same month, but they were recovered by a party from the Presidio del Príncipe. . . .
> The Enemies robbed on the 23rd of January eight beasts near the Hacienda de Encinillas. . . .

That such robberies occurred in the midst of and even at the very locations at which the Spaniards had mobilized large military forces must have been extremely frustrating for Nava. This fact also confirmed the belief of many Spanish military officers that the perpetrators were Apaches de paz, who simply could not or would not stop raiding.[25]

Yet Nava realized that the continued small-scale raiding conducted by the Apaches would pale in significance in the face of any large-scale invasion that the Mescaleros at war might initiate. As such, he was adamant that the Spaniards keep up the pressure by continuing to attack the enemy in their own lands beyond the line of presidios that marked the frontier. Nava described the situation succinctly: "Constantly pursued in their own lands they have retreated to the most rugged mountains in the front of the Line abandoning those nearby in order to free themselves from the punishment deserved by their disloyalty." Nava was clearly far from satisfied that the Mescaleros had been punished sufficiently. Thus, he would continue to launch multiple attacks from all the provinces under his command into the Mescalero heartlands and disrupt their ability to feed themselves. Until Commandant General Nava received satisfaction, the war would go on.[26]

10

WAR IN THEIR OWN LANDS

Villa de Chihuahua, January 6, 1796—His work as a scribe required that he write not only legibly and gracefully but rapidly as well. Such speed was essential given the voluminous amount of reports that he regularly had to transcribe from a variety of individuals, many of whom had atrocious penmanship or a poor grasp of spelling, or both. Speed was also essential if he had to take dictation, though in many cases several assistants would help him, each one writing specific sections for later compilation into a final document. Yet, for the scribe, the most recent documents he worked on were already completed and he merely needed to copy them. Nevertheless, there were five separate items that totaled forty-four pages, and their consecutive numbering required special care in his margins and order. Fortunately, at least one aide helped, and he had the documents ready a day before they were needed. His superior, the secretary of the commandant general of the Interior Provinces Manuel Merino, reviewed the scribe's copy and gave formal approval by signing and dating it.

The next day, Commandant General Pedro de Nava reviewed the papers prepared by the scribe and assented to their quality. He would include them in the packet of letters and reports he was dispatching to the Spanish minister of war, Miguel José de Azanza, in Madrid. In all likelihood, the reports' contents would reach the king, and the possibility existed that his majesty himself might even read them. For the scribe, this might be the closest any of the many works dispatched to Spain might ever come before royalty. But for Pedro de Nava these papers were yet another reminder that after five months, he had not yet brought the war against the Mescaleros to a successful close.

It had not been for lack of effort. Between the outbreak of war in August 1795 until the end of the year, Nava's soldiers from Nueva Vizcaya, New Mexico, and Coahuila had killed or captured almost 150 Mescaleros of all ages and both sexes, seized hundreds of horses and mules, and destroyed great quantities of food and other necessities vital to the Mescaleros' survival. But still it did not seem enough. Those identified by the Spaniards as the leaders of the uprising had not been punished, and many of the rancherías of the Mescaleros de paz remained at best sullenly aloof, if not openly hostile. Still, Nava felt the need to offer explanations to his superiors to prove that he was doing everything in his power to defeat them.

On January 6, 1796, Nava sent a report to the Spanish court demonstrating that he had not neglected even the smallest details. In this, he included a document entitled "Dispositions that are to be observed by the Commanders of Companies and Detachments for Campaign Service." This contained thirty-one points of practical and useful directives on how the troopers were to engage the Apaches, ranging from the formation of detachments to the correct use of weapons in combat. Originally composed in 1793, over the following years Nava had augmented this document with several others, all of which he had circulated to the officers of his command with the punctilious micromanagement typical of the eighteenth-century Spanish military. He now sent copies of these instructions to his superiors as proof that his men were performing their duties effectively and to demonstrate that he had the situation well under control. Now it only remained for him to convince the Mescaleros.[1]

As the year 1796 began, Nava determined to intensify his military operations and try different tactics in a new effort to finish the war. First, he would maintain the offensive initiative by keeping large campaign detachments from Nueva Vizcaya and Coahuila continuously in the field. These forces were to operate exclusively beyond the frontier, constantly striking at the Mescalero homelands. Simultaneously he would station smaller units in a defensive perimeter around the Bolsón de Mapimí to guard against any Apaches infiltrating through it and launching counterstrikes. Next, he would entertain no peace negotiations with any ranchería unless they unconditionally accepted

Spanish terms. Finally, he would not agree to any exchange or redemption of captives. He would consider all those captured as prisoners of war and deport them into permanent exile to Veracruz, Mexico, and Havana, Cuba. If they had not learned already, Nava was determined to teach the Mescaleros the brutal consequences of starting the war in the first place.

Nava again turned to Lieutenant Colonel Antonio Cordero to initiate these new tactics, and on January 25 Cordero led a detachment of two hundred men into the Mescalero homelands. Despite the snow and ice, he doggedly searched the numerous mountains beyond El Paso for almost two months, with little luck. Then on March 14, he located and attacked a ranchería in the Sacramento Mountains, "killing a gandul, wounding many, and making nine prisoners and taking from them twenty-five horses." However, this limited success also alerted the Mescaleros to Cordero's presence, and consequently, they took measures to thwart him. The scattered rancherías in the Sacramentos and nearby ranges began to send out smoke signals that warned of the Spaniards' movements. After three more weeks of fruitless pursuit, Cordero decided to end operations, because "they knew from the smoke signals that they made in those mountains and environs that it would be useless to pursue them." He headed out of the mountains on April 9.[2]

Despite these poor results, the constant Spanish harassment did convince some Mescaleros to choose a more stable life. At the same time that Cordero was campaigning in the Sacramentos, a ranchería under a capitancillo named Joagosun approached El Paso and requested to make peace. Nava said that he would allow this, but sternly warned that if Joagosun and his people "moved away from there, our troops would go out and attack and I arranged that if they left that land, this would be immediately obeyed." Unfortunately, other Mescaleros still at war threatened Joagosun about cooperating with the Spaniards, and he and his ranchería appear to have been caught in the middle of precarious neutrality.[3]

Still other Mescaleros clearly favored remaining on the warpath. In late February, Nava received reports that some Mescaleros had attacked in the province of Coahuila, where "they seized seventy-five animals, killing two shepherds, but the troops dispatched in pursuit of them recovered all the theft, wounding an Apache." In response to this raid, the Spaniards launched a counterstrike. On March 2, troops from Coahuila began a reconnaissance of the mountains across the Rio Grande in the Big Bend vicinity. They entered into the Sierra del Carmen along the eastern flank of the great bend, where the river flowed north. On March 11, during a routine break from searching, the soldiers came down to the river bank "in order that their horse herd could drink," when they suddenly spied two Indians in the hills above them. The commandant of the detachment ordered a sergeant and twenty-five troopers "to scale a nearby height in order to see if they could discover more enemies." The commander warned the sergeant that if he found any Indians, he was not to pursue them, but the sergeant disregarded his orders. After making contact, he led his men straight into a Mescalero ambush. The sergeant quickly paid for his disobedience, being killed along with six of his men. Fearing the worst, the Spanish commander rode up with the rest of his men in the nick of time, as "the bulk of the detachment hurried to succor them and fought for more than an hour until night fell. Favored by the darkness and the roughness of the mountain the enemies dispersed." The Spaniards attempted to pursue the Mescaleros the following day, but to no avail. Eventually, the soldiers ignominiously returned to their posts.[4]

In the wake of this defeat, Commandant General Nava insisted on sending out more expeditions to harry the Mescaleros in their own country. On April 30, another detachment commanded by the alférez of the Presidio of San Buenaventura, Nicolás Madrid, set out from San Elizario. Madrid and his men had moved for several days toward the Guadalupe Mountains northeast of the presidio, before turning west. By May 4 the Spaniards entered the Cornudas Mountains, about seventy-five miles east of El Paso, where they camped for the night.

The next morning Madrid dispatched a small advance guard heading west, while he followed with the bulk of the party some distance behind. After having covered about thirty miles, the Spaniards were close to the Hueco Mountians, when Madrid "heard in the field a lively fire of escopetas." Putting spurs to their horses, Madrid and the main body of troopers rode hard and soon caught up to the advanced guard, "which he found had recovered nineteen animals, warring with the Enemies." The troopers had stumbled upon a significant body of Mescaleros who were encamped in the mountains and had seemingly been taken unawares by the advanced guard. Yet despite this, the Apaches appeared determined to fight. "These were entrenched in a cave of the Cerro Hueco," reports later said, "from where the advantage of the terrain and the superiority of their numbers, convinced them that they could destroy our detachment."

Granite Masses—Waco [Hueco] Mountains, Texas, by John Russell Bartlett, 1851.
Courtesy of the John Carter Brown Library at Brown University, John Russell Bartlett Collection.

But Alférez Madrid had other ideas, and "trusting in his skill and that of the Troop," he quickly realized that the Mescaleros had put themselves in an untenable position. Dismounting his men, Madrid had them push forward, driving the Apaches back toward the mouth of the cave, which soon became a death trap. For several hours the Spaniards fired into the cave, where the ricocheting musket balls and splinters of rock rained down on the defenders. Eventually, the Mescaleros' resolve broke. "In spite of the resistance of the Indians and of their vigor in shooting arrows and bullets from the mouth and openings of the cave, they were obliged to abandon the terrain as soon as night came on."

If Madrid and his men believed that the Apaches might surrender, they were soon disappointed when it became clear that the Mescaleros had managed to escape "via an almost inaccessible precipice." When the soldiers finally were able to enter the cave is not clear, but it may not have been until the light of morning. Nevertheless, they had clear evidence of the battle's carnage, noting that in addition to "the lamentations and cries of the wounded, they left in testimony of the great calamity they had suffered, the bodies of nine Gandules and great pools of blood that indicated how large the number of them they carried away." Later reports stated that ten Indians had died and one was captured, which may indicate that two Apaches were left behind, one of whom died later. For their part, the Spaniards suffered six soldados wounded. Following up this action, Madrid pushed his troops in pursuit, and soon "the same detachment had a second action with the same Indians, and in that they killed two gandules made sixteen prisoners and took ten horses."[5]

When Commandant General Nava learned of the victory achieved by Alférez Madrid and his men, he was clearly delighted. He ordered the account of the operation transcribed and had it sent to all the presidios in the Interior Provinces. There, the commanders at each post assembled their troopers and read the account before them in an attempt to bolster their morale and to demonstrate the superiority of Spanish arms. Yet despite this success, Nava knew that the back and forth cycle of violence between Spaniard and Mescalero would continue with a tedium that must have seemed wearisome if not for its deadly consequences.[6]

As the summer of 1796 approached, the Mescalero continued small-scale livestock raids throughout Nueva Vizcaya, which were invariably counterattacked by the Spanish troops. For example, after one such raid near the Presidio of San Buenaventura, Apaches "that intended to penetrate our Lands" were overtaken by troops from that post who "succeeded in ruining their ideas, killing three gandules and imprisoning an equal number." In similar fashion, after the rustling of some cattle and horses near El Paso, the Spaniards managed to seize "an Indian Caudillo of the Mescalero *parcialidad* [faction]." Perhaps seeking to inflate the importance of this capture, Nava claimed that this unnamed warrior "deserved greater estimation by his talents and resolution and was the director of their operations of war."[7]

As had become the pattern, soon after these raids, a large force from the Presidio del Príncipe set out to harry "the Enemy Country," searching the Guadalupe and Mogano Mountains and then moving east all the way to the Pecos River. Over the course of sixty-five days between May and July, the expedition "found no more than one ranchería that they attacked and punished, having made five prisoners and recovered eighty-three horses." The Spaniards suffered no casualties during the combats, but one soldado died when he incautiously mingled with the captured prisoners. With what was characterized as "blind confidence," the soldado, whether because he knew the Mescalero or was engaging in foolish braggadocio, "placed his escopeta in the hands of one of the prisoners." The captive immediately turned the weapon around and shot the soldado dead. The Apache's fate is not recorded.[8]

As Nava feared, several groups of Mescaleros responded to the Spanish invasions of their homelands by striking back in kind on a large scale. Entering through the Bolsón de Mapimí, Mescalero raiders slipped undetected south of the frontier line and emerged into the heart of Nueva Vizcaya. There they killed "three men they encountered undefended, robbed one hundred and eight horses and captured two muchachos." In response, the troopers from the First, Third, and Fourth Compañías Volantes chased after the raiders, "threw them out of the interior part of the Frontier," and recovered one of the captive boys.[9]

However, these pursuits merely pushed the raiders eastward into the province of Coahuila as the Mescaleros fled before the Spanish strikes and out of the bolsón. In Coahuila the Mescaleros broke up into several small parties, and "from May 3 until the second of this June the Enemy killed in the said Province four Paisanos that they found defenseless and without any warning along its roads, and robbed two herds of mares, and three horses." Troopers from the province pursued the Apaches "as far as the interior of their country and succeeded in recovering all the cited robbery with more than fifty-five horses and mules."[10]

But like a series of dominos falling against each other, every Spanish attack seemed to trigger another Mescalero raid. As had happened in Nueva Vizcaya, so now in Coahuila the troopers merely pushed the Indians farther eastward to the border of the Nuevo León province. On May 11, First Lieutenant Juan Ygnacio Ramón of the Volante Company stationed at Punta de Lampazos in Nuevo León received word that enemy Indians had stolen a large number of horses and mules from the Hacienda de Carrizal just across the western border of his province.

Ramón immediately set out with thirty men in pursuit on the best horses available and chased the raiders for several days. Unfortunately, he was unable to overtake them as they rode back into the Bolsón de Mapími. With his horses exhausted and suffering from a lack of water, Ramón decided to end the pursuit and return to his post at Punta de Lampazos.

Upon arrival he met a large force of troopers from Coahuila led by Lieutenant Casimiro Valdez from the Presidio of Monclova. Valdez reported that there had been "a large junta the Enemy had made in the Sierra del Carmen" on the eastern side of the Big Bend. Valdez and his men had attacked this gathering, "scattering them in many parts" as they fled into the Bolsón de Mapímí. Valdez informed Ramón that his superiors in Coahuila had taken the precaution of stationing five detachments of troops to guard the watering holes leading out of the bolsón "in order to punish the evils that they intended in the entrada."

The raiders that Ramón encountered were most likely some of those that had escaped from Valdez; consequently Ramón could expect more attacks into Nuevo León. Within days this prediction came true as another group or raiders attacked and carried off more than three hundred horses and mules from Punta de Lampazos and the mining community of Real de Boca de Leones. Driving their stolen stock west into Coahuila, the raiders unexpectedly ran into troopers from that province. The Indians immediately abandoned their plunder and managed to flee unscathed, and the soldados were eventually able to return the horses and mules to their owners in Nuevo León. But despite this lucky outcome, more livestock raids continued throughout the summer.[11]

The spread of violence into Nuevo León, a province under the direct control of the Viceroy Branciforte, compelled Commandant General Nava to explain why he had failed to contain the hostilities. Writing to Branciforte in July, Nava pointed out that his soldiers were constantly in the field and were doing everything possible to defeat the Mescaleros. However, he stressed that "it is not difficult for them to pass through the Seño or Bolsón de Mapímí" as they had in May, "where they executed many hostilities." Nava went on that "the multitude of mountains" that formed "an uninterrupted chain" encircling the bolsón and forming the border between Coahuila and Nuevo León, combined with the distances between populated places, "made it most difficult to know in time when they entered with the result that in many cases there is no news until after the damage has been caused." Somewhat defensively, Nava also pointed out that while he was required by orders from Madrid to communicate directly with the viceroy regarding any items that might affect the viceroy's provinces, he was not given the same courtesy. Then, striking a more conciliatory tone, Nava concluded that if officials from both areas communicated with each other regularly, it might help prevent these attacks.

As if to show that the spike in violence in Nuevo León was not symptomatic of the rest of the frontier, Nava also pointed out to Branciforte that he had successfully disrupted the Mescaleros' relations with their erstwhile allies and kinsmen, the Lipan. He informed the viceroy that "the Lipan Apaches continue to be calm, entering in peace daily at San Antonio de Bexar, where they have given no aide or allowed into their rancherías, the Mescaleros." This same pattern occurred in Coahuila, with other Lipan groups that had approached the Presidios of Rio Grande and Aguaverde. Likewise, Nava noted that he continued to cultivate alliances with the Comanches and other Nations of the North, whom he claimed would support the Spaniards as a result of their "ancient and natural hatred of . . . all Indians of the Apache race."[12]

Believing he had satisfied the viceroy's concerns about the attack on the frontier, Nava now turned to seeking the latter's support in driving home to the Mescaleros the cost they would pay for challenging the Spaniards. During May and June Spanish forces had killed sixteen Mescaleros and captured another thirty-five. When adding these to the casualties inflicted since the war began in August 1795, the Spaniards claimed to have killed 111 Apaches of all ages and both sexes and captured another 104, almost all them Mescaleros. In early August Nava decided to deport seventy-nine of these prisoners from the Interior Provinces into exile in Havana, and for this he would need the logistical support of Viceroy Branciforte.[13]

On August 3, 1796, Nava wrote to the viceroy that he was dispatching the alférez of the Third Compañía Volante, Andrés Mateos, with an escort of twenty-five troopers to deliver a collera of captured Indians to Mexico City, from where they would be exiled to Cuba. The collera was to consist of "seventy-nine Apache Piezas, prisoners of war . . . which number is composed of twenty Gandules of eighteen to forty years of ages, five muchachos of twelve to fourteen, and fifty-four women of twenty to forty years, which should be delivered by the cited Alférez where Your Excellency orders." Nava had made arrangements to entrust Alférez Mateos with more than two thousand pesos to provide daily rations for the prisoners and for the use of seventy mules to carry them on the anticipated sixty-day journey. In addition, the military advanced the soldiers of the escort four months' pay to defray their personal expenses. Once arrived in Mexico City, the collera would become the responsibility of Viceroy Branciforte, and Nava anticipated his close cooperation.[14]

However, despite careful preparations, the prisoners experienced a harrowing ordeal. During the many weeks of travel, only sixty-one of the prisoners reportedly reached Mexico City. Judging from the data of other colleras, it is most likely that the eighteen unaccounted for either died from illness or exhaustion or were left behind in one of the many cities along the route, too ill to finish the trek. Yet, for the remaining sixty-one captives, the worst was yet to come. After recuperating for about a month in the capital, they were dispatched to the port city of Veracruz, arriving in November. But Veracruz was notorious for its unhealthy climate, which bred the dreaded *vómito negro*, and in the weeks they waited for a ship to take them to Cuba, twenty-four of the sixty-one prisoners died and eleven more were hospitalized. By the time they boarded a vessel for their final exile, only twenty-eight of the Apaches remained.[15]

Whether or not the Mescaleros along the northern frontier ever learned the particulars of their exiled kinsmen's terrible fate is unknown, but they understood the finality of their removal. As for the Spaniards, they remained determined to ensure that the war's brutal consequences were made abundantly clear to the Apaches, so much so that Commandant General Pedro de Nava wrote that he considered it an "urgent necessity to continue beating down the pride of the Mescalero Apaches." And one of the main instruments in Nava's arsenal would continue to be Lieutenant Colonel Antonio Cordero.[16]

By early September 1796, Nava directed that Cordero organize a force of two hundred troopers from the presidios and volante companies of Nueva Vizcaya to attack the Mescaleros "in the lands that are outside of the frontier between the said Province and that of Coahuila." Cordero was to sweep the border region between Coahuila and Nueva Vizcaya from south to north as far as the Rio Grande. The plan called for the troopers from Nueva Vizcaya to receive reinforcements from detachments from Coahuila, which would bring in supplies and remounts. The combined force would then head east, covering the mountains on both sides of the river, between the Big Bend and the regions near present-day Eagle Pass, Texas. Cordero's men were to exert relentless pressure on the Mescaleros so that "the operations can be vigorous and continuous in the present season of the year and that can occur when they go on the Buffalo hunt." By disrupting the Apaches' efforts to resupply themselves, Cordero would deliver a punishing blow to the Indians, even if he failed to engage significant numbers of them.[17]

Having by this point in his career overseen operations against the Apaches for six years, Nava's plan unfolded as he had generally foreseen. Throughout the rest of September and October, Antonio Cordero led his forces relentlessly in what some would come to call the Expedition of Coahuila. Although no detailed reports of the expedition have come to light, Nava provided a terse summary in a letter to his superiors in Madrid: "The detachment that was put under the command of Lieutenant Colonel Dn Antonio Cordero that was searching for the Enemies in part of the Frontier of Coahuila, carefully reconnoitered the Sierras and Parages where they lived; and over the course of forty-six days that were involved in these operations, attacked four divisions of Mescaleros and succeeded in taking from them all that they possessed, killed four individuals, made sixteen prisoners, and recaptured one hundred ten horses, without our Troops having suffered any losses other than one soldado lightly wounded."[18]

Though many details are lacking, records show that the "one soldado lightly wounded" was twenty-eight-year-old Mariano Madrid of Presidio del Norte. In a fight that took place on October 10, Madrid had been "wounded in two places on the body by gunshots from the Enemy." Whether Madrid considered getting shot twice as "lightly wounded," he nevertheless had the satisfaction of his superiors noting that he had "conducted himself with the greatest bravery," and received a certification of that fact from none other than Lieutenant Colonel Cordero.[19]

If Cordero was at all dissatisfied with the achievements of the Expedition of Coahuila up to that point, events soon unfolded that would allow him ample opportunity to try and obtain greater results. On October 22, 1796, he received word of his appointment as interim governor of Texas. The incumbent, Manuel Muñoz, had been requesting retirement for some time because of his advanced age and ill health, and it had finally been granted. However, both Muñoz and Cordero were quickly disappointed in their hopes for new horizons when soon thereafter Commandant General Nava, wishing to retain his most effective officer in the field, delayed the transfer in order to have Cordero continue directing "the Operations of War over the Frontier of Coahuila." Never one to hesitate, Cordero quickly organized his forces for more strikes and in early November, the Expedition of Coahuila set out once more to seek out and attack the Mescaleros in their homelands north of the Rio Grande.[20]

During the same period in which Cordero had been bringing pressure to bear on the Mescaleros out of Coahuila, Commandant General Nava was determined not to allow those Indians to the west any respite. Fortunately, Nava had found in Captain Manuel Rengel another officer with the same tenacity and determination.

Born in the Spanish city of Málaga around 1764, Rengel was not originally destined for a military career. However, his uncle was Colonel José Antonio Rengel, a veteran army officer who had distinguished himself at the sieges of Menorca and Gibraltar in 1782 during Spain's campaigns against the British in the American Revolution. As a reward for his services in 1784, the elder Rengel was appointed as commandant inspector of the Interior Provinces, and when he traveled to Mexico he decided to bring his twenty-year-old nephew with him. Colonel Rengel quickly obtained a captaincy for Manuel in the Regiment of Provincial Dragoons del Príncipe in the central Mexican city of Guanajuato. But when the colonel moved north to take up his position in the Interior Provinces, Manuel decided to stay close to his uncle. Once again Colonel Rengel used his influence and arranged a transfer for Manuel as lieutenant of the Third Compañía Volante of Nueva Vizcaya.[21]

Despite benefiting from the nepotism showered on him by his powerful relative, on the northern frontier Manuel Rengel soon proved his own worth in situations not influenced by familial connections, namely in the face of continuous combats against the Apaches. Between 1784 and 1790 Rengel served in a total of eleven major campaigns throughout Nueva Vizcaya and into the Apache homelands beyond. In five of these he served directly under Antonio Cordero, who clearly imparted his immense knowledge of frontier warfare to the young officer. By 1791 Rengel's actions had won him a promotion to captain of the Third Volante, and he served with distinction, leading campaigns rather than following the orders of others.[22]

Rengel's abilities were further honed after 1794, upon his appointment as captain of the Presidio of Janos. Here, he found himself not only responsible for the troopers under his command, but also for a large establishment of several hundred Chiricahua Apaches de paz. Like Antonio Cordero before him, Captain Rengel seized this opportunity to familiarize himself with the Apaches and their customs, if for no other reason than to better understand his enemy.

The knowledge gained through contact with the Chiricahuas at Janos would stand Rengel in good stead when it came to dealing with other Apaches. Like many officers, he realized that the constant application of military force, combined with the safety and sustenance that settling at the peace establishments promised, would prove crucial in containing the Apaches. In the summer of 1794, he saw a clear example of this when after a campaign he led against the Mescaleros in which his men took sixty prisoners, the immediate result was the "putting under peace . . . the capitancillos Barrios [Nzazen] and Mayá with their numerous rancherías." Despite being supposedly at peace outside El Paso, the on-again, off-again attitude of these two Mescalero leaders clearly proved to Rengel that the force of Spanish arms would be the ultimate guarantee of peace.[23]

In a show of force perhaps designed to overawe the Mescaleros around El Paso, in the summer of 1796 Commandant General Nava ordered Captain Rengel to organize a detachment of about three hundred troopers from throughout Nueva Vizcaya and to gather them in a cantonment outside that town. Between the end of July and the middle of October, Rengel would lead his men from this base of operations in hopes of, as Nava described it, "making incessant war on the Enemy that inhabit the vast lands of that Frontier." Moving out at the end of July, Rengel and his forces swept across the frontier on a sustained operation that lasted almost seventy-five days. His target seems to have been into the area north of the Big Bend and east to the Pecos River. By the middle of October his troopers had found and engaged the Mescaleros in three separate fights with impressive results in spite of the Apaches' "great numbers and stratagems." Altogether, Rengel's men killed thirteen Apaches, captured fifty-three, and recovered ninety-eight horses while suffering no casualties themselves.[24]

After only a few weeks respite, Rengel soon put his men again into the field. This time Commandant General Nava had ordered Rengel "to punish and route the Tribes of Faraónes Apaches." The Spanish regarded the Faraónes as either a branch of the Mescaleros or as closely allied kinsmen. Regardless of their actual affiliation, the regime recognized that their homelands were the mountains to the north of El Paso and west of the Rio Grande above the Jornada del Muerto.

Rengel launched his campaign in November and for the next two months scoured the region. Over this period he located and attacked three gatherings of Apaches and "succeeded in killing six, capturing fifty-three, and taking from them fifteen horses, without more loss on ours than two soldados lightly wounded." One of the wounded was apparently Captain Rengel himself, who recorded on his service record that during one of these fights, "he came out wounded by a lance thrust." Despite his wound, or perhaps because of it, Rengel determined to press ahead with his pursuit of the Apaches. However, it appears that he received orders from Commandant General Nava to suspend the campaign, "because with the abundant snows that blotted out the tracks and covered the pastures, freezing the rivers, lakes, and other watering places, such that the horse herds would perish if they continued their operations." Rengel opposed ending the campaign, but "despite his resistance" when Nava insisted, the captain reluctantly complied, "consequent to my orders."[25]

If the fierce winter thwarted the operations of Captain Rengel in the west, similar conditions did not stop Lieutenant Colonel Antonio Cordero farther to the east from continuing operations in the Expedition of Coahuila. Like Rengel, Cordero had launched an attack into the Mescalero lands north of Coahuila in early November in pursuit of "the Barbarian Indians." Nava recorded that although "the winter is so severe in those Countries," Cordero and his troopers "have continued their operations with the greatest tenacity." Over the course of two months, the Spaniards located and attacked "into the broken terrain contiguous to the Province seven of their large rancherías that had occupied the most rugged mountains." Although the number of Mescaleros killed and captured was apparently very low, "in the different skirmishes they lost all they possessed and fifty-four horses." Amid the cold and snow, the loss of their winter food supplies would have been crippling to these Mescaleros, and starvation may have been a greater blow than any battle casualties inflicted by the Spaniards. Cordero's troopers were mainly drawn from the presidios of Nueva Vizcaya, not Coahuila, and Cordero "felt that their successes would have been greater if those lands and water holes were better known by the Troops." Despite this, Commandant General Nava was satisfied with Cordero's performance and wrote assuredly to his superiors in Madrid that they would continue to batter the Mescaleros, "pushing out those that remain on our Frontier, or humbling them to make peace." Lauding Cordero and his men, Nava proclaimed, "The troops will not cease to pursue them at the example of their indefatigable Commandant."[26]

The relentless determination of Lieutenant Colonel Antonio Cordero and Captain Manuel Rengel throughout the winter of 1796 had, to a large measure, brought the war beyond the Rio Grande into the homelands of the Mescalero Apaches. Between the latter part of July and the end of December, Spanish forces had continuously hunted and harassed the Apaches over almost the entire expanse of their range from the Rio Grande in the west, through the Big Bend country, to the Pecos River in Texas in the east. At the same time, the garrisons of the Provinces of Nueva Vizcaya and Coahuila had responded with alacrity to the entrance of Apache raiders into Spanish territory, and despite the infiltration into Nuevo León and areas farther to the east, troopers' efforts were generally successful. Over the course of the year, Nava's forces had killed 55 Mescaleros of all ages and both sexes, made 231 others prisoners, and seized or recovered 866 animals. However, these successes did not come without cost, as at least eight Spanish soldiers were killed and several wounded in action, along with at least ten civilians killed.

Yet, in spite of the large numbers of casualties the Spaniards inflicted, there had not been a general return of large numbers of Mescaleros to the peace establishments. Only a very few rancherías had remained "loyal," and after fourteen months of open warfare, the number of groups that had sought peace, even temporarily, was even smaller. Despite the violence, the loss of life, and the disruption of their hunting cycles that the Spanish had unleashed upon the Mescaleros, it seemed to Commandant General Nava and his officers that they were either unwilling or incapable of curtailing their propensity for raiding. The atomized nature of Mescalero society made it almost impossible for any of their leaders to control the actions of their diverse and independent people and all but ensured that attacks for revenge and gain would never cease. Whether or not Pedro de Nava and his commanders knew, or even cared, about the intricacies of Mescalero society had by now become irrelevant. In the end, the Mescaleros would either make peace or they would be destroyed. It had come down to that.

11

INVASIONS REAL AND IMAGINED

ISLAND OF TRINIDAD, THE CARIBBEAN, FEBRUARY 16, 1797—The appearance of the British fleet had come as a total surprise late that morning. The flotilla included nine ships of the line, three frigates, six sloops, a bomb vessel, and fourteen armed transports carrying almost seven thousand soldiers. Rear Admiral Sebastián Ruiz de Apodaca's small squadron of four ships of the line and one frigate had been at their anchorage at Chaguaramus Bay, some five miles north of Puerto España, the capital city of Trinidad, for several weeks. The majority of his sailors and marines were on shore, many lying sick from the ravages of an epidemic of malaria that had swept over them. Over the course of the day the British men-of-war drew up just beyond cannon range from Apodaca's ships. Word had been sent to Governor José María Chacón in the capital, but the situation there was chaotic. The battery of twenty cannons on Gaspar Grande Island, just to the east of Apodacas's anchorage, was precipitously abandoned by its small garrison, who fled at the first sight of the British. In Puerto España the battalion of five hundred regular soldiers had been assembled, but more than two thousand of the island's militiamen and volunteers had thrown down their arms and scattered back to their homes. With no word from the governor, Apodaca was at a loss for what to do next.

By sunset the British fleet had spread out all along the bay and had effectively blockaded both the anchorage of the Spanish ships and the harbor at Puerto

The Capture of Trinidad, 17 February 1797, by Nicholas Pocock.
Courtesy National Maritime Museum, Greenwich, London, United Kingdom.

España. At eight that night Admiral Apodaca called a council of war with his captains. They were outnumbered and outgunned by the British over two to one, and even had they wished to attempt a breakout, their crews were in such poor condition that the attempt would be suicidal. The only option left seemed to be to deny their ships to the enemy. The council voted to scuttle the fleet, and Apodaca accepted the decision.[1]

At midnight, small groups of Spanish sailors began to lay incendiary materials throughout the four ships of the line and one frigate. Several hours later the British admiral, Sir Henry Harvey, and his men witnessed a strange light that appeared in the Spanish fleet. Harvey later reported: "At two o'clock in the morning of the 17th we discovered one of their ships on fire, and soon after three others, all of which burnt with great fury until near daylight, when they were entirely consumed." Though the British were surprised by the fires, they soon noticed that one of the Spanish ships of the line, the seventy-four-gun *San Damaso*, had failed to ignite, and as Harvey noted, "One of them having escaped the conflagration, the boats were sent from the squadron and she was brought out without having received any damage."[2]

The failure of Admiral Apodaca to completely scuttle his own fleet was perhaps the least of the humiliations heaped upon the Spaniards. On the morning of February 18, as the British began landing marines and soldiers at several points around the city, Governor Chacón's spirit collapsed. He issued no orders, and when the first British soldiers entered the capital, he immediately requested terms of surrender. By that afternoon, the British had formally taken possession of the Island of Trinidad without having suffered a single casualty. With this one blow, they demonstrated that they could attack the Spanish empire anywhere they chose, whenever they chose, perhaps in Mexico and perhaps even in the Interior Provinces. The bitter truth was that the Spaniards knew the British were right.[3]

For many residents of Mexico City, the corruption of the Viceroy the Marqués de Branciforte was reputed to have no bounds. When he had assumed office in July 1794, Spain was at war with revolutionary France and the new viceroy had used the opportunity to seize the property of many French residents in Mexico City, much of which he pocketed for himself. Then in 1796, when Spain had switched sides and gone to war with Britain, Branciforte again used the opportunity to enrich himself by confiscating the personal property of British subjects then in the capital. Despite the disgust of many citizens for their opportunistic and venal viceroy, there seemed little they could do.

Branciforte was the brother-in-law of Manuel Godoy, first minister of the Spanish court. Godoy himself was a consummate opportunist. As a member of the Spanish Royal Guards, he had used his striking good looks to become the queen of Spain's lover. With Queen María Louisa's support, the young guardsmen advanced rapidly, amazingly becoming a trusted advisor of the cuckold King Charles IV. Soon, the reins of government passed into Godoy's hands, and he quickly placed his own men, like Branciforte, into key positions. But despite his pretensions, Godoy's skills were no match for the turbulent events that threatened to engulf Spain. In 1794 and 1795 the French had inflicted a humiliating defeat on the Spanish armies in the so-called War of the Pyrenees and invaded the north of the country. Godoy sued for terms to quickly end the war by promising to ally with France. A relieved Charles IV awarded Godoy with the pompous title of "the Prince of the Peace" and entrusted him with virtually absolute control of the government. But the new title did little to protect Spain, and by October 1796 the nation found itself dragged into a new war against Britain as a French satellite.

Miguel de la Grúa Talamanca, 1st Marqués de Branciforte,
Viceroy of New Spain, 1794–1798.
From Manuel Rivera Cambas, Los Gobernantes de México,
Vol. 1 *(Mexico, 1872), between pp. 488 and 489.*

When news of the war's outbreak reached Mexico City, rumors flew that Viceroy Branciforte planned to once again line his own pockets. He had ordered the expansion of the viceregal army, and some alleged that he would make a handsome profit by selling commissions to prospective officers. But as reports began to filter in of the awesome power of Britain, Branciforte began to fear that they might attack his own viceroyalty of New Spain. His fear soon bested his greed, and he seemingly began to take his responsibilities for defending the country seriously.[4]

For their own part, the British were deadly serious. Within four months of the outbreak of war, they had launched a series of massive blows designed to cripple Spain's economic underpinnings. On February 14, 1797, the British defeated the main Spanish battle fleet off the coast of Portugal at the Battle of Cape St. Vincent. The Spaniards lost four ships of the line, with two captured by the renowned British commander Horatio Nelson himself. The British drove the remaining Spanish ships back into home ports, where the victors managed to bottle them up.

A scant four days after the victory at Cape St. Vincent, another British expedition under the command of General Sir Ralph Abercromby invaded and captured the island of Trinidad off the Venezuelan coast. Capitalizing on this dramatic success, almost exactly two months later, on April 17, 1797, Abercromby led a force of four thousand soldiers and almost sixty warships and transports in another lightning assault on the island of Puerto Rico.

This time the British met stiffer resistance. The governor of Puerto Rico was none other than Ramón de Castro, the former commandant general of the Eastern Interior Provinces. Despite his questionable tenure along the Apache frontier, Castro found his moment in the face of the British assault on the city of San Juan and its series of massive fortifications constructed in anticipation of just such an attack. Rallying the regular garrison, and backed up manfully by the militia and civilian population of the island, Castro and his *puertorriqueños* fought fiercely for the next thirteen days. Despite the shelling from the British fleet, Castro's soldiers contained and repelled several amphibious landings. By April 30 the British had had enough and withdrew, having lost 250 men killed and captured and abandoning a large quantity of cannon and munitions on the beach.[5]

Despite the setback at Puerto Rico, the massive British naval power ensured that the offensive initiative continued to lay with Great Britain. Soon after the outbreak of the war, Spanish intelligence picked up reports that the British were contemplating an attack directly on the viceroyalty of New Spain. Such a move would cripple the shipment of silver produced in Mexico and regularly sent back to the mother country and would prove fatal to the economy of the empire.

For Pedro de Nava, the power of British arms was half a world away. Early 1797 still saw him earnestly directing the war against the Mescalero Apaches, maintaining the strategy of disrupting the Indians' winter encampments. During the winter of 1796–1797 he had organized a strategic shift to the eastern theater of operations against the Mescaleros, with detachments of troops from Sonora sent into Nueva Vizcaya to replace squadrons from the latter province that had been grouped into a special cantonment around Presidio San Elizario commanded by Captain Manuel Rengel. At the same time, the army detached a large numbers of soldados from Nueva Vizcaya for the Expedition of Coahuila commanded by Lieutenant Colonel Antonio Cordero, which had been sent into eastern Nueva Vizcaya and from there entered Coahuila. Utilizing forces from both the western and eastern Interior Provinces, the commandant general ordered continued attacks against them into April. In reporting to Madrid, Nava boasted, "The repeated blows [that his troopers had inflicted on the Mescalero] have obliged them to retire to the interior of the deserted countries . . . as they are heavily pressed by the constancy with which the Troops of the King search for them." He continued that from the end of January until April, the Apaches "have not made any attacks in our territories" and that the Interior Provinces had "experienced a peace and tranquility which possession I believed before to be very remote." Yet if Nava was gratified by the quiet that the region was enjoying, he also knew that it owed to the relentless military pressure his forces were applying against the Apaches. To maintain that pressure, he authorized more invasions into the Mescalero heartlands.[6]

In late January, Nava ordered Lieutenant Colonel Antonio Cordero and his Expedition of Coahuila to again cross the Rio Grande. Cordero divided his forces into three columns, which penetrated "to the interior by different routes in the Country of the Enemy, examining most carefully their plains, mountains, cañadas, and the rest of the sites where they might hide." Over the course of forty-six days, Cordero's forces swept the regions north of Coahuila, most likely from the Big Bend eastward to the Pecos River in Texas. Altogether, they accounted for "the death of six Gandules, imprisoning thirteen Enemies, recovering one hundred fifty-six horses and restoring two captive Spaniards." Despite the relatively low number of casualties, Nava was satisfied with the results, claiming that they had assured "the calmness of our territories, and bloodying the Barbarians in their own places where they had always considered themselves free from experiencing punishment."[7]

Cordero's forces remained in the field into the spring of 1797. On April 8, one of his detachments, under the command of Lieutenant Miguel Francisco Múzquiz from the Presidio of Monclova, located and attacked a large number of Mescaleros in the Sierra de los Taraises. Despite the Apaches being ensconced in difficult terrain, Múzquiz and his troopers "dislodged them from their position, taking from them all of their tents, ranchos, equipment, and horses."

The troops did not ascertain the number of killed or wounded, but the field was "left inundated with blood." The Spaniards felt that "a certain sign of how much they suffered" was that the Mescaleros had fled from battle, "dragging many wounded that were near death as well as others very hurt." Although the troopers recovered one captive after the attack, they also lost one Ópata soldado killed and another wounded.

Ten days later, another of Cordero's detachments, this one under Alférez Antonio Griego of Presidio San Juan Bautista de Rio Grande, also located and attacked a group of Mescaleros. On April 18, Griego's men came upon "a numerous body of Mescalero Apaches in the paraje de los Encinos." In the fight that followed, the Spaniards succeeded in "killing two Gandules and taking seven prisoners, wounding many of the Enemy, part of them mortally, who saved themselves by a precipitous flight in the most broken part of that terrain; and they also recovered a Spanish captive."[8]

During the same period in which he had unleashed Cordero's expedition, Nava also ordered forces from Nueva Vizcaya under Captain Manuel Rengel stationed in a cantonment at Presidio San Elizario to invade the region's Mescalero territory, "with the end of castigating the Enemies that live to the north of this Province." From late January through the end of March, Rengel conducted a lengthy "examination and reconnaissance of the lands that are in between that and New Mexico, penetrating into the Sierras where they hide." Despite their dogged pursuit into the Sacramento Mountains and adjoining areas, Rengel's men "did not find any more Indians than one ranchería, which he attacked, killing five individuals in it, making one captive and taking four horses." Rengel held forth that the lack of success owed to the Mescaleros having abandoned the region, and he assured Nava that "the Indians of those countries have absented themselves from them, as he did not see anything other than the vestiges of their retreat."[9]

By early June 1797, Commandant General Nava reported that the invasion "against the Mescalero Indians were executed in their own territories, beyond the Line of Presidios" was having an effect. In a letter to his superiors in Madrid, he noted that the Indians "had already sent emissaries soliciting peace, which I think to concede to them." However, recalling the numerous times that the Apaches had requested peace only to break it soon thereafter, Nava believed he still needed to "finish battering them," so that it would be impossible for the Mescalero to quickly recover and once again "harm that part of territory inhabited by the loyal vassals of His Majesty." Taken together,

Nava hoped that Cordero's and Rengel's invasions would finally break the will of the various Mescalero groups at war and lead them to sue for peace.¹⁰

But the commandant general's hopes were soon dashed. On June 27, a force of sixty men led by Captain Pedro Nolasco Carrasco from the Volante Company of San Carlos de Parras in eastern Nueva Vizcaya set out on a routine scout. At a location identified as the Río de Teria somewhere in Coahuila, Carrasco and his men were ambushed by a force exceeding two hundred Mescaleros. For nine hours the outnumbered Spaniards fought desperately, killing five Indians and wounding many more until the Apaches finally withdrew. Captain Carrasco himself was wounded by a gunshot that broke his leg, while soldados Francisco Flores of the Presidio of La Bábia was killed and Joseph Valentín Quesada of the Volante de Parras died two days later of his wounds. Leadership considered the battle of such import that all the troopers involved were allowed to cite it on their service records, and the widows of the slain were awarded a monthly pension of eight pesos.¹¹

Despite the Spanish victory, Nava reluctantly realized that the fighting spirit of the Mescaleros remained far from broken. The war was not over and would require the Spaniards to prepare for even more campaigns. But within weeks of Captain Carrasco's fight, the commandant general received reports that made his efforts against the Apaches pale to seeming insignificance when he received a dire warning from Viceroy Branciforte. The British were planning an invasion of Mexico, and Spanish officials considered the Interior Provinces a possible target.

In June 1797 Viceroy Branciforte wrote to Commandant General Nava with a series of warnings about the rumored British invasion. The viceroy had received word from Spain that the British had recruited the services of Francisco Miranda, a one-time Spanish officer who had become the focal point of the growing independence movement in Spain's American colonies. Miranda, who would come to be known as *el precursor* in Latin America, was reportedly set to embark from England for Mexico. At the same time, the Spanish ambassador in Philadelphia, the capital of the United States, had sent word of ominous preparations that he believed would be directed against New Spain, writing "that the English were going to make an attack on that Kingdom by the Mississippi, from Canada with ten thousand men." He continued, "It appeared that there was no doubt in the intent as there had arrived in the past days three English frigates with troops from Jamaica to Halifax from where they were going to begin the Expedition." This movement of troops seemed to confirm the idea that a British invasion out of Canada was imminent. In addition, the ambassador also noted that "six ships and eight frigates were loaded with supplies in Baltimore and were passing to Santo Domingo to take troops and make a landing on those coasts," meaning the Gulf of Mexico coast. The Spanish ambassador was so convinced of this intelligence that he sent warning not only to the court in Madrid, but directly to the Spanish governor of Louisiana and to Viceroy Branciforte to save time.[12]

Galvanized by the specter of an invasion, Branciforte had immediately sent reinforcements to strengthen the port city of Veracruz, the most likely target of any invasion and the key defensive point for New Spain. He also issued orders to protect other sections of the coast north of the port, and had commissioned Lieutenant Colonel Felix María de Calleja to organize a force of militiamen and regulars to guard the shorelines of Nuevo Santander all the way north to Texas. Finally, he issued orders to the governor of Louisiana, the Baron de Carondolet, to prepare for a British invasion from Canada that might descend the Mississippi River and assault New Orleans, possibly in conjunction with an amphibious assault on that city.

Branciforte also believed that the Interior Provinces might be attacked. When he wrote to Commandant General Pedro de Nava, the viceroy began by claiming that he had already undertaken "all that is possible and that is considered necessary for the defense of Vera Cruz, its lateral coasts and the Castillo de San Juan de Ulúa." He also asserted that if the English attacked Veracruz, "the enemy will find the most vigorous resistance which will disrupt their designs . . . and force them to invade this kingdom by other points." Though Louisiana appeared as a most likely target, the viceroy deemed that the Provinces of Coahuila and Texas were also vulnerable. British forces might set out across the Mississippi or they might make a landing on the Gulf Coast and move inland. The possibility also existed that they might come down the Missouri River and cross over into New Mexico and attack there.

The viceroy knew that any British move across the northern plains would prove difficult, as they would "have to cross great and deserted lands, where it is not possible to bring artillery, or provisions to maintain themselves." Nevertheless, given their resources, such a move was not impossible. He also expressed concerns about the nature of the Spanish subjects under Nava's control, cautioning against "carelessness or indolence on our part," and that the

English might discover "shelter and protection in the peoples of our Provinces that are already seen not covered in its characteristic loyalty." Regardless of the locals' patriotism, the viceroy much more realistically worried about the actions of powerful Indian nations, foreseeing "the friendship and alliance that the Enemy would try and procure with the Nations of the North bordering on our frontiers, and with the Apaches that live or encamp below them." Leaving no eventuality unstated, he concluded by cautioning that British landings along the coast of Sonora and more likely on the coasts of Alta or Baja California were also possible.[13]

For the previous six months Commandant General Pedro de Nava had focused much of his energy on directing the war against the Mescalero Apaches. When he received the frantic warnings from the viceroy about a British invasion, Nava concluded that finishing the war against the Mescaleros took on a greater importance in the face of the growing foreign threat. He responded to Branciforte by stating that while he was aware of the rumors of an invasion, he would not be able to detach any large force immediately, because his soldiers were "indispensable for the active war in which they are engaged against the Apache Indians that have attacked it."

Despite his determination to finish dealing with the Mescaleros, Nava did not discount the dangers posed by the British. Nevertheless, he felt that any British expedition would not be directed against the Provincias Internas: "If the English realize the announced expedition from Canada I consider that their principle gaze will be directed against the Province of Louisiana, as it is closer and because it presents greater objects that will animate their greed." He speculated that the British might send forces down the Missouri and Mississippi Rivers, "enabling them to go down this to the capital New Orleans, until it flows out into the Gulf of Mexico, working thus to combine the expedition by land with that by sea that they prepared in Baltimore."

Nava next sought to discount the possibility of a direct attack on the Provinces of New Mexico, Texas, and Coahuila by the British stating, "it does not appear credible that they would direct it against any of the three cited provinces because of their small dispersed populations, the poverty of their citizenry, the distance, and the little facility conducive for them crossing over immense terrain. . . . [T]hese are in my opinion obstacles they would not be able to overcome from that direction."

However, should the British approach the frontier, Nava sought to assure the viceroy that he would be able to personally move to Texas or Coahuila and within a few days "raise in them the veteran Troops, Militia, and armed citizenry." With these he could aid the Spanish forces in Nuevo Santander under Lieutenant Colonel Felix Calleja in defending that area, or even head eastward to Nacogdoches and Louisiana if necessary. Nava maintained that he would have "at my disposition a heavy [force] capable of opposing the Enemies, reinforced with the Indios Amigos del Norte and with part of the Apaches that exist in Peace."

The commandant general recognized the importance of maintaining good relations with the Native peoples of the plains and encouraged the viceroy that these Indians would serve Spain's needs. "It is not possible for the Expedition from Canada to march without noise," he told Branciforte. Nava remained confident that "the Indios Amigos that live on the Frontiers of New Mexico are in communication with others more distant," and they would give the Spaniards warning. Similarly, Nava optimistically and naively also believed the allied Nations of the North including the Comanche, would aid the Spaniards. "The Indians of the divisions Amigos del Norte, including the Comanche already have the office of spies," he wrote; and because of the good treatment and gifts given them by the Spaniards, "they will not only conserve their loyalty, but they will serve us on the occasion as good auxiliaries," especially if they received even more gifts, which Nava intended to dole out.

In the interim while he waited for more certain news, the commandant general would maintain himself in the center of his provinces. This would ensure his immediate availability wherever necessary with a competent force, whether toward New Mexico, Coahuila, and Texas, and even westward should something occur along the coast of the Province of Sonora or in California. He believed that a more likely danger lay in a British attack along the Gulf Coast, and he ordered the governor of Texas to increase surveillance with patrols twice a month and to enlist "the Carancaguaces and the rest of the Indians that inhabit the area to bring news of any ships."[14]

Although he may have believed that he had managed to calm Viceroy Branciforte's fears, Nava also took the precaution of directly reassuring the court in Madrid as well. On August 1, he sent a separate letter to Manuel Godoy, "the Prince of the Peace," reiterating his contention that Louisiana, not the Interior Provinces, were the most likely British targets. "I am with the greatest vigilance prepared to avoid a surprise if the English . . . direct it against some of the internal territories of my command," he told Godoy. Nava reiterated that he had taken all precautions for "being able to cover the Provinces of the Colonia del Nuevo Santander and Nuevo Reyno de León, dependencies of the Viceroyalty and that border upon those of Coahuila and Texas subject to this Comandancía General." He had also directed his officers in New Mexico and Texas to "advise him of any news they might acquire by means of the Indios Amigos," so that he might quickly learn "the true designs of the Enemy and destination of the Expedition."

Finally, Nava again stressed that he could move quickly wherever danger threatened, but for now he would stay in Chihuahua, because it was the center of the Interior Provinces. From there he could go to either New Mexico if word came that they need help there, "or to Sonora if the Enemy works to land on the undefended coast some part of the naval or land forces they have in their possessions in India, and to California which could also be invaded according to the misgivings of the Viceroy of New Spain." Subtly distancing himself from the nervous reports of Branciforte, Nava assured Godoy that he could respond to a British attack wherever it might materialize, and that he would not spare any "hardship or diligence . . . for the conservation of these Countries."[15]

While attempting to calm somewhat the apprehensions of his superiors, Nava nevertheless remained on his guard for any possible British movements. Responding to the rumored British threat, in June 1797, Nava ordered the Sonoran troops serving in Nueva Vizcaya to return to their home presidios, from where he could dispatch them to aid Spanish forces in California. Nava believed that a British sea-borne invasion against Alta or Baja California was a distinct possibility. Therefore, he decided to head west to Sonora to conduct an inspection and review of that province's military to ensure they were prepared for any contingency.[16]

Despite the cloud of the British threat, as the heat of the summer of 1797 increased, the commandant general, having made what preparations he could, was again able to focus on the ongoing war against the Mescalero Apaches. While the campaigns in the field from Nueva Vizcaya and Coahuila continued, Nava also ensured that those Apaches at peace remained quiescent. In late June his attention fell upon the Chiricahua Apaches de paz settled near the Presidio of Janos, who were engaged in an internal struggle. One of their capitancillos, named Vívora, had come into conflict with another leader named Güero. Whatever particulars led to the strife, it soon reached a level that the commander at Janos requested assistance from Commandant General Nava in sorting it all out. For his part Nava was concerned that the rivalry might disrupt "the tranquility they have been offered" at the peace establishment, which would cause some of the Apaches de paz to leave, either because of "bad inclinations or as a result of their chimerical disputes and rivalries."

Fortunately, Nava proposed a solution he believed would not only solve the rivalry between Vívora and Güero, but also aid in the war against the Mescaleros. This was to have one of the capitancillos relocate with his people to the Presidio of Príncipe south of the junction of the Río Conchos and Rio Grande, where they could aid the Spaniards. Nava wrote the Janos commandant, "In order to avoid . . . another offence between the said capitancillo Güero, Vívora and their factions. . . . Your Honor should make known to the first that if he moves he will be accommodated at the Presidio del Príncipe with all his ranchería . . . to the Frontier of Coahuila in order to be employed in the War against the Mescaleros." In exchange for this service, Güero would be regularly issued with supplies, including "cattle for giving rations of meat to his people."[17]

Whether or not capitancillo Güero and his followers actually relocated to Presidio del Príncipe is not known, but the intervention by Nava seems to have reduced tensions among the Chiricahuas at Janos. Indeed, there seemed to be an increased eagerness among them to assist the Spaniards. For example, capitancillo Vívora told the officers at the post that an Apache leader named Pasqualillo, who was possibly a Mescalero, along with four other warriors had come to Janos to enlist aid for an attack, and "they called juntas for the Sierras de Sacramento and San Mateo," where all the Apaches of the region were to gather.[18]

Armed with this information, the Spaniards launched a preemptive strike when "a party of troops from the Presidio of Janos with some Apaches from there that exist in Peace . . . succeeded in killing Pasqualillo and another two Gandules, and taking one prisoner along with eight more piezas." As if this were not enough, Vívora also reported that some Mescaleros had been involved in the planning, saying "that he knew that the one named Mayá who is found at peace at some distance in the Jurisdiction of El Paso not only sheltered in his ranchería Pasqualillo and other Indians that had come to attack, but that he even united with the Apaches that are at war in the Sierras de San Mateo, Magdalena, Sacramento and others nearby."

Mayá had long been identified as one of the war's instigators and had only recently agreed to terms with the Spaniards. Yet, most regarded him with deep suspicion. Now not only had Vívora implicated him, but so had the captured compatriot of the slain Pasqualillo. This man claimed that many Apaches had planned to "join in Robledo [Mountains] at the beginning of the moon and that he knew for certain that Mayá would rise up with all his people and retire to the Mogollons."

Word of these suspected plans immediately went to Lieutenant José María de la Riva, the commandant of the Presidio of San Elizario. Riva in turn passed on these warnings to the lieutenant governor of El Paso in order to guard "against whatever surprise may be intended by the reputedly loyal Indians of the rancherías of Joagusum and Mayá and the damages that might follow." Though Lieutenant Riva stressed the need to verify the truth of these allegations, he believed that Captain Manuel Rengel, who was currently on campaign in the region, should also receive word, and "if the bad faith of both capitancillos and their communication with the enemies" was confirmed, then "they are to be pursued and attacked where they are found."[19]

For his own part, Captain Rengel had continued his operations north of the Rio Grande between El Paso and Presidio del Norte throughout early 1797. During this time, he had issued a constant call to El Paso citizens to provide militiamen to help guard the large *caballada*, or horse herd, belonging to the troopers stationed in the special cantonment he commanded. This service by the militiamen would allow more of Rengel's men to stay in the field in constant pursuit of the Mescaleros. But such duty could prove onerous to the citizens, and after complaining that it was harming their ability to plant their crops, they received a reprieve. In early May, Rengel wrote to the authorities in El Paso, "The Commandant General accedes that there not join in the campaign I go to make, any people of that jurisdiction . . . it being the legitimate time of that citizenry to have their sowing." Nevertheless, Rengel warned that the citizen must still maintain an armed detachment "ready for any invasion or notice of the Enemies."[20]

The constant campaigning by Rengel and other Spanish forces into the Mescalero lands across the Rio Grande appeared to have finally begun producing results. Reports from El Paso indicated that the area was quiet for many months, with no hostilities or fatalities reported between December 1796 and

May 1797. Instead, the Spaniards received further word of growing tension among the Mescaleros. In May, news came of intertribal fighting among the Mescalero when the Spaniards received a report "of the attack suffered . . . by the ranchería of Jagosum from the Apaches commanded by Arrieta for not having wished to unite with them in order to attack us." These reports clearly indicated that many Mescaleros were torn between making peace and waging war. Only a few weeks after this report, the Chiricahuas de paz from Janos tracked down and killed the hostile leader Pasqualillo and accused the Mescalero Mayá of joining him.[21]

After suffering almost no losses, at least in the vicinity of El Paso, during the first five months of 1797, the summer saw an upturn in minor thefts committed by the Mescaleros in the region. Surprisingly, the Spaniards responded with a marked degree of restraint. For example, in June the citizens of El Paso complained to Captain Rengel that enemy Apaches had carried off eight horses and mules. However, when Rengel found out that the animals had been allowed to cross to the far bank of the Rio Grande, he refused to get involved, declaring this "a very good punishment for those [the citizens] for having them [the cattle] maintained on the other side of the river against what he advised."[22]

Another incident occurred when the son of a Mescalero de paz was accused of stealing clothing from two El Paso women. Rather than the Spaniards retaliating, they apparently complained to the Apache leaders of the establishment and requested punishment of the culprit and restitution. A report surfaced of three horses being stolen by the enemy from the Mescaleros de paz themselves. Again, the Spanish responded in a measured manner, with a small party of nine troopers being sent out with a similar number of Apaches to try and recover the animals.[23]

Indeed, things appeared quiet enough for the authorities in El Paso to begin construction of a bridge by requisitioning labor from the citizens and mission Indians of Senecú and Ysleta for wood cutting and work parties. Nevertheless, continuous calls came for the militia and citizens of the area to assist with ongoing military expeditions beyond the frontier, either by riding out with the soldiers or helping to guard the remount herds of the presidios. For example, on August 1, Rengel ordered Lieutenant Governor Francisco Xavier de Uranga to have the citizenry provide forty men fully supplied and ready to set out on a two-month campaign. Rengel cautioned Uranga that he planned to inspect these men to ensure they were "very apt for war," and not to allow the citizens to send out "unfit peons as they are accustomed, which by close examination I warn Your Honor to prevent."[24]

Yet if the situation outside El Paso was relatively quiescent, the same could not be said for other areas of the frontier. Spanish forces in Coahuila continued their incessant incursions across that province's northern frontier. However, a rapid change in the command structure of the province did slow operations somewhat. Lieutenant Colonel Antonio Cordero had been appointed interim governor of Texas on October 22, 1796, but Commandant General Nava ordered Cordero to delay assuming office until the following year. Despite this pause, Cordero began to wind down the formal operations of the Expedition of Coahuila, and the majority of troopers from Nueva Vizcaya returned to their posts. But then on March 13, 1797, the governor of Coahuila, Juan Gutiérrez de la Cueva, died unexpectedly. Because Cordero had not yet left for Texas, Commandant General Nava used his discretion and ordered that Cordero take over as interim governor in Coahuila rather than Texas, most likely to avoid losing the initiative in the war against the Mescaleros. In fact, Cordero upon assuming his new role immediately again pressed forward with operations in Coahuila. In October he received reports that several parties of "Enemy Indians" had attempted to attack across the frontier and "one of them succeeded in penetrating into the territories of Nuevo Reyno de León." Responding quickly, he "dispatched a competent detachment to march out and punish the aggressors," with the result of the Apaches being driven off.[25]

Maintaining the strategy of striking at the Indians' food supplies, Commandant General Nava then ordered Cordero "to continue the punishment of the factions of Mescalero and Lipiyanes Indians . . . to the end that a body of troops . . . [be] directed to reconnoiter the lands where the said Barbarians annually have their Buffalo Hunt." Cordero responded aggressively. On October 26, 1797, he ordered Captain Josef Menchaca, the commandant of the Presidio of Aguaverde in eastern Coahuila, to sally out with a force of 217 men on a search-and-destroy mission targeting the Mescaleros' semiannual excursion to hunt buffalo. Menchaca remained in the field until December 18, "examining most closely the Sierras and the rest of the terrain where the Enemy live in the present season." Over the course of seven weeks, his troopers "attacked different bands having succeeded in killing one Gandul, imprisoning another six, with seven women and ten infants of both sexes, recovering ninety-two horses." In addition, Menchaca was approached by "five Gandules with nine women and four infants of the referred to Mescalero faction requesting surrender as to be admitted to peace." Menchaca took the surrendered Indians back with him to his post, from where he sent to Governor Cordero asking what was to be done with them. Cordero in turn referred the matter to Commandant General Nava. The latter ruled that these Mescaleros should be allowed to remain on the frontier to see if any more Apaches voluntarily surrendered. At that point, he planned "to impose on them the conditions that lead to their subjugation."[26]

Yet even as this small group of Mescaleros waited to see if they would be granted terms, their kin taken captive during this campaign and others were being prepared for deportation, in line with Nava's draconian policies. By late fall, another collera or chain-gang of Apache prisoners of war exiled these Indians to forced labor in Cuba. Setting out from the frontier on November 7, 1797, the collera contained seventy-one prisoners, including eleven men and boys, fifty-seven women and girls, and three small children. It is certain that almost all of the prisoners were Mescaleros captured during the year. Their journey from the frontier was remarkably uneventful, and when they reached Mexico City on December 26, the collera had only suffered a single loss, one woman left behind too sick to travel. But their luck ran out within weeks of their arrival, when smallpox broke out in the capital, with devastating results. After two months in Mexico City, and despite the authorities sending the sick to hospitals, only nineteen of the fifty-seven Apache women survived, while the fates of the men and boys are unknown. Despite these losses, the surviving women were soon marched to Veracruz, bound ultimately for shipment to Havana and the oblivion of exile.[27]

While the terrible fate of the deported Mescaleros unfolded, Nava also decided to break up the special cantonment of troopers that Captain Manuel Rengel commanded at Presidio San Elizario. In November he ordered that the soldados from the various detachments in Nueva Vizcaya and Sonora be sent back to their home posts, and the defense of the region returned solely to the garrisons in each of the frontier's jurisdictions. The commandant general's dispersal of his forces to their regular duty station may have been a result of his preparations for any potential British invasion.

However, while fear of the English may have been dimming by the end of 1797, Nava was convinced that the invasions he had launched into the Mescalero lands across the frontier had pushed the Apaches to the brink. Over the year, his forces had killed or captured approximately seventy-six Mescalero men, women, and children, including at least twenty-two warriors slain against the loss of only three soldados killed. More importantly, eighteen Mescaleros had voluntarily surrendered, and Nava clearly hoped that this was a signal that other Apaches at war would follow suit. In addition, his allies among the Chiricahuas de paz at Janos had purportedly broken up a nascent counterattack led by Pasqualillo and the Mescalero leader Mayá. This action had seemingly resulted in an unexpected quiescence in the regions around El Paso. But more incursions would prove necessary to impose peace throughout the frontier. As the winter of 1797 set in, Pedro de Nava believed that the war against the Mescalero remained far from finished.[28]

12

THE CALAMITIES OF WAR

Sierra de Guadalupe, January 29, 1798—The first light of Monday morning had not yet broken when Lieutenant Zozoya's scouts located the enemy. There ahead lay the camp described as "a dense assembly of Apaches made up of one hundred and forty-seven tents and two hundred and fifty gandules or men at arms." His entire force totaled only 154 troopers and six Indian auxiliaries, and he had left 53 of his men farther back to secure the supply train. Now, in what his soldados may have regarded as either foolhardy bravado or an excess of caution, he detailed another 26 troops to separate and guard the horse herd. Selecting the best 75 mounts, he ordered his remaining men to prepare to charge despite being outnumbered at least three to one. As they tightened the cinches of their saddles and prepared their weapons, the soldados placed their fate in the hands of God and the orders of their commander.[1]

The confidence displayed by Lieutenant Joseph Francisco Zozoya had come from a lifetime of Indian fighting. A thirty-five-year-old native of El Valle del Pilón in Nuevo León, locals regarded him of noble status, but he had enlisted as common soldier in the First Compañía Volante of Nuevo Santander in 1783. He had gained his spurs fighting the tribes that inhabited the Sierra de Tamaulipas and who had violently and successfully resisted Spanish conquest for decades. Despite the perilous nature of the war, Zozoya proved himself and in less than two years won a commission as an alférez. After four more years of steady service, he received promotion to second lieutenant of the Presidio of Monclova, where he now turned to fighting the Apaches. Whether owing to his skill or the accidents of fate, in less than three months, superiors promoted him to first lieutenant of the Presidio of Aguaverde on Coahuila's eastern border, hard by the Mescalero lands.

Over the course of his career, Zozoya had distinguished himself in more than a dozen major campaigns and in numerous raids, pursuits, and small combats. No armchair officer, he always led from the front. In one action, he had taken a lance thrust in the right hand, but the wound did not deter him. He had killed two warriors in single combat and captured three more "by his own hands." With his hard-won knowledge of Indian warfare, Lieutenant Zozoya was supremely confident of his own abilities, and on this Monday morning, despite the enemy's numbers and the strength of their position, he still believed he had the upper hand. As the light of day broke over the Guadalupe Mountains, Zozoya and his seventy-five troopers put spurs to their horses and charged into the Mescalero encampment. Almost immediately the fortunes of war turned.[2]

Although the lieutenant thought he had caught the Mescaleros by surprise, they were in fact waiting for him, "as there went out to meet him more than two hundred of them protected by a trench that they had formed from rocks, making from it two consecutive discharges of fusils and arrows." The volleys of the Mescaleros slightly wounded three soldados and an Indian auxiliary, and one Apache archer succeeded in "putting an arrow into the mount of the Commander." Atop his wounded horse, Lieutenant Zozoya was momentarily confounded by the Apaches' field fortifications. At the same time, he was now presented with an unexpected counterattack, when suddenly "left [from] the cañadas and outcroppings in which another portion of Gandules were hidden, making against the rearguard of our troop a heavy fire."

Showing the ability to respond to the vagaries of combat, in an instant Zozoya "ordered thirty men under command of a sergeant to dismount in order to contain them, which was executed with the best order and resolution." With this threat at least temporarily halted, Zozoya pressed forward, and with forty-five men, the lieutenant "with the rest of the Troop and Alférez Don Joseph de Rabago, despising the fire that they made from the trench, penetrated into them, he and ours using their lances." The soldados de cuera of Zozoya's command were trained and equipped as heavy lancers in the European model of warfare that almost never occurred along the frontier of northern New

Guadalupe Mountains, Texas, by John Russell Bartlett, 1850.
Courtesy of the John Carter Brown Library at Brown University, John Russell Bartlett Collection.

Spain. Yet here, in this instance, they finally had an opportunity to employ the tactics they had so often trained for, but had so seldom ever used. In a matter of moments, the impetus of the lancers "penetrated to the very heart of the ranchería where they evicted the numerous *Indiada* from their defenses."

With their field fortifications broken and their village about to be overrun, the Mescaleros began to scatter to the winds. In a desperate move to impede the Spanish, they slaughtered more than two hundred horses, "seeing that it would be impossible to avoid these falling into the hands of the Troop that pursued them." As the Indians vanished into the broken terrain surrounding their village, Lieutenant Zozoya recalled his men. Surveying the field, they found the bodies of nine dead Mescaleros. They also seized thirteen prisoners, including two warriors, and had taken seventy-six horses, the majority of them saddled. In addition, "the great amount of blood which they found in the nearby *barrancas*, showed how much the enemy had suffered."

The battle completed, the Spaniards began to gather the spoils and plunder found within the 147 lodges the Mescaleros had abandoned. In the midst of all this, the soldados were surprised when "there presented themselves to the Commandant of the detachment, dutifully soliciting peace, five Mescalero Indians with their families comprising eighteen persons." Faced with the loss of all their worldly goods, these five warriors realized that their families could not face the rest of the winter without food, shelter, and horses. Unlike their compatriots who could not or would not surrender, they gambled on Spanish clemency. At least for the moment, their gamble paid off as Zozoya ordered his men not to molest the Apaches. Instead, they were to accompany the lieutenant and his victorious detachment being "freely conducted to the Presidio of Aguaverde." Upon arrival, the Apaches would be left to either the tender mercies or draconian harshness of Commandant General Pedro de Nava.[3]

Winter in Chihuahua City could be cold, especially for one born and raised in the moderate climate of the Canary Islands. Still, in February 1798 Pedro de Nava found things to warm his spirits, if not his body, not the least of which was his conviction that the war against the Mescalero Apaches was finally nearing an end. Nava had received word of Lieutenant Zozoya's victory over the Mescaleros in the Sierra de Guadalupe, and he was convinced that it was a portent of good things ahead. He saw a special significance in the voluntary surrender of eighteen Apaches after the battle. This marked the second time in less than six weeks that groups of Mescaleros at war had placed themselves into the hands of the Spaniards and requested peace. Clearly, Nava hoped that this was the beginning of a trend.

In early April, he wrote to Juan Manuel Alvarez, the Spanish minister of war in Madrid, detailing the battle waged by Zozoya in the Guadalupe Mountains. Nava lauded the lieutenant, declaring that he "proved anew his intelligence and bravery, which with his previous merits of war, I consider him worthy of the grade of Captain of Cavalry." But even more than the merits of Zozoya, the commandant general proclaimed the significance of the voluntary surrender of the eighteen Mescaleros brought to Presidio Aguaverde. "This number," Nava wrote, "along with those existing there already at peace, and the repeated instances … conceded this to diverse capitancillos of the Mescalero and Lipiyana tribes, makes me express that briefly there will be reduced the greater part of these two tribes." Looking forward, Nava promised to inform Alvarez "of the conditions that are imposed on them to secure as soon as possible future tranquility."[4]

Despite his hopes, or perhaps because of them, the commandant general determined to escalate his incursions into the Mescalero heartlands. Nava informed the Spanish court: "Knowing that for the Barbarians of this Frontier to submit, nothing is as conducive as much as that they experience in their own Countries the calamities of war, I directed to sally out from the Province of Coahuila a Detachment of one hundred seventy-nine men at the command of Lieutenant Miguel Múzquiz in pursuit of the Mescalero and Lipiyanes Tribes that are the only ones that are found in open war."[5]

In other words, Nava had once again turned to the forces under the command of Lieutenant Colonel Antonio Cordero, who continued as interim governor of Coahuila and who had emerged throughout the war as a veritable flail against the Apaches. Spanish troops in Coahuila under Lieutenant Múzquiz of the Presidio of Monclova crossed the Rio Grande and headed northwest, only three months after Lieutenant Zozoya's foray. For forty-five days, Múzquiz and his men scoured the lands from the Pecos River westward to the Sacramento Mountains. Finally, on April 24, "after hard marches, crossing rugged mountains and swift running rivers," the lieutenant's scouts located a large number of Mescaleros encamped at Sierra Blanca, the largest mountain in the Sacramento chain. Realizing he had caught the Apaches unawares, Múzquiz dispatched seventy-one men to guard his supply train, and with the remaining 108 troopers prepared for combat.[6]

At daybreak, apparently using the same tactics Lieutenant Zozoya had employed successfully, Múzquiz formed his men for a mounted charge into the Indian ranchería. The lieutenant and his lancers "trampled down the many Apaches that presented themselves for the defense" and rapidly swept through the encampment. The Spaniards killed eleven Mescaleros in the fight. In addition, they captured another fifty-four Natives of both sexes and all ages, an astoundingly high number for a single engagement and an indication of the overwhelming nature of the Spanish attack. Immediately thereafter, another twenty Mescaleros, including nine warriors, approached Lieutenant Múzquiz and voluntarily surrendered. The troopers also seized 240 horses and a large amount of spoils from the camp. For their own part, Múzquiz and his men only had "three soldados wounded by gunshot, but not dangerously."[7]

Although fatigued by the combat, Múzquiz and his troopers would have continued the action, but "the hindrance caused by the great number of prisoners impeded the pursuit of the rest of the Enemies that dispersed, fleeing precipitously." Realizing he would not be able to catch them, the lieutenant ordered his detachment to break off the engagement. The next day they withdrew from the Sierra Blanca and began the return trip back to Spanish territory, "where they delivered the prisoners and the rest of the spoils."[8]

When word of the battle reached Commandant General Nava, he was undoubtedly pleased. In reporting the news to his superiors in Madrid, he lauded Lieutenant Múzquiz and his men, noting that the lieutenant "conducted himself with the valor and good judgment he had already proven, and the troop comported themselves with the greatest courage." But of greater import was that his forces had delivered two telling blows against the Mescaleros in a little less than three months. When quantifying the results of both operations, the Spanish troopers out of Coahuila had killed twenty Indians, captured sixty-seven, and accepted the voluntary surrender of thirty-eight others. The total of 125 Mescaleros accounted for in these two battles alone greatly exceeded the seventy-six reported in the previous year of 1797. Nava proclaimed, "With this blow and those previous that they have suffered the Mescalero Indians have promised me their submission as they do not want to suffer their total extermination in the subsequent expeditions that I will prepare against them." Just which and how many Mescaleros had promised to submit to Nava and accept Spanish control, he did not make clear. But clearly, he was indeed preparing more attacks, which he hoped would prove as successful as the previous two.[9]

Within only a few days of the battle at Sierra Blanca, Nava ordered Antonio Cordero to send yet another expedition into the field. This time, the Spaniards concentrated on the Mescalero homelands in the mountains around the Big Bend. At the beginning of May, the captain of the Volante Company of San Carlos de Parras, Pedro Nolasco Carrasco, led a large force into the region. On May 9, his scouts located a ranchería in the Sierra Rica, south of the Rio Grande, opposite the imposing Chisos Mountains. Carrasco attacked immediately, and his soldados, "killed three gandules and one woman and imprisoned thirteen piezas including three gandules, [and] they recovered seventy-four animals, and took all of their goods." A single Spaniard suffered light wounds in the fight.[10]

One of the slain warriors was identified as Dayél, a capitancillo who had resided with his people outside Presidio del Norte for several years and who was regarded by the Spaniards as an Apache de paz who had been "disloyal."

Though Captain Carrasco and his men might have taken some satisfaction in revenge, the dryness of the season had taken its toll on his men and animals. As summarized later by Commandant General Nava, "The scarcity of pasture and waters from the lack of rain impeded Carrasco to continue the operations that he had been detailed to, and made him retire with the prisoners to the Presidio from which he set out." Nevertheless, Nava issued orders for Carrasco to prepare for further action, noting, "After the rains begin he will continue in battering the Mescaleros until they submit or are destroyed."[11]

The rainy season began in July, and soon thereafter Nava ordered another Spanish detachment from Coahuila to head into the Mescalero lands. However, this force was not led by Captain Carrasco, but by his lieutenant, Antonio Griego, a fifty-seven-year-old veteran who had risen through the ranks. Not only had Griego proven himself "a very good officer for war," as his superiors characterized him, but as a native of Presidio del Norte, he had intimate knowledge of all the frontier regions between that post and his current station at Presidio Rio Grande. Utilizing his vast experience in the terrain, Lieutenant Griego hounded the Mescaleros. Despite "the troop making many days' journeys without water, which lack resulted in the loss of some horses," somewhere in the vast region of the Big Bend, they found their quarry and attacked. In the fight that followed, Griego and his men "killed one Gandul, imprisoned fourteen piezas including five Gandules and recovered sixty animals."[12]

Griego and his soldados also discovered they "had the luck to kill their *Jefe Principal*, named Volante." Since about 1790 Volante and his ranchería had been among the most prominent of the Mescaleros de paz established outside Presidio del Norte. In 1792 Volante had been among the capitancillos who had assassinated several Lipans visiting the presidio after the Spaniards had grown suspicious. Leadership long regarded him as "loyal," and he appeared not to have joined in the war's initial outbreak in August 1795. Under what circumstances Volante had come to be regarded as an enemy is unclear. He may have been hostile or he might have merely moved outside the limits that the Spaniards had imposed on the peace establishments. Regardless of the circumstances, Volante paid with his life.

It had long been standard practice among the Spaniards to show proof of their killing of an enemy by taking the head, ears, or other body parts from the slain. In this capacity, Griego ordered his men to scalp Volante. The Apache believed that being in the presence of a dead body, body parts, or even the possessions of the deceased opened them up to spiritual contamination. For the companions of Volante, the long-haired scalp of their capitancillo not only brought home the terrible reality of their capture, but delivered a demoralizing shock to their entire belief system. Armed with this grisly trophy and fourteen prisoners, Lieutenant Griego and his detachment headed home.[13]

On September 4, 1798, Pedro de Nava sat down in his office in the Villa de Chihuahua to compose for Minister of War Juan Manuel Alvarez in Madrid an update on the war against the Mescaleros. Overall, he felt the conflict was going well. Most recently he had received reports from Governor Cordero of Coahuila that the Mescaleros had lost "their principal support by their having separated themselves entirely [from] the faction of the Apaches Lipiyanes that contain a sufficient number of very warlike gandules." Nava maintained that the Lipiyanes had decided to come to terms as a "result of the clashes they have received from us." He also boasted, "They have submitted to peace almost at discretion, as they have surrendered as hostages of their fidelity the sons of their principle capitancillos." In addition, the Lipiyanes agreed to move their rancherías into areas where the Spanish could register them and "to never treat with our Enemies, and serve us as auxiliaries in such expeditions as may be arranged." Perhaps most importantly, these Apaches had agreed to surrender to the Spaniards a Mescalero leader, "one of their principle capitancillos named Alegre." This leader, like Volante, the Spaniards regarded as among the principal capitancillos of the Mescaleros de paz, and his capture would have been considered a great success. Whether this exchange actually occurred is uncertain, but Nava was convinced that the offer itself would help drive a wedge between the Mescaleros and Lipiyanes and increase "the rancor that this has occasioned them."

At least some of these Lipiyanes had previously been led by the redoubtable Picax-andé, whom the Spaniards feared and mistrusted. However, Commandant General Nava made no mention of him or any other particular leader in claiming that the Lipiyanes were requesting terms for peace. This most likely indicates that only some members of this Apache group had approached the Spaniards and probably only as a temporary cessation of hostilities rather than an actual determination to accept Spanish terms.[14]

As he was finishing this report, Nava received word that mail pouches had arrived with important contents about recent actions against the Mescaleros. Upon his return to Coahuila, Lieutenant Antonio Griego had forwarded the scalp of Volante along with a diary of the expedition to Governor Cordero at the Presidio of Monclova. In turn, Cordero sent both items to Commandant General Nava in the Villa de Chihuahua. Upon receiving the scalp of Volante and the diary of Griego, Nava decided to compose a second letter to Minister of War Alvarez. In this he heralded that there was "sufficient importance . . . in depriving the Mescalero faction of the cited *caudillo* Volante, by his great fame and experience in war, and to whom all those Indians respected as its principal captain." He held forth that "it is very probable" that with the death of Volante, the Mescaleros might "cease the tenacious obstinacy with which that Tribe has remained without submitting." Yet, having consistently underestimated the Mescaleros' will to fight, Nava remained cautious. He informed Alvarez that he would continue to send out detachments of troopers "to finish the destruction of said nation," but warned that "some desperate parties of them, errant and without horses in which to mount will procure some losses in our territories."[15]

The disaffection between the Mescaleros and the Lipiyanes appeared to portend a general movement toward accommodation on the part of many Apaches. Farther to the east, the Lipans, or at least a substantial number of them, had begun to send out peace feelers as early as January 1798. In response, Nava had drawn up a series of "Articles of Capitulation and the Celebration of Peace" that he presented to several Lipan groups residing west of San Antonio, Texas. Whether the Lipans actually accepted these terms is unclear, but the movement toward peace soon spread. In a letter to the court at Madrid dated August 27, 1798, Branciforte's successor, Viceroy Miguel José de Azanza, who was directly responsible for the provinces of Nuevo León and Nuevo Santander, recorded that "the Lipan Captains Canoso, Moreno and Chiquito have set up their rancherías at the return from the Buffalo hunt in the environs of the Presidio of Laredo without causing any attacks." Despite the Lipans' subsequent unauthorized movement south of the Rio Grande, and a brief scare that they would go on the warpath after one of them was killed trying to steal corn from a vecino at Laredo, the peace held.

Yet Spanish officials remained wary, not fully trusting the Lipans, who had violated numerous past peace treaties. In September, Azanza informed Madrid that the Lipans were "mitigating their rancor [with] good faith" and had even returned eight horses and a mule some of them had stolen as proof of this. "However" the viceroy cautioned, "we ought not to give confidence in the good disposition shown by these Indians, because it is necessary for them to rob in order to subsist," and whether at peace or at war, the troops of the frontier

Miguel José de Azanza Alegría, Duke of Santa Fe, Viceroy of New Spain, 1798–1800.
From Manuel Rivera Cambas, Los Gobernantes de México,
Vol. 1 (Mexico, 1872), between pp. 496 and 497.

should live with the greatest vigilance. Recalling the admonitions of Gálvez's Instructions of 1786, Azanza harkened back to the maxim of a bad peace being better than a good war, writing, "all of the evils caused by the Barbarians . . . will be much less and more easy to contain than those of a determined war."[16]

While the bad peace had been reestablished in the eastern provinces under viceregal control, Pedro de Nava continued his unrelenting assaults upon the Mescaleros. In addition, Nava also continued his policies of deporting captured prisoners of war from the Interior Provinces into permanent exile in regions far removed, and from where they would never return.

Having previously launched attacks against the Mescalero homelands from Coahuila to their southeast, Nava now sent forces from the southwest. In mid-September he ordered Captain Joseph de Ochoa at Presidio del Norte to head out with 180 men from the garrisons in Nueva Vizcaya "in order to continue the destruction of the Mescalero Apache Nation." Ochoa's force included a limited number of Ópata Indian soldiers from Sonora, who may have helped him track down an enemy encampment after only ten days in the field. Although the exact location was not recorded, Ochoa's men discovered and attacked a large ranchería of Mescaleros "commanded by the head man Múzquiz, who they killed and two gandules, making another prisoner, five women with three boys." According to the Spaniards, the bulk of the Indians "retreated with precipitation," including "many wounded Indians, according to the signs they left." The troopers also seized fifty-seven horses and "whatever else they had for their maintenance, which was enough to divide up among the Ópatas and the rest of the people." The soldiers' victory was swift and complete and the only casualty was Captain Ochoa, who "took an arrow in the body which passed through his cuera but without injuring him." Perhaps motivated by this close call, Ochoa ordered his men to pursue the fugitives, and "in a second clash with the Enemies imprisoned thirteen men at arms, five women and boys and took from them three horses."

Simultaneously with this attack, Nava had ordered another force from the Presidio of Guajoquilla in Nueva Vizcaya to also invade the Mescalero lands. They left on September 16, and although many of the details went unrecorded, Nava stated that within a few days of setting out, the detachment "attacked a ranchería of Mescaleros situated most advantageously, [and] succeeded in killing one Gandul, imprisoning five piezas, and taking from them twenty-one horses without our suffering any loss. They executed these actions in the enemy country outside the frontier line."[17]

After these clashes, Nava once again found himself in possession of a substantial number of Mescalero prisoners of war; so many in fact that he decided to send out two separate colleras. He dispatched the first collera in late August, and it contained forty-nine Apaches, including fifteen men and thirty-four women. The collera was commanded by Alférez Nicolás Lemeé of Presidio Aguaverde, who had as an escort a cavo and twenty-four troopers. Departing from the villa of Santa Rosa in Coahuila, the collera was dogged by mismanagement and ill-luck from the start. For some reason, the soldiers of the escort were not provided with the usual daily stipend. As a result, they were soon at short rations, receiving each day only "a handful of thinly sliced bread, one tortilla and two small morsels of meat."

The scarcity of food for the escort may also have affected the Apaches prisoners, and might explain the illness that attacked them. After a journey of approximately fifty days, Alférez Lemeé arrived in Mexico City. On October 15, 1798, Viceroy Azanza recorded the delivery of the collera, noting that of the "15 men of all ages and 34 women, there died on the road three of these and 17 of those as was proven by the expressed officer with the documents respecting those that died in populated places and the ears of those that finished their lives in the field." Despite almost half of the prisoners having died, the viceroy unmercifully ordered that "all should be transported to the Plaza de la Havana."[18]

Mercy was similarly absent when less than a month later, Commandant General Nava sent out a second collera of prisoners, of whom it seems certain all were recently captured Mescaleros. In a letter of November 6 to Viceroy Azanza, Nava succinctly summarized the details: "The Alférez of the Presidial Company of Príncipe, Dn Valentín Moreno with a party of twenty-eight men of the troop conducting to enter into that City by disposition of Your Excellency ninety-eight Apaches piezas, prisoners of war that existed in the Cuartel of Pilar de Conchos, which number is composed of twenty-five Gandules, four muchachos, and sixty-nine women, which I hope it will serve Your Excellency to receive; and that they be transported, most particularly the *Indios*, to overseas destinations with the useful end of avoiding their returning to the countries of their origin."[19]

Alférez Moreno arrived in Mexico City in early January and turned over the collera to the commander of the capital's garrison. On January 16, Viceroy Azanza wrote back to Commandant General Nava and tersely recorded the arrival and subsequent fate of the prisoners: "The Alférez Dn Valentín Moreno in charge by Your Honor of conducting to this Capital a collera composed of 98 Apache piezas, prisoners of war, of all ages and sex has deposited 96 of these, having had die on the road one old woman and having left behind sick another of the same class in Rancho Grande." In keeping with standard practices, the viceroy had assured Nava that the Apaches "all will be most absolutely transported to La Havana . . . as dispensed with the previous collera conducted by Alférez Dn Nicolás Lemeé." But this time things would not proceed as planned, and events unfolded that proved the spirit of resistance among these Mescaleros was far from broken.[20]

In the waning days of 1798, Spanish officials in Mexico City had made preparations to dispatch a large number of convicted criminals to Veracruz, where they would serve their sentences of forced labor at the public works. These *presidarios,* as the convicts were labeled, were to be escorted by an officer and forty-six soldiers. For greater security, each of the prisoners would wear a pair of iron manacles, euphemistically called *esposas,* or "wives." At this same time, Alférez Moreno had delivered his collera of ninety-six Mescalero Apache prisoners of war to the capital. For the sake of efficiency, Viceroy Azanza approved that the presidarios should be joined with the collera, which consisted of twenty-six men, sixty-six women, and four young boys.

The combined collera of criminals and Apache prisoners of war departed Mexico City on January 19, 1799. Thirteen days later, the collera reached the city of Perote, a strategic military post along the highway leading from the capital to the port of Veracruz. Here, Lieutenant Juan de Díos Cos of the Regiment of the Dragoons of Mexico assumed command of the prisoners. Lieutenant Cos would take responsibility for the collera's final delivery into Veracruz. His command would include a sergeant, two corporals, and seventeen dragoons from his own regiment, along with a sergeant, two corporals, and eighteen men from the Second Company of the Voluntarios de Cataluña, drawn from the garrison of Perote.

On February 5 at four o'clock in the afternoon, Lieutenant Cos and his charges arrived at the Venta de la Rinconada, a traveler's inn several leagues outside Veracruz, where he received a reinforcement of ten mounted lancers from the port's garrison. The inn consisted of several large rooms, or *galerías,* each with cane walls and thatched roofs, windowless, and with a single door fronting a common patio. Lieutenant Cos herded all the presidarios and adult male Mescalero Apaches, or *mecos,* as the Spaniards termed them, into a single room, which must have been substantial enough to contain all 112 men. The sixty-six females, or *mecas,* along with one small boy, were split up into two other rooms. After feeding them dinner, at about seven, the soldiers performed a routine search of the prisoners and then secured all the men with their manacles, or esposas. The women were also restrained, tied together at the wrist in pairs with leather cords, called *mancuerdas.* As night came on, Lieutenant Cos posted sentinels, two inside the men's quarters with two more at the door. Each of the women's quarters contained one sentinel inside and another at the door. Five more men took positions behind the quarters. In addition to the eleven sentinels, a corporal's guard of four men made the rounds as the watch. The overcast night featured strong, gusty winds that constantly blew out the lanterns carried by the sentinels, making it difficult to see clearly inside the prisoners' quarters.

Between midnight and one in the morning, one of sentinels in the galería noticed that a Mescalero had slipped out of his manacles. In an instant, the Apache jumped up and lunged at the sentinel; the latter raised his weapon to strike and yelled for the watch. Simultaneously, all the Apache men began shouting, while the eighty-six presidarios seemingly stood by in confusion and amazement. The soldiers of the watch and several of the sentinels ran to the room and discovered that six of the Apache had managed to get out of their manacles and were preparing for a fight. Lieutenant Cos quickly arrived on the scene with sword and pistol in hand, and immediately ordered that the Mescaleros be tied up with riatas fetched from the soldiers' horses. The Spaniards began to strike at the Apaches with their weapons and with wooden sticks to try to regain control.

At the same instant, the Mescalero women in the two adjoining galerías seized their chance. Screaming in answer to the shouts of their men, all the women in both rooms rushed the sentinels. In one room, soldier Manuel Carpintero of the Voluntarios de Cataluña "called out for the Guard, but it availed nothing as all of that troop ran to the gallery of the men." Carpintero shot one woman dead and tried to bayonet another, but the rest of the Apache women, "some casting blows with the hand and others clawing," simply pushed passed him. Outside, they ran over three dragoons and trampled their firearms into the ground. One of the dragoons received several blows to the head, seriously wounding him. In the other room, the Mescalero women had rushed the sentinels as well, but the soldiers had grabbed the leather thongs holding some of the women's wrist and managed to hold on to fourteen of them, but the remainder broke free. According to Lieutenant Cos, within a short time after the first outcry, "all of the Mecas [were] in the patio of the Venta with furious outcries and . . . as they could not get the weapons from the sentinels the Mecas made for the Mountains."

Daybreak revealed that fifty-one Mescalero women and one boy about six years old had managed to flee from the Venta de la Rinconada, most while remaining tied together in pairs. Lieutenant Cos sent out several mounted lancers in pursuit, but these managed to recapture only one woman, and even she did not go back easily. The soldier who captured her had to strike her with his machete, wounding her severely. In the meantime, Cos sent news of the outbreak to military authorities in Veracruz and the surrounding regions. When Viceroy Azanza heard of the escape, he became furious and ordered Lieutenant Cos tried for dereliction of duty. But a court-martial in July 1799 found him not guilty, mainly because jurors determined that he had been given too few troops to properly escort such a large number of prisoners.

For the Mescalero women, records indicate that out of the group of fifty-one females and one boy that escaped, soldiers eventually recaptured twenty-nine. The fate of the remaining twenty-three Mescaleros is unknown. They would have had to negotiate their way over hostile terrain filled with enemies, although breaking up into smaller groups may have increased their chances. Still, the distance home would have been at least a thousand miles, and they lacked food, water, weapons, and other essential supplies. Even if they managed to elude pursuit and apprehension by the military and civil authorities, the women would have been prey to bandits and other outlaws that infested the highways in many parts of New Spain. Yet, the Spaniards themselves reported that many Apaches over the years had succeeded in finding their way back to the northern frontier, so it is not inconceivable that at least some of the women succeeded in reaching their homeland. Regardless of their ultimate fate, the determination evidenced by these Mescalero women demonstrated that the Mescalero spirit was not yet completely broken, and reflected a tenacity that permeated many of their kin along the northern frontier.[21]

For Commandant General Pedro de Nava, his focus lay not on the ultimate fate of the recently deported Mescaleros, but on the recent victories his forces had achieved in August and September 1798. Hope for victory and peace again waxed large. On November 8 Nava composed a report for his superiors in Madrid. He maintained that "the latest successes that have been achieved by the Campaign Detachments" had contained the Mescaleros and that these Apaches "have not caused damage anywhere in the Provinces under my command." But Nava stressed, "This quiet depends on the constancy with which they are sought for in their own Countries by the Troops of the operations and there are some presently employed in this service."[22]

The quiet that Nava observed in the provinces under his command likewise extended eastward into the viceregal provinces of Nuevo León and Nuevo Santander. In reports of October 27 and November 28, 1798, Viceroy Azanza noted that the Lipans continued at peace and that "consequently there live with quietude the vassals of the King, vecinos of both Provinces." Indeed in a missive of January 5, 1799, the viceroy noted that the Lipans had even helped the soldiers pursue some *Indios bárbaros* after the latter had run off fifty mules from an arriero while traveling from San Antonio to Laredo. Further, he recorded that the governors of the two provinces were still negotiating with several Lipan capitancillos to settle their people outside Laredo. The peace lasted for the remainder of the spring and summer of 1799 as Azanza continued to receive reports about the generally tranquil conditions in these two provinces.[23]

However, though the Lipans and Lipiyanes may have been cowed into quiescence, at least temporarily, many Mescaleros were not. As he told his superiors, Nava believed that to maintain the relative quiet after the victories in August and September, he must continue deploying incursions into the Mescalero homelands. Therefore, despite his hopes that victory lay within his grasp, the commandant general refused to slacken his efforts. Even before sending his report to Madrid, Nava launched more campaigns. Around the end of October 1798, a force of sixty-six troopers from Coahuila, led once more by Lieutenant Antonio Griego of Aguaverde, moved once again into the trans-Pecos region toward the Big Bend. After searching for "thirty-three days in the Country of the enemy," at an unidentified location, Griego and his men "found situated in advantageous terrain, sixty gandules, which defended themselves in it." The lieutenant and his men launched an attack, but this encounter proved much different than the quick victory Griego had won earlier that summer. The Mescalero warriors defended themselves stoutly and managed to escape with their families and possessions, losing only one man killed and twenty-five horses captured, in spite of "the constancy with which the troop fired on them and successively pursued them." On the other hand, the Spaniards suffered two soldados from Presidio Aguaverde killed in the combat.[24]

Soon after this foray from Coahuila, another force invaded from Nueva Vizcaya. On November 29, Lieutenant Colonel Joseph Tovar led 110 men from Presidio del Norte heading north into the Mescalero lands. On December 5, the Spaniards surprised a small ranchería that contained fifteen gandules and their families somewhere in the mountains. Tovar's men killed three Mescalero warriors, three women, and one youth, and seized thirty-six horses. Not satisfied with this result, the captain and his men "maintained themselves in the field until 24 January reconnoitering with great exactness all of the Sierras and terrain . . . not finding any other enemies that those they had fought."[25]

Almost simultaneous with Tovar's incursion, yet another force from Coahuila under Captain Bernardo Fernández left Aguaverde on November 26, "looking to engage the Mescaleros." Clearly hoping to revenge the loss suffered by Lieutenant Griego a few weeks previous, Captain Fernández doggedly hunted the Apaches. However, after "having subsisted in the field two and a half months, it was not possible to encounter them." Still Commandant General Nava put the best possible spin on the situation, concluding that Fernández's vain search had been efficacious in that he had disrupted the Mescaleros' winter encampments by "reconnoitering the parajes in which they are accustomed to inhabit."[26]

The inability of the Spaniards to locate substantial numbers of Mescaleros at war was a clear indication that Nava's coordinated invasions of their homelands had at long last produced results. During the year 1798 the Mescaleros had suffered a mounting stream of losses at the hands of troopers invading from Coahuila and Nueva Vizcaya. In total, they had suffered thirty-seven killed, including at least eleven warriors, and 126 men, women, and children of all ages captured, among whom were at least another eleven warriors. They had also lost 592 horses taken by the Spaniards. Perhaps most tellingly, another thirty-eight Mescaleros, including fourteen adult male warriors, had voluntarily surrendered, seeking admission to the peace establishments.

Another indication of peace was the quiet among the Spanish settlements in the Interior Provinces in spring 1799. In April, Nava reported only two relatively minor incidents involving the Chiricahuas and Western Apaches, with no reports of any raids by the Mescaleros. For the majority of the frontier provinces, there simply were no hostilities, and Nava concluded that "the interior tranquility occasioned that prosperity followed in those territories."[27]

Nevertheless, not convinced the Mescaleros were truly quiescent, the Spanish continued to launch their forays. In May 1799 Nava reported that his troopers "had succeeded to kill three Gandules . . . to imprison eight persons and to take from them one hundred thirty four horses, with many spoils." These blows further demoralized the Mescaleros, so much so that the commandant general claimed, "The said Enemies have withdrawn, so much filled with fear of our Arms that they dread to present themselves in considerable bodies." The fear among the Mescaleros had resulted in "the solid good to preserve these territories (as well as those of the Viceroyalty) from their previous incursions in which they devastated all." For the rest of the spring an almost surreal calm settled upon the Spanish territories. In a letter of June 11, 1799, Nava maintained that the Mescaleros "have not caused any loss in the Provinces under my charge, according to the reports that I have lately been given by their governors and *Comandantes de Armas*; they having retired to the most distant sierras of the Frontier where they have found hiding places, dividing in small bands to the end to avoid being surprised by the frequent strikes the troop detachments make in their country, with the useful object of increasing their dismay in which they find themselves as a result of the blows they have experienced, and to preserve from incursions our territories, populations, haciendas and ranchos, which inhabitants go breathing now [free] from the bloody destructions and robberies of cattle that they suffered previously."[28]

Three months later, in another letter dated September 10, 1799, Nava again noted that quiet still reigned throughout the Provincias Internas. He informed his superiors in Madrid that the frontier had not "experienced any hostilities on the part of the Enemy Indians in the territories of my command; and there continued the same calmness . . . and I have been advised [of no] hostility that perturbed it." As the year 1799 drew to a close, the stillness that Nava reported remained, and although the commandant general and officers remained wary and vigilant, it became increasingly evident that the war against the Mescaleros had finally come to an end.[29]

13

CHASING THE SHADOW OF PEACE

Presidio del Norte, June 4, 1800—Among the Mescaleros de paz, the capitancillo Esquin-yoé, along with two other men and two young boys, were the first to fall sick. He had been one of those who had stubbornly fought against the Spaniards over the four years of war and had only brought his people to live at the peace establishment when there was seemingly no other choice. Now, as the heat of summer came on, he undoubtedly had developed a fever and nausea. He may have contracted the disease almost a fortnight before he noticed the rash and the pustules forming on his face and body. By then it was clear that it was the dreaded *viruela*—smallpox.

The sickness had been prevalent in eastern Sonora and western Nueva Vizcaya for some time, and it was probably inevitable that it would reach Presidio del Norte. While many residents of the presidio, especially the young, were endangered by the disease, some of their older siblings and parents had likely been exposed previously and had developed some resistance. But among Esquin-yoé and his people, the disease enjoyed a host population with little or no immunity.

On the same day that Esquin-yoé's symptoms clearly emerged, the commander at Presidio del Norte, Captain Blas de Aramburu, authorized several attempts to provide relief. The captain had personally led many expeditions against the Mescaleros during the course of the war, but now he struggled to help them survive. Aramburu contracted the services of some *sangrados*, or blood-letters, to treat Esquin-yoé and another Apache man. In addition, he arranged that all the patients be given a special diet of rice, mutton, and sugar and that their bed sheets be freshly washed. A large number of candles allowed that the sick could be tended to at night. But the ministrations provided by the Spaniards proved ineffective. The unnamed Apache man died on June 6, and two days later, Esquin-yoe himself passed away. The Spaniards paid for the making of *mortajas*, or shrouds, for the bodies, an indication that the two Mescalero men may have been buried according to Christian ceremony.

For almost ten days the situation appeared stable, but then on June 17 the epidemic exploded again, with two more Apache men, two women, and five children all falling ill. In what may have been an attempt at quarantine, the Spaniards arranged for the sick Mescaleros to be moved into several different houses at the presidio where they would receive individualized care. Caregivers provided candles, sweets, and clean blankets, but these were of little avail. Illustrating the clear pattern of transmission between family members, two days later came reports that "the *India*, wife of Esquin-yoé" died. Seeking to avail themselves of every possible source of relief, on June 25 Captain Aramburu had some folk healers brought in, paying one *peso*, four *reales* to hire "the women *curanderas* that assisted the sick." Yet that same day, reflecting the harsh reality of the epidemic, they also paid for the washing of more material to be used for burial shrouds.

By July 11, the sickness seems to have stabilized, and a sheep had been butchered to provide meat "for five persons convalescing from smallpox." Treatment of the disease also seems to have evolved, with another charge noted "for lard for rubbing the smallpox," as well as for three curanderas to ply their trade. Still, the disease continued to claim victims, with two more Mescalero women dying the following day. By this point at least one man and two or three women remained ill, and for the remainder of July they received a variety of goods in hopes of aiding their convalescence. Rice, maize, wheat, mutton, and sugar were all prepared for special meals, while helpers used lard and vinegar for unguents and medicine. Caregivers purchased candles and fresh blankets, and again washed their bed sheets. The services of the three woman curanderas were renewed once again. For several days the situation appeared hopeful, but at the beginning of August, the final reckoning began. On August 3 one of the Mescalero women died, and ten days later the last remaining victim, an unnamed man, finally succumbed. By the middle of the month the disease seems to have burned itself out, and the remaining victims began to recover.[1]

During the course of the epidemic, at least fourteen of the Apaches at the peace establishment at Presidio del Norte contracted the disease and five died from it. Given that the entire population of Mescaleros de paz living there was only about forty-seven individuals, this was a staggering blow. Among the survivors were several children and women relatives, one labeled as "the widow" of the dead capitancillo Esquin-Yoé. They continued to draw rations of food and goods from the presidio's store, paid for by a special account known as the *gastos de Apaches*—Apache expenses. Deprived of their leader, these women and children may have had no other means of support and nowhere else to go.

Another Mescalero family at Presidio del Norte may have been in similar straits. El Carpintero was one of several sons of Volante, who had led a substantial ranchería. Volante had first brought his people to settle at del Norte about 1790 and for many years was regarded as among those leaders most "loyal" to the Spaniards. Even after the outbreak of war in August 1795, Volante had managed to steer clear of much of the violence for more than three years. But in the late summer of 1798, he and his people were ensconced somewhere in the mountains of the Big Bend in a region the Spaniards held to be within the war zone. Here the Mescaleros were surprised and attacked by Spanish forces, and Volante had been killed. Soldiers then scalped him and sent his long hair to Commandant General Pedro de Nava as proof of his death. Whether or not the grisly trophy ever made its way back to Presidio del Norte, Volante's family were allowed to return to the post and settled as Apaches de paz.

At some point El Carpintero became recognized as a capitancillo of his own small family group, which appears to have included his mother and several siblings. Over several months they also drew a steady supply of food rations, blankets, and other items from the gastos de Apache. The ranchería of El Carpintero, and the ranchería of another capitancillo named Yscané, appeared to be the only remaining Mescaleros at Presidio del Norte after the smallpox epidemic—all told they numbered fewer than twenty souls. Five years earlier, before the war, there may have been as many as eight hundred men, women, and children at the peace establishment. In many ways El Carpintero and his family represented the last pitiful remnant of those Mescaleros who had sought to reach an accommodation with the Spaniards. Over the course of the war, they had suffered dislocation and despair. Death and hunger had been their constant companions as much as freedom and independence. Now, even after they had returned to the harsh embrace of Spanish control, they had been subjected to disease and more death. But despite these tribulations, for the moment they all had enough to eat, and they lived in relative safety and, for the moment, that was enough.²

The desperate conditions of El Carpintero and his companions at Presidio del Norte during the first half of 1800 provided a clear indication that many Mescaleros were again willing to acquiesce to the regulated lifeways imposed by the dictates of "a bad peace." The situation also reflected how the Spaniards had waged "a good war" with ruthless efficiency. Although they suffered a stunning pair of initial defeats, by relying on professional leadership and a centralized quartermaster and commissariat, the Spaniards were quickly able to regain and maintain the offensive initiative. Through four years of war, the forces of Pedro de Nava had clearly been able to reassert their military superiority over the Apaches. Indeed, this had been achieved fairly early on in the conflict and had been accomplished with relative ease, mainly because the Spaniards had been able to launch centrally planned and coordinated operations, a feat the Indians could almost never achieve.

Man for man, the Mescaleros may have been more than a match for the soldados, but the Spaniards' command and control proved insurmountable. With a strategy conceived by Pedro de Nava and executed by competent officers such as Antonio Cordero, the Spaniards methodically and aggressively invaded the Mescalero heartlands with forces operating mainly from Nueva Vizcaya and Coahuila. These invasions achieved maximum effect by attacking during the late fall and early spring, when the Indians were poised to enter the Llano Estacado on their twice-yearly buffalo hunts. By striking at the Mescaleros' primary means of feeding themselves, the Spanish victory was inevitable. They added to their effectiveness by sending out smaller assaults during other times of the year and by encouraging the Comanches and other Nations of the North to attack the Mescaleros whenever possible. Nava and his men also ably employed a divide-and-rule policy with other Apaches groups, especially the Lipan and Lipiyanes, to use them both overtly and covertly against the Mescaleros. Finally, the policy of deporting captured Apache prisoners of war from the frontier made brutally clear to the Mescaleros that they would not be able to recover their captives or engage in negotiations for exchanges, as they had in previous years. In effect, the Spaniards unleashed all the power and subtleties available to a modern nation-state against a tribal society.

While the war allowed the Spaniards to decisively reaffirm their military superiority, for the Mescaleros the conflict proved an unmitigated disaster. Over the course of four years, the unrelenting Spanish invasions into their lands across the Rio Grande pushed these Indians further and further toward the brink of destruction. Breaking up into ever-smaller contingents to avoid being discovered by the Spaniards became an untenable strategy. The smaller parties might escape detection, but they lacked the solidity necessary to successfully venture onto the plains of the Llano Estacado, where they needed to simultaneously hunt buffalo and repel any potential Comanche attacks. Unable to provide security for their families, the Mescalero rancherías were given the choice to either seek accommodation with the Spaniards or to risk capture and death at the hands of their enemies.

For many, agreeing to settle in peace establishments near Spanish presidios was the best option. By the late spring of 1800, between 250 and three hundred Mescaleros, including about eighty-five warriors, had established themselves outside five presidios in the Province of Nueva Vizcaya. These included approximately forty-five at Presidio del Norte, fifteen at Guajoquilla, forty-five at Coyamé, and fifty-five at Cerro Gordo. The largest contingent by far was that administered from Presidio San Elizario, with 185 Mescaleros residing alongside approximately another one hundred Chiricahuas. A number of these Mescaleros may have been among those deemed "loyal" at the beginning of the war in 1795, but many of the capitancillos listed by the Spaniards had different names. The greatest change appeared in the peace establishment administered outside Presidio del Norte. Where at the beginning of the war, there may have been as many as eight hundred Mescaleros, five years later there were fewer than fifty.[3]

Though the diminution in Mescalero numbers at the peace establishments clearly reflected that many still chose to live in freedom beyond the pale of Spanish control, another more immediate cause was the extremely high number of casualties they had suffered. Over the course of the war, between August 1795 and the end of 1799, the Mescalero had lost more than seven hundred men, women, and children killed or captured and deported from the frontier. The mortality rate of the latter group was very high, and the majority of those shipped out in colleras never returned to their homelands. The estimates of the Mescalero population as a whole during this period range from three thousand to five thousand persons. As such, the losses they endured during the four years of conflict may have approached a staggering one-quarter of the population.⁴

Yet if the consequences of war for the Mescalero were overwhelmingly negative, for the Spaniards they soon became more ambiguous. For a brief period, Pedro de Nava and other Spanish officials were convinced that their crushing of the Mescalero outbreak had produced tangible benefits. The demonstration of military power in such a powerful and sustained fashion clearly signaled to other Apaches that the Spaniards remained more than able and willing to deal with any opposition to the systems they had imposed on the region. Now, Nava and his officers sought to return to the cost-saving maxims of Bernardo de Gálvez and the Instructions of 1786, in which a bad peace was better than a good war. After the Mescalero outbreak, however, Nava may have wished to add the caveat that the power of Spanish arms would of necessity have to be manifested with vigorous regularity.

Though the Spaniards had clearly waged and won a "good war," the question now remained if they would be able to manage a good or a bad peace. Throughout 1800, issues concerning the true status of the Mescaleros continued to bedevil Pedro de Nava. The blurred lines between Mescaleros de paz and Mescaleros at war was in some ways a conundrum of his own making. The cost-savings measures that he had ordered implemented in 1794 requiring peaceful Apaches to locate in designated areas about thirty leagues beyond the frontier remained in effect. However, many rancherías routinely ignored this directive and established themselves directly opposite the posts. Thus several presidios were responsible for administering Apaches who could be close at hand one month and far removed the next. Not unnaturally, these fluctuations led to great confusion about exactly which Apaches were peaceful and which were not.

Taking full advantage of this, some Apaches regarded themselves bound only to "their" presidio and believed they were free to raid into areas beyond this range. A prime example of this situation consists of the Mescaleros de paz administered from Presidio San Elizario. During the first few months of the year, Nava received several reports that hostile Apaches from the San Mateo and Magdalena Mountains, located in the long stretch of territory between El Paso and the Villa de Albuquerque, had been involved in raids on both those Spanish towns. The raiders were most likely Gileño Chiricahuas, but some may have been from the Sacramento Mountains, and these had been identified as

Mescaleros. To make matters worse, after one attack, claims surfaced that the raiders were actually Mescaleros de paz from outside Presidio San Elizario, as they had left behind packages of *cigaros* issued from that post.[5]

The confusion surrounding peaceful and warlike Mescaleros around Presidio San Elizario was exacerbated by the movements of other Apaches. During the last half of 1800, there were two large Mescalero rancherías under capitancillos named Visenegotean and Cluyé, living near the presidio. These men led forty married gandules, fifty-three women, and eighty-eight children, for a total of 185 individuals, all registered at the peace establishment at San Elizario. However, throughout this same period, they were joined by varying numbers of Chiricahuas de paz that were officially associated with other peace establishments. The first was led by capitancillo Jasquedegá from Carrizal and the other by capitancillo Vívora from Janos. These Chiricahuas were continuously moving back and forth and their total numbers fluctuated between seventy-nine and 123 individuals. Nevertheless, during this period the Mescaleros remained constantly near San Elizario, and the presence of the Chiricahuas may have had the effect of restraining the Mescaleros' movements.[6]

Yet if the Mescaleros remained attached to their establishment at San Elizario, this did not prevent them from moving into the hinterland, often at the Spaniards' behest. Many of the Apaches de paz went out either as warriors in Spanish punitive campaigns, as spies to report on the Indians beyond the frontier, or as couriers. For example, on July 2, 1800, a report stated that "the paymaster officer gave to the seven Apache friends that went on campaign a serape to each one and to one of them a bit and to another an adarga." Three weeks later, a more complete listing noted that seven Apaches were recruited to go out on a thirty-day campaign with Captain Manuel Ochoa. These seven men enjoyed the advantage of "indispensable items for their sally," which included not only rations of beef, pinole, piloncillos, and cigars, but also hats, breeches, changes of clothing, a saddle tree with rigging, and even "to the capitancillo Puquienete, money to buy arrows."[7]

Following up on orders to conduct monthly campaigns into the regions north of San Elizario, in late August Captain Ochoa again solicited the Apaches de paz for fighting men. In addition to three warriors, probably Mescaleros, from the peace establishment, others came in from different presidios. These included several Chiricahuas from Janos, described as "Apache friends that have arrived to campaign with Captain Dn Manuel de Ochoa." Specifically mentioned was a leader held in high regard by the Spaniards, "capitancillo Jasquenelté, who was in this presidio to concur to the campaign operations." The presence of these Chiricahuas may indicate that the Spaniards felt uncertain about the loyalty of some of the San Elizario Mescaleros. Nevertheless, the monthly levy of warriors continued, with eight Apaches setting out on campaign in September and another sixteen in November.[8]

Not all the Apaches' travel in the hinterlands at San Elizario was overtly warlike. In July the Spaniards fitted out "two Indian friends that went as spies to the Sacramento Mountains." In early September another small party of "three Apache friends" received supplies so that they could ostensibly "explore the Enemy Country." A few weeks later, this time described with a bit more honesty, three more Apaches were sent "to go out as spies to the frontier." On October 1, one of these apparently returned, and the paymaster at San Elizario gave "to the Indian Fuerte that came with news from the Sacramentos, one blanket and one real of puros." This terse notation may indicate that the Spaniards were also employing other Apaches as well as Mescaleros de paz as spies into the Mescalero heartlands, as Fuerte was the name applied to a man who later became famous as the great Chiricahua leader Mangas Coloradas.[9]

But travels between the Mescalero lands and the peace establishments were not all one way. In several instances Mescaleros either outside or on the edges of Spanish control interacted with the authorities at San Elizario. In late July there had been given "to the Capitancillo Botas of those established at peace in the Sacramento Mountains" one serape, cigars, and two sweets, charged against the gastos de Apaches. In late August another Mescalero leader from beyond the frontier came in, and the paymaster at San Elizario gave "to the capitancillo of the Sacramento, Ystlebacinla a change of clothing and a blanket."[10]

While the Spaniards were willing to deal with the Mescaleros beyond the pale of their authority, they also demonstrated a willingness to admit back into their fold those that had strayed. Their treatment of the capitancillo Mayá was a prime example. Authorities believed him among those leaders that had initiated the rebellion in August 1795; however, after having suffered a severe wound during a Spanish attack on his ranchería, he had attempted to win back his status as a "loyal" Mescalero de paz. In September 1800 the paymaster at San Elizario gave "to the capitancillo Mayá a serape and a blanket this to his wife." This gift portended an apparent return of sincere loyalty, as Mayá would be reckoned among the "loyal" Mescaleros until his death some twenty years later.[11]

The Spaniards also looked after the relatives of those that had proven their loyalty. The capitancillo Francisco had been among the most steadfast of those

Mescaleros in accommodating with the white men. At the outbreak of war, he had personally seized several Apache involved in the initial attacks. Over the next four years he had assiduously cultivated this relationship with the Spaniards, and won for his ranchería an undoubted reputation as the most loyal of the Mescaleros at San Elizario. But during the course of the war he had died, either from natural causes, disease, or violence. Regardless of the cause, Francisco left his ranchería and his immediate family into the care of the Spaniards, even as the leadership of his people technically passed to another successor, a capitancillo named El Cautivo. Still, the Spaniards awarded a small mercy to his memory when in December there had been "given by the Paymaster officer three blankets to the three Indian widows of the ranchería of Francisco that came with El Cautivo."[12]

But the dark side of the relationship between Spaniard and Mescalero also manifested in the continued deportation of Apache prisoners of war. Although the massive coordinated campaigns launched from Coahuila and Nueva Vizcaya over the length of the frontier had ceased, Commandant General Nava still ordered localized monthly punitive raids to continue, especially along the Rio Grande in the region between the Spanish villas of El Paso and Albuquerque. Although the targets of these raids were generally the Chiricahua Gileños that lived to the west of the Rio Grande, Spanish soldiers also engaged the Mescaleros east of the river.[13]

In late August and early September 1800, soldados operating out of San Elizario launched just such a raid into the Sacramento Mountains, where groups of Mescaleros de paz and those at war routinely intermingled. Although details of the operation are unclear, the Spaniards captured twenty-five Mescaleros, who were doomed to deportation. Spanish reports coldly recorded a few instances concerning the prisoners' treatment. On September 4 one of the troopers, Mariano Trujillo from the Presidio of Buenavista, was slated to be reimbursed for giving up "a horse that he gave in order to feed on campaign the Prisoners of War." Soon thereafter, the prisoners again dined from "a yearling calf that Alférez Dn Ignacio Sotelo killed in the Sacramento for those being conducted to Chihuahua for their maintenance."[14]

As had been the case for many years, these captured Mescaleros faced deportation to Mexico City and from there to Havana, Cuba, for a period of ten years. The records of the first leg of their journey read: "The Paymaster of the Company of San Elizario will satisfy the arrieros that conducted the collera for Chihuahua, one hundred pesos, two reales, imported for the freighting of eighteen mules, on which were mounted twenty five piezas and the rations corresponding, as far as that Villa making this charge on the Cuenta de Prisioneros." On the same day, officials also distributed a series of rations for the prisoners. "Given from this paymaster store one and a half fanegas of pinole and two bulls for the rations of the twenty five Prisoners that are to be conducted to Chihuahua." These twenty-five Mescaleros were eventually placed among a larger group of Apache prisoners of war shipped south to Mexico City toward the end of 1800.[15]

The Mescaleros' constant losses from Spanish raids into regions beyond the frontier, and the terrible certainty of deportation, ensured that a substantial number of Indians remained attached to the peace establishments. By the end of the year 1800, approximately three hundred men, women, and children remained officially registered outside five presidios in Nueva Vizcaya, but exactly what percentage these Mescaleros de paz represented of the entire tribe is difficult to calculate. But the actual numbers did not reflect accurately the impact the Spaniards exerted on these people. For every individual registered in the peace establishments, there were probably an equal or greater number that remained in the hinterland. Yet these "free" Mescaleros were continuously subjected to overwhelming pressure from Spanish bases. Whether having to confront, repel, or elude military raiders, or having to engage in licit or illicit trade and exchanges of goods, these Mescaleros lived firmly within the reach of Spanish power. And often that power, both peaceful and aggressive, was increasingly aided and abetted by other Mescaleros allied with the Spaniards. To many the lesson was clear and had been driven home by the dreadful four years of war they had recently endured—accept the terms of the bad peace rather than risk the terrors of the good war.

In the end, what had the war accomplished? The four years of coordinated strikes into Mescalero heartlands by the forces of Pedro de Nava clearly diminished the Indians' ability to attack Spanish territory. While sporadic and localized small-scale raids continued, the Mescaleros ceased almost all of their larger attacks into the Provincias Internas south of the Rio Grande. Further, the admittedly diminished numbers of Mescaleros entering into the peace establishments near San Elizario, Presidio del Norte, and other frontier posts indicated a newfound, albeit transitory, willingness of some in the tribe to accept Spanish terms.

Somewhat surprisingly, for many of the Mescaleros that agreed to registration at peace establishments outside Spanish military posts, there was an unexpected benefit. Before the outbreak, the Apaches de paz had lived principally outside El Paso, San Elizario, and Presidio del Norte on the river's northern bank. While many remained in these locations, now some of them were allowed to gather at Coyamé, San Geronimo, and Guajoquilla, in areas far south of the great river and in regions close to their traditional raiding paths into Spanish territory. This accommodation on the part of the Spaniards may have been seen as efficiency for the distribution of rations or as a military necessity in keeping the Indians under the close control of nearby troopers. Nevertheless, it also would have fostered the notion among the Mescaleros that "their lands" had now come to include the regions near the peace establishments, and a seeming territorial expansion, from their point of view.

But, tragically, even with this development, the overall conditions were essentially those of *status quo ante bellum*. As they had been before the war, the Mescalero Apaches as a people remained firmly within the Spanish sphere of influence, militarily, economically, and culturally. Among the various individuals, families, and rancherías the only difference was a matter of degree. Some of their warriors still aided the Spaniards as scouts and fighting men against other Mescaleros who refused to fight for the white men. A number of Mescalero women and children still came in for rations of Spanish food, tools, clothing, and trinkets, while others sought to steal or trade for the same. Some Mescaleros adopted Spanish language, profanities, vices, and sometimes religious practices, while other despised and rejected the same. As they had before the conflict started, the Mescaleros as a people still lived balanced upon the edge of a knife.

EPILOGUE

The Turns of History

THE SUMMER OF 1800 found Pedro de Nava exhausted. He was now sixty-two and the years had begun to wear on him. He had been in command along the northern edge of the empire for almost ten years, longer than any of his predecessors. He had struggled mightily to subdue the Apaches all along the frontier and had achieved some notable successes. In Sonora significant numbers of Chiricahuas and Western Apaches had been subsumed into the Spanish orbit and settled in peace establishments outside several presidios. In the east, the Lipan Apaches had recently agreed to a formal treaty with the authorities in Nuevo León and Nuevo Santander, complementing the peace they had agreed to previously with the Spanish governor in San Antonio, Texas.

But conditions in the central provinces of Nueva Vizcaya and Coahuila were more ambiguous. Since August 1795 Nava had directed a protracted, bloody, and, by all the metrics of the eighteenth century, generally successful war against the Mescalero Apaches in those regions. Hundreds of the "Barbarian Indians" had been captured and killed, and his soldados had proven their superiority in numerous engagements, full-scale battles, and small skirmishes. As a result, substantial number of Mescaleros had even agreed to reside outside several peace establishments throughout Nueva Vizcaya.

The level of violence throughout the Interior Provinces had abated remarkably over the year's early months, and hopes for peace had returned. Yet for

Pedro de Nava, it was not enough. For every Apache that was killed or that agreed to an accommodation at the peace establishments, another one seemed to rise up to fight and raid. The constant cycle of strike and counterstrike and the machinations of maintaining a "bad peace" rather than a "good war" had consumed the last decade of Nava's life. Nava was worn out and had had enough. He had already supplicated the king a few years before to allow him to return to Spain. Now, his request would finally be answered, as on August 29, 1800, King Charles IV signed an order finally relieving Pedro de Nava as commandant general of the Interior Provinces.[1]

Yet despite Nava's seeming containment of the Apaches, the security of the Interior Provinces remained questionable, and not just from the Native peoples. A more ominous threat had emerged from across the great Mississippi River. Citizens of the United States of America were beginning to cross the river in great numbers into Spanish Louisiana, some legally by swearing allegiance to Spain, but many others clandestinely and illegally. The Americans came searching for trading opportunities with the region's numerous Indian nations, ever hungry for muskets, gunpowder, and iron tools. In 1795 Spanish authorities had granted the Americans free trading rights at the port of New Orleans, Louisiana. However, within a few years the Spaniards became alarmed by the burgeoning numbers of Americans and reversed course, restricting the trade. Outraged, the Americans howled at their government and demanded war. Watching and waiting in the wings, the British from their base in Canada appeared more than willing to stoke the fires of discontent, and rumors abounded that they would launch an invasion to seize the Mississippi themselves. From there, they would threaten the Interior Provinces and perhaps the silver mines of Mexico that they shielded.[2]

Pedro de Nava had allowed himself to be drawn into these intrigues by carelessly sending out a letter. In 1797, he received word from the governor of Texas, the aged and infirm Manuel Muñoz, that a party of foreigners led by one Philip Nolan had come to San Antonio to corral mustangs. The region proliferated with these wild horses, and Nolan wanted to procure them ostensibly for the use of Spanish dragoons in Louisiana. When he arrived at San Antonio, Nolan presented a passport he had been issued by the governor of Louisiana, the Baron de Carondelet. At this point, Nava was not too concerned about the matter, as he had dealt with Nolan before. Indeed, this was the third time

Nolan had traveled to Texas. In 1791 and 1795 Spanish authorities had allowed him to enter and obtain horses, and each time he had conducted his business and departed without causing trouble. Being an Irishman and a Catholic with a mastery of Spanish, Nolan had ingratiated himself with many Spaniards in the region. Therefore, when in 1797 Nolan appeared again in San Antonio, Governor Muñoz vouched for him and asked for Commandant General Nava's permission to allow Nolan to again hunt mustangs. Nava quickly, and in hindsight, carelessly obliged.

Armed with permission from the commandant general, Nolan began his operations, and eventually gathered a considerable number of horses that he would sell in Louisiana. However, his activities had begun to arouse suspicion. Unlike his first two visits, this time he had overstayed his welcome in Spanish territory, lingering around San Antonio for more than a year before finally heading back across the Mississippi River. Afterward, rumors circulated that he had been acting as an agent of the British or for the United States government, and that he had been secretly mapping the region in anticipation of an invasion. When word came that Nolan was a protégé of the American General James Wilkinson, Spanish authorities concluded that Nolan was involved in attempts to undermine their possessions.

In the early months of 1800, Nolan again entered Spanish territory, with some thirty followers on another expedition to round up mustangs. But this time, the Spaniards were determined to prevent his activities. A force exceeding one hundred soldados and militia departed from the Presidio of Nacogdoches to arrest him. On March 21, they came upon Nolan and his party gathering horses near the area of present-day Waco, Texas. Nolan defiantly chose to fight, but was killed almost immediately. The rest of his men were forced to surrender and were later imprisoned for many years. Whatever his true intentions, Nolan's actions sent a clear message to the Spaniards that they would continue to face American aggression, both covert and overt, against their provinces.[3]

For Commandant General Nava, Nolan's activities may have reflected poorly on his judgment. Yet, even had he handled the situation more effectively, the political situation evolving around the Interior Provinces clearly demanded a reevaluation of Spanish strategy. For almost a decade, Nava had concentrated much of his energy on confronting the Native peoples that lived along the northern frontier, especially the Apaches. In this he had continued the policies of his predecessors of the last thirty years, alternating the mailed fist of military power with the velvet glove of forced acculturation and accommodation. He had especially adhered to the maxims of Bernardo de Gálvez's Instructions of 1786, advocating that a bad peace was better than a good war. Yet during the last several years, he had waged "a good war" against the Mescaleros, only to have the situation return to what it had been before the war, with all the frustrations surrounding "a bad peace."

But now Spanish policies regarding the Apaches and other Native peoples were becoming increasingly irrelevant in light of these new threats. Spain needed new policies to deal with the intentions of Great Britain and the aspirations of the United States, and for these Pedro de Nava may have felt himself unsuited. By the end of 1800, he received word that the king had granted his wish to be relieved of duty and would replace him with a younger man, one perhaps more suited to the new challenges swirling about the Interior Provinces. But the wheels of government ground but slowly, and two years would pass before his relief arrived. In the meanwhile, as he had for more than ten years, Pedro de Nava continuously monitored the frontier, guarding against enemies old and new.

For the Mescaleros de paz gathered outside the peace establishments at San Elizario, Presidio del Norte, and other posts in Nueva Vizcaya, the year 1800 had marked a return to a tense existence. Over the last four years, they had suffered tremendously at the hands of the Spaniards in a general war that seemingly engulfed all of their people. Many had died, many were maimed, and many were exiled, never to be heard from again. But for those remaining, a hard lesson had been learned. They could continue to move their rancherías about yearly, as they always had; they could continue their great buffalo hunts and seasonal farming and harvesting; they could continue to raid and trade for horses, weapons, and material goods; they could continue many of their traditional lifeways and at the same time receive Spanish rations to sustain them and Spanish protection from their enemies. They could do all these things—as long as they did not push the Spaniards too far.

And that posed the greatest challenge. Given their society's decentralized nature, the Mescaleros had to constantly negotiate their terms of accommodation with the Spaniards outside the peace establishments. They had to accept some level of control over, or at least knowledge of, their movements. They would have to accept the small disciplines of being counted and registered in order to receive their rations; and they had to accept some level of Spanish authority as they set out to raid and make war on other "free" Mescaleros in the hinterland. Although they would not articulate it as such, the Mescaleros de paz had to accept the Spanish maxim of the bad peace and the good war.

As the months passed, it appeared that the Apaches de paz had learned the lesson. For the Mescaleros in Nueva Vizcaya, for the Chiricahuas in the west, and for the Lipans in the east, peace, or at least the absence of war, became the norm over most of the Interior Provinces. For the foreseeable future, the accommodation of the Apaches de paz at the various establishments would continue under Spanish rules and under the threat of Spanish military power. While small-scale livestock raiding and occasional violent encounters continued, there would be no more outbreaks on the scale undertaken by the Mescalero. Indeed, in many areas, especially Sonora and Nueva Vizcaya, many would come to view the decade after 1800 as among the most productive. Spanish towns and settlements grew in population and prosperity, farms and ranches increased production, and even mining expanded with the opening of copper mines at Santa Rita del Cobre, in the midst of traditional Apache homelands.[4]

Yet, regardless of the outcome of the struggle against the Mescaleros, the Spaniards soon found themselves in a markedly different situation as a result of forces far more powerful than all the peoples along the northern frontier could imagine. While various groups of Apaches still struggled to decide whether or not to accommodate outside Spanish peace establishments, the continent's fate had already been decided half a world away.

In October 1800 Napoleon Bonaparte, now military dictator of France, browbeat the Spaniards into signing a secret treaty to return the province of Louisiana to his government. Though the parties would not make the treaty public for many months thereafter, the ultimate result was the Louisiana Purchase of 1803, wherein the French sold more than eight hundred million acres of territory to the United States under the leadership of President Thomas Jefferson. For Spain the loss of Louisiana placed the Interior Provinces in direct contact with the burgeoning economic and demographic power of the young American republic. As the official border between the two nations shifted to the west, the Interior Provinces, especially New Mexico and Texas, were now confronted with an aggressive and belligerent people with resources far beyond anything ever dreamed of by the Mescalero or Chiricahua Apaches.[5]

Within a short period of time, the Americans were threatening Spain's control over the entire northern frontier. In the wake of several years of official and covert aggressions launched from American soil, during the fall of 1810

Father Miguel Hidalgo cried out for independence and justice, unleashing forces that would sweep Spain from North America. By 1821, the newly independent Mexico now stood alone and unsteadily in the path of a United States infused with a sense of expansion. As the two nations gradually lurched inexorably toward war, the Mescaleros de paz and their kinsmen living free in the hinterlands were trying to maintain their lifeways within the understandable confines of their recent past. But this would prove a vain conceit. Although it would take several decades, the forces unleashed between Mexico and the United States would enormously impact the paths the Mescalero Apaches were able to follow. They would find themselves ever more constrained by situations that allowed for neither a bad peace nor a good war, but only for the bare hope of survival.

NOTES

Abbreviations

AGS   Archivo General de Simancas
AGN   Archivo General de la Nación, Mexico
JA   Juarez Archives Collection
PI   Provincias Internas
SGU   Secretaria de Guerra
UTEP University of Texas at El Paso

Introduction

1. For the sense of peace and the central role of Gálvez, see Weber, *Spanish Frontier*, 234: "In the last decade of the eighteenth century, then, the northern frontier of New Spain entered a period of relative peace . . . mainly because Spanish and Indian leaders had come to believe, as Bernardo de Gálvez hoped they would, that they had more to gain from peace than from war." Historians using the concept *establecimiento de paz* include Griffen, *Apaches at War and Peace*, 14; Hämäläinen, *Comanche Empire*, 129; Jacoby, *Shadows at Dawn*, 55–57, 60, 64, 82, 157, 159, 161; Kessell, *Spain in the Southwest*, 311; Matson and Fontana (eds.) in Bringas, *Friar Bringas Reports*, 123; Officer, *Hispanic Arizona*, 64, 79, 87; Sweeney, *Mangas Coloradas*, 17; and Weber, *Spanish Frontier*, 233–34, and *Bárbaros*, 185, 193–94, 219. Historians characterizing these establishments as reservations include Weber, *Bárbaros*, 185, 193–94, while Moorhead, in *Presidio*, 243–66, devotes an entire chapter describing these entities as reservations, though he does not use the term *establecimiento de paz*. Babcock, in *Apache Adaptation*, 8, 17n18, notes that the term was not used by the Spaniards

contemporaneously, but was a creation of Mexican historians from whom U.S. historians borrowed the term. He uses *establecimiento,* or establishment, as more historically correct and does characterize the system as a reservation, though he maintains that the term does not always adequately express the nuances of the system.

2. Gálvez, *Instructions for Governing the Interior Provinces,* 38–39; Weber, *Bárbaros,* 165.
3. Navarro García describes the beginning of the war in *José de Gálvez,* 493; Babcock, in *Apache Adaptation,* 192–93, gives a brief account of the conflict.
4. Griffen, *Apaches at War and Peace,* 14, 69–116; Blyth, *Chiricahua and Janos,* 87–121; Bringas, *Friar Bringas Reports,* 121–30; Dobyns, *Spanish Colonial Tucson,* 97–105.
5. McGown Minor, *Turning Adversity to Advantage,* 110–30.
6. Hendricks and Timmons in *San Elizario,* 137n11, note the lack of records for San Elizario. Nevertheless, they draw on the Juarez Archives Collection at the University of Texas at El Paso for items dealing with the establishments around El Paso and San Elizario. Jones, "Settlements and Settlers at La Junta de los Rios," 43–44, notes the scarcity of records for Presidio del Norte, but uses pertinent records from the archives of El Templo de Nuestro Padre Jesus Nazareno, and the parish church of Ojinaga, Chihuahua, with copies at Sul Ross State University.
7. Bringas, *Friar Bringas Reports,* 120, wrote the Mescaleros "rose up." Lieutenant Colonel Cordero referred to "a general irruption" in "Diario seguido por el Teniente Coronel Cordero de las Operaciones del Destacamento de su cargo desde el día 16 de Agosto hasta el de la fecha" (hereafter cited as Cordero, "Diario Seguido"), enclosed with Antonio Cordero to Pedro de Nava, Paso del Rio del Norte, August 27, 1795, while Pedro de Nava characterized it as an "uprising" or "revolt." Pedro de Nava to Exc^{mo} S^{or}. Dn Miguel Joseph de Azanza, Chihuahua, July 5, 1796, both in Archivo General de Simancas, Secretaria de Guerra (hereinafter cited as AGS, SGU), Provincias Internas, Indios 7025, 1. For "just war," see Weber, *Bárbaros,* 144–45; Santiago, *Jar of Severed Hands,* 34–35.
8. Bringas, *Friar Bringas Reports,* 120.
9. Navarro García, *José de Gálvez,* 493; Babcock, *Apache Adaptation,* 192–93.
10. Moorhead, *Presidio,* 47–114.
11. For Spain's dealings with revolutionary France and Great Britain, see Bergamini, *Spanish Bourbons,* 114–21.

Chapter 1. A General Irruption

1. Kessell, *Spain in the Southwest,* 325–29, 331, 343–44; Weber, *Spanish Frontier,* 271–75.
2. Hendricks and Timmons, *San Elizario,* 29–38; Babcock, *Apache Adaptation,* 142–43, 177–83.
3. El Coronel Dn Pedro de Nava por medio de Apoderado, Madrid, July 23, 1787, in Pedro de Nava, Informe, 7166, 44, AGS, SGU; Pedro de Nava, Hoja de Servicio through December 1791, enclosed with El Conde de Revillagigedo to Conde del Campo de Alange México, June 29, 1793, AGS, SGU, Provincias Internas, Nueva España, 7278, 7.

4. Pedro de Nava to Exc^mo S^or. Conde del Alange, Chihuahua, 6 August 1795—No. 211—"El Comandante General de las Provincias Internas. Refiere varias ocurrencias de Indios que pretenden aproximarse a la Frontera de Texas huyendo de los Americanos," AGS, SGU, Provincias Internas, Indios, 7025, 1.
5. Hoja de Sevicio of Alférez Dn Josef de Urías, December 31, 1794, enclosed with Pedro de Nava to Exc^mo Sor Conde del Alange, Chihuahua, August 6, 1795, AGS, SGU, Provincias Internas, Nueva España, 7278, 4.
6. Moorhead, *Presidio*, 90, 92.
7. San Carlos was located at present-day Chorerras, Chihuahua, approximately twenty-one miles northeast of Chihuahua City; Moorhead, *Presidio*, 90, 92. The details for these events and the two battles that followed are found in Pedro de Nava to Conde del Campo de Alange, Chihuahua, September 1, 1795, No. 217, "El Comandante General de Provincias Internas Refiere hostilidades de Enemigos y sus disposiciones para escarmentarlos"; and Pedro de Nava to Conde del Campo de Alange, Chihuahua, November 3, 1795, No. 230, "El Comandante General de Provincias Internas de Nueva España Remite Extracto de hostilidades," both in AGS, SGU, Provincias Internas, Indios, 7025, 1. In the later, Nava states that "The Indians robbed on the 25th of July twenty animals from the Rancho de Santa Cruz, and Pueblo de la Joya, jurisdiction of la Ciénega de los Olivos and were pursued with vigor by two parties of Troops from the Presidios of San Carlos, Príncipe, Tercera, and Quarta Compañías Volantes." Ciénega de los Olivos is the modern Valle de Rosario, Chihuahua.
8. Nava to Alange, Chihuahua, September 1, 1795, No. 217, and Nava to Alange, Chihuahua, November 3, 1795, No. 230, AGS, SGU, Provincias Internas, Indios, 7025, 1.
9. Ibid.
10. Moorhead, *Presidio*, 182–84, 199. Captain Antonio García de Texada, Coyamé, December 15, 1797, "Extracto de Revista y Inspección . . . Real Presidio del Príncipe," AGS, SGU, Provincias Internas, Premios y retiros, 7027, 12.
11. Nava to Campo de Alange, Chihuahua, September 1, 1795, No. 217, AGS, SGU, Provincias Internas, Indios, 7025, 1.
12. Captain Antonio Garcia de Texada, Coyamé, December 15, 1797, "Extracto de . . . Príncipe," AGS, SGU, Provincias Internas, Premios y retiros, 7027, 12; Nava to Campo de Alange, Chihuahua, September 1, 1795, No. 217, and Nava to Campo de Alange, Chihuahua, November 3, 1795, No. 230, AGS, SGU, Provincias Internas, Indios 7025, 1.
13. Texada, Coyamé, December 15, 1797, "Extracto de . . . Príncipe," AGS, SGU, 7027, 12.
14. Hojas de Servcios of each, enclosed in Manuel Antonio Flores to Frey Dn Antonio Valdés, México, November 21, 1788, AGS, SGU, Provinicias Internas, Nueva España, 7278, 9.
15. Hoja de Servicio of Cayetano Limón, in Pedro de Nava to Excmo. Señor Conde de Campo de Alange, Chihuahua, August 6, 1795, AGS, SGU, Provincias Internas, Nueva España, 7278, 4.

16. Hoja de Sevicio of Alférez Dn Juan Fernández, December 31, 1794, enclosed with Pedro de Nava to Conde del Alange, Chihuahua, August 6, 1795, AGS, SGU, Provincias Internas, Nueva España, 7278, 4.
17. Moorhead, *Presidio*, 70n55. From San Carlos to Los Pilares is approximately 150 miles as the crow flies. However, given the course of events, it appears that Limón and Fernández were following a more circuitous route that may have added another fifty or more miles. This is not unusual considering that they were engaged in tracking, a rather intensive and thus slow process.
18. The Sierra de los Ojos Calientes is the southern extension of the Quitman Mountains in Hudspeth County, Texas, containing the modern Indian Hot Springs. Cloud, "Indian Hot Springs."
19. Nava to Campo de Alange, Chihuahua, September 1, 1795, No. 217, AGS, SGU, Provincias Internas, Indios 7025, 1.
20. Antonio Vargas to the Señor Teniente Gobernador del Paso, San Eleazario, August 8, 1795, University of Texas at El Paso, Juarez Archives Collection (hereinafter cited as UTEP, JA), Roll 13.
21. Ibid.
22. Ibid.
23. Ibid.; Griffen, *Apaches at War and Peace*, 5–6; "Cordero's Description of the Apache," 341–43.
24. Antonio Vargas to the Señor Teniente Gobernador del Paso, Dn Francisco Xavier de Uranga, San Eleazario, August 13, 1795, UTEP, JA, Roll 13.
25. Hart and Hulbert, eds., *Journals of Zebulon Pike*, 233. Cordero's 1795 Hoja de Servicio, enclosed in Pedro de Nava to Miguel de Azanza, Quartel de las 1ª Compañía Volante en Guajoquilla, August 3, 1796, N. 301, El Comandante General de Provincias Internas de N.E. Remite ojas de servicios del año de 1795, AGS, SGU, Provincias Internas, Nueva España, 7278, 4.
26. Cordero's 1795 Hoja de Servicio, AGS, SGU, Provincias Internas, Nueva España, 7278, 4.
27. Matson and Schroeder, "Cordero's Description of the Apache," 339, 349–50.
28. Ibid., 339, 341.
29. Santiago, *Jar of Severed Hands*, 99–108, 115–16. Cordero to Revillagigedo, Chihuahua, February 15, 1791, Archivo General de la Nación, Mexico, Provincias Internas, 142 (hereinafter cited as AGN, PI).
30. Cordero's 1796 Hoja de Servicio, Pedro de Nava to Dn Juan Manuel Albarez, Chihuahua, July 4, 1797, No. 374, "El Comandante General del Provincias Internas de N.E Remite ojas de servicios pertenecientes afín del año de 1796," AGS, SGU, Nueva España, Provincias Internas, 7278, 2.

Chapter 2. Origins of Conflict

1. Cordero, "Diario seguido."
2. Carter, *Indian Alliances*, 3–79.
3. Ibid.

4. Cook and Lovell, *Secret Judgments of God*, 3–19, 213–42.
5. Forbes, *Apache, Navaho, and Spaniard*; Carter, *Indian Alliances*, 118–208.
6. Anderson, *Indian Southwest*, 57–66, 105–27; Parrott Hickerson, *Jumanos*, 199–208. Weber, *Spanish Frontier*, 206.
7. Santiago, *Jar of Severed Hands*, 207–8. Opler, "The Apachean Culture Pattern," 388–89; "Chiricahua Apache," 416–18; "Mescalero Apache," 420, 437–38; Veronica E. Tiller, "Jicarilla Apache," 447–50, all in *Southwest*, ed. Alfonso Ortiz, *Handbook of North American Indians*. Throughout this work, I use the modern classification *Chiricahua* to describe those groups labeled by the Spaniards as *Gileño*, *Mimbreño*, and *Chiricagui* when referring to them in general. I use the Spanish terms if greater specificity is required or in relation to a historical quotation or description. Similarly, I refer to groups distinguished by the Spaniards as *Faraón* and *Mescalero* together as Mescalero under the same circumstances.
8. Opler, "Mescalero Apache," 420, 437–38.
9. Ibid.
10. Ibid.
11. Sonnichsen, *Mescalero Apaches*, 17–52; Dunn, "Apache Relations in Texas," 202–3, 220–22, 264–69.
12. Hämäläinen, *Comanche Empire*, 18–67.
13. John, *Storms Brewed*, 60–62; Weber, *Bárbaros*, 80–81.
14. Santiago, *Jar of Severed Hands*, 18-21; Opler, "Apachean Culture Pattern," 368–76; Basso, *Western Apache Raiding*, 14–18, 253–63; John, *Storms Brewed*, 57–64; Griffen, *Apaches at War and Peace*, 1–18.
15. Scholes, Simmons, and Esquibel, eds., *Juan Domínguez de Mendoza*, 25–26, 112–42; Forbes, *Apache, Navaho, and Spaniard*, 145–75; Murphy, *Salinas Pueblo Missions*, 57–60.
16. Carter, *Indian Alliances*, 184–208. Forbes, *Apache, Navaho, and Spaniard*, 145–75;
17. Parrott Hickerson, *Jumanos*, 152–53, 203–4, Dunn, "Apache Relations in Texas," 202–3, 220–22, 264–69.
18. Hämäläinen, *Comanche Empire*, 35–36.
19. Weddle, *San Sabá Mission*.

Chapter 3. War, Peace, War

1. Moore and Beene, "O'Conor's Report," 269, identifies these as the present-day Davis Mountains in west Texas. Moorhead, *Apache Frontier*, 216, 219, 243, calls them Sierra del Movano.
2. Hugo O'Conor to Viceroy Antonio María de Bucareli, "Diario seguido desde el día 18 de Noviembre próximo anterior en que se dio cuenta con el último al Excmo. Señor Virrey hasta el día 8 del corriente," Real Presidio de las Juntas de los Ríos Grande del Norte y Conchos, December 8, 1773, enclosed with Bucareli to Julian de Arriaga, No. 1247, El Virrey de Nueva España remite extracto de las últimas novedades acaecidas en las Provincias Internas, Mexico, January 27, 1774, Archivo General de las Indias, Sevilla, Audiencia de Guadalajara, 513 (hereinafter cited as AGI, Guad.).

3. Torres Ramírez *Alejandro O'Reilly en las Indias*, 31–48. Kuethe, *Cuba*, pp. 33–40; Santiago, *Jar of Severed Hands*, 21–25.
4. Robles, *Nicolás de Lafora*; Jackson, *Imaginary Kingdom*, 71–228.
5. Brinckerhoff and Faulk, *Lancers for the King*. Santiago, *Red Captain*, 1–35.
6. Hadley, Naylor, and Schuetz-Miller, *Presidio and Militia, Central Corridor*, 9–14.
7. For Apache utilization of the Bolsón de Mapimí, see "Berroteran's Report on the Condition of Nueva Vizcaya," in ibid., 167–204; Moorhead, *Apache Frontier*, 26–27.
8. Santiago, *Red Captain*, 43–53.
9. Ibid., 54–65.
10. Santiago, *Jar of Severed Hands*, 35–48.
11. Hugo O'Conor to Viceroy Antonio María de Bucareli, attached with "Plan de Operación," Presidio de Carrizal, March 24, 1775, AGN, PI 88.
12. O'Conor to Bucareli, attached with "Diario seguido el día siete de Septiembre en que se ha dado cuenta con el ultimo al Excm. Sr.," Carrizal, December 1, 1775, AGN, PI 88.
13. Ibid.
14. Ibid.
15. Santiago, *Red Captain*, 65–67.
16. Ibid., 70–76.
17. Jansen, *Charles et Théodore de Croix*, 37–41, 65–80. Moorhead, *Presidio*, 76–94.
18. Moorhead, *Presidio*, 77–82, 84–85.
19. Babcock, *Apache Adaptation*, 61–65.
20. Moorhead, *Apache Frontier*, 203–4; Thomas, *Teodoro de Croix*, 89.
21. Thomas, *Teodoro de Croix*, 90–93; Hämäläinen, *Comanche Empire*, 98.
22. Thomas, *Teodoro de Croix*, 89–92, 125–27. For Buena Esperanza, Babcock, *Apache Adaptation*, 61, 63–65, 84–94; also, Babcock's earlier dissertation, "Turning Apaches into Spaniards," 20–27, 66–87.
23. Babcock, "Turning Apaches into Spaniards," 20–27, 66–87; Thomas, *Teodoro de Croix*, 89–92, 125–27; Moorhead, *Apache Frontier*, 204–6; Santiago, *Jar of Severed Hands*, 51–52.
24. Ibid.
25. Jansen, *Charles et Théodore de Croix*, 68–74; Moorhead, *Presidio*, 85–94.
26. Moorhead, *Presidio*, 95–98.
27. Ibid., 100–108.
28. Ibid. Navarro García, *José de Gálvez*, 450–57.
29. Gálvez, *Instructions for Governing the Interior Provinces*, 37–38; Weber, *Bárbaros*, 165.
30. Moorhead, *Presidio*, 101
31. Ibid., 102–3.

Chapter 4. Between Two Fires

1. This account is based on Cruz Barney, "Derecho Indiano Local," 103–18, 125–28.
2. Moorhead, *Apache Frontier*, 64–86. Weber, *Spanish Frontier*, 227–30. Weber, *Bárbaros*, 183–85. Babcock, *Apache Adaptation*, 106–7.

3. Díaz to Ugarte, Presidio del Norte, March 29, 1787, enclosed with Jacobo Ugarte y Loyola to the Marqués de Sonora, Arizpe, April 16, 1787, AGS, SGU 6952, 4, Negociaciones de paz con Indios Apaches. Moorhead, *Apache Frontier*, 207, 212–13. Moorhead, *Presidio*, 250–53.
4. Moorhead, *Apache Frontier*, 207–13. The Spaniards identified the eight Mescalero capitancillos as Domingo Alegre, Volante, Patule El Grande, Bigotes el Bermejo, Zapato Tuerto, El Quemado, Montera Blanca, and Cuerno Verde. Two other headmen, El Natagé and the powerful Lipiyan leader, Picax-andé, had pledged to join the other capitancillos. Babcock, *Apache Adaptation*, 87–93.
5. Moorhead, *Apache Frontier*, 206. Cruz Barney, "Derecho Indiano Local," 126.
6. Moorhead, *Apache Frontier*, 207–13. Nelson, "Campaigning in the Big Bend," 200–27.
7. Griffen, *Apaches at War and Peace*, 57–58.
8. Nelson, "Juan de Ugalde and Picax-andé Ins-Tinsle," 438-64.
9. Santiago, *Jar of Severed Hands*, 87–88; Juan de Ugalde to Flores, Valle de Santa Rosa, March 4 and April 1, 1789, AGN, PI, 159.
10. Santiago, *Jar of Severed Hands*, 88; El Conde de Revillagigedo to Exmo. Señor Conde del Campo de Alange, Mexico, 15 January 1791 AGS SGU. Indios Provincias Internas, 7020, 8.
11. Revillagigedo to Campo de Alange, Mexico, 15 January 1791, AGS SGU, Indios Provincias Internas, 7020, 8.
12. Ibid.
13. Moorhead, *Apache Frontier*, 254–56.
14. Ibid. Cordero's 1787 hoja enclosed in Manuel Antonio Flores to Frey Dn Antonio Valdes, Mexico, November 21, 1788, N. 659, El Virrey de Nueva España Remite Libretas de Servicios de Oficiales, Cadetes, y Sargentos de las Provincias de la Comandancía General del Poniente respectivas al año último, AGS, SGU, Provincias Internas, Nueva España, 7278, 9.
15. "Dn Antonio Cordero y Bustamante, Teniente Coronel de las Reales Ejércitos y Capitán del Presidio de Janos. Certifico que las servicios contenidos en esta libro esta arreglados a los despachos certificaciones que me han presentado las interesadas a las hojas de servicios anteriores y publica notoriedad," Chihuahua, February 28, 1791, AGS, SGU, Provincias Internas, Nueva España, 7278, 8.
16. Cordero most likely crossed the Rio Grande at San Diego Crossing between Rincon and Radium Springs, New Mexico. "Copias que contiene los partes Justificados del Capitán Dn Antonio Cordero sobre efectos de su campaña y varias órdenes comunicadas a este oficial." Containing: Cordero to Ugarte, two letters, Campamento de San Diego en el Rió Grande del Norte, September 11 and September 14, 1789, AGN, PI 193.
17. Cordero to Ugarte, Campamento del Muerto en el Rió Grande del Norte, September 25, 1789, AGN, PI 193. Cordero noted that "there is a river they named the Rio Salado, and a mountain to where they proceeded that they named that of La Sal; as far as the center of another Sierra Madre that they knew as La del Piñon." According to New Mexico anthropologist Karl Laumbach (personal communication, April 16, 2009), the

Rio Salado is the same as the present-day river of the same name, while the Sierra La Sal may be the Bear Mountains and those of La del Piñon the Gallinas Mountains.

18. Cordero to Ugarte, Campamento del Muerto en el Rió Grande del Norte. September 25, 1789, AGN, PI, 193.
19. Ugarte to Cordero, Chihuahua, October 3, 1789, AGN, PI, 193.
20. Cordero to Ugarte, Paso del Norte, November 18, 1789; Certification, Manuel Rengel, Juan Sartorio, and Juan Juárez, Laguna de la Victoria within the Sierra del Sacramento, November 12, 1789, AGN, PI, 193.
21. Ugarte to Cordero, Chihuahua, November 22, 1789, certified copy, November 27, 1789, by Juan Gassiot y Morales; "Relación de las Ventajas logradas sobre los Enemigos por los Destacamentos del mando de los Capitanes Dn. Antonio Cordero y Dn. Manuel de Carrasco," Chihuahua, November 27, 1789, AGN, PI, 193.

Chapter 5. Forging a Bad Peace

1. Hendricks and Timmons, *San Elizario*, 25–26.
2. Hoja de Servicio of Francisco Xavier de Uranga, Presidio del Norte, December 31, 1787, enclosed in Manuel Antonio Flores to Excmo. Sor. Bo. Frey Don Antonio Valdés, Mexico, November 21, 1788, AGS, SGU, Provincias Internas, Nueva España, 7278, 9; and Uranga, Hoja de Servicio, December 31, 1798, enclosed in Pedro de Nava to Excmo. Sor. Don Antonio Cornel, Chihuahua, April 8, 1800, AGS, SGU, Provincias Internas, Nueva España 7279, 3; in the latter, it was noted that Uranga helped move "the populations at the Ciénega del Coyamé, and San Antonio de Chorreras."
3. Hendricks and Timmons, *San Elizario*, 25–26.
4. Moorhead, *Apache Frontier*, 257–61.
5. Moorhead, *Presidio*, 258; Declaración del Alférez Dn Nicolás Villaroel, Presidio del Norte, June 23, 1792; Declaración del 10 Teniente Dn Joaquin Peru, Presidio del Norte, June 23, 1792; Declaración del Sargento Andrés Naranjo, Presidio del Norte, June 25, 1792; Declaración del Soldado Interprete Francisco Perez, Presidio del Norte, June 23, 1792; all enclosed with Antonio Cordero to Pedro de Nava, Pueblo del Paso, July 20, 1792, AGN, PI, 170. McGown Minor argues that Bigotes el Bermejo was actually a Lipan leader, McGown Minor, *Turning Adversity to Advantage*, 85–86.
6. Moorhead, *Presidio*, 261; Griffen, "Chiricahua Apache Population," 191–92.
7. Declaración del Capitán de Milicia Dn Francisco Xavier Bernal, El Paso del Norte, July 13, 1792; Declaración del Capitán de Milicia Dn Miguel de Espinosa, El Paso del Norte, July 13, 1792; Declaración del Soldado Interprete Juan Pedro Rivera, El Paso del Norte, July 14, 1792 Declaración del Alcalde de Real Diego Antonio Candelario, El Paso del Norte, July 14, 1792 Declaración del Teniente del Pueblo de Senecú Juan Antonio Narvaez, El Paso del Norte, July 14, 1792; all enclosed with Antonio Cordero to Pedro de Nava, Pueblo del Paso, July 20, 1792, AGN, PI, 170.
8. Declaración del Capitán de Milicia Dn Francisco Xavier Bernal, El Paso del Norte, July 13, 1792; Declaración del Soldado Interprete Juan Pedro Rivera, El Paso del

Norte, July 14, 1792, both enclosed with Antonio Cordero to Pedro de Nava, Pueblo del Paso, July 20, 1792, AGN, PI, 170.
9. Hämäläinen, *Comanche Empire*, 127.
10. Moorhead, *Apache Frontier*, 86, 256.
11. Ibid., 254–58; Revillagigedo to Conde de Campo de Alange, Mexico, January 15, 1791, AGS, SGU, Indios Provincias Internas, 7020, 8.
12. Miguel José de Emparan to Exmo Señor Virrey Conde de Revillagigedo, Monclova, March 23, 1790, AGN, PI, 160.
13. Emparan to Revillgigedo, Monclova, March 24, 1790, AGN, PI, 160.
14. Emparan, "Estado que manifiesta las hostilidades que ha sufrido la Provincia en el mes ultimo de Marzo de 1790," Monclova, April 8, 1790, enclosed with Emparan to Revillagigedo, Monclova, April 6, 1790, quotes from, the latter. Revillagigedo to Emparan, México, 14 April 1790; Revillagigedo to Emparan, Mexico, April 27, 1790; Revillagigedo to Emparan, Mexico, May 24, 1790, all in AGN, PI, 160.
15. "Extracto de las novedades de Enemigos ocurridas en la Jurisdicción del Saltillo y la del Presidio del Rio Grande en los días que de declaran," enclosed with Emparan to Revillagigedo, Monclova, 15 July 1790, AGN, PI, 160.
16. Emparan to Revillagigedo, Monclova, July 15, 1790, AGN, PI, 160.
17. Emparan to Revillagigedo, Monclova, 29 July 1790, AGN, PI, 160.
18. Revillagigedo to Conde de Campo de Alange, Mexico, January 15, 1791, AGS, SGU, Indios Provincias Internas, 7020, 8.
19. Moorhead, *Apache Frontier*, 279–83; El Coronel Dn Pedro de Nava por medio de Apoderado, Madrid July 23, 1787, in Pedro de Nava, Informe, 7166, 44, AGS, SGU; Pedro de Nava, Hoja de Servicio through December 1791, enclosed with El Conde de Revillagigedo to Conde del Campo de Alange México, June 29, 1793, AGS, SGU, Provincias Internas, Nueva España, 7278, 7. Pozo Redondo, "Funcionarios Canarios en América," 866–74.
20. Revillagigedo to Conde de Alange, September 26, 1790, Mexico, "El Virrey de Nueva España avisa la llegada de Comte. Gral. de Provincias del Poniente Dn Pedro de Nava, y remite copia de oficio instructivo que le ha pasado"; Nava to Revillagigedo, September 17, 1790, Mexico, certified copy, September 26 1790, Mexico, AGS, SGU, Correspondencia de Pedro de Nava, 7045, 6.
21. "Convenio ajustado por el Brigadier Don Pedro de Nava Comandante General de Provincias Internas con los Indios de la Nación Lipana conocidos por los Arriba..." Pedro de Nava, Villa de San Fernando, February 8, 1791, AGS, SGU, Provincias Internas de Oriente, Indios Lipanes, 7021, 2.
22. Hendricks and Timmons, *San Elizario*, 25.
23. Ibid., 26–27.
24. Ibid., 28–29.
25. Ibid., 29. The Jornada del Muerto is an approximately ninety-mile stretch on the route along the Rio Grande north of El Paso along which there were no watering holes, only barren land and rocks.

26. Santiago, *Jar of Severed Hands*, 149–50; Hendricks and Timmons, *San Elizario*, 102–9.
27. Santiago, *Jar of Severed Hands*, 178–79. Castro to Revillagigedo, April 16, 1791, Valle de Santa Rosa, No. 32. Revillagigedo, no recipient, México, May 27, 1791, Juan Gutiérrez de la Cueva to Revillagigedo, Valle de Santa Rosa, May 2, 1791, AGS, SGU, Provincias de Internas Oriente, Indios Lipanes, 7021, 2.
28. Castro to Revillagigedo, Valle de Santa Rosa, August 11, 1791, AGS, SGU, Provincias Internas de Oriente, Auxilios; Revillagigedo to Campo de Alange, Mexico, November 27, 1791, both in AGS, SGU, Provincias Internas de Oriente, Auxilios, 7020, 15.

Chapter 6. Threats to Fragile Peace

1. Edgeworth, *Authentic Memoires of the Revolution in France*, 289–95; Durant and Durant, *Age of Napoleon*, 51–52.
2. Extracto de las hostilidades ejecutadas por los Lipanes y Mescaleros en el Comandancía General de las Provincias de Oriente desde el mes de Noviembre de 1791 hasta fin de Marzo de 1792, enclosed with Castro to Revillagigedo, Valle de Santa Rosa, April 9, 1792, Revillagigedo to Nava, Mexico, April 25, 1792, AGN, PI 170.
3. Antonio Cordero, "Decreto," Presidio del Norte, June 23, 1792, enclosed with Cordero to Pedro de Nava, Pueblo del Paso, July 20, 1792, AGN, PI, 170.
4. Ibid.
5. Those interviewed were Alférez Nicolás Villaroel of Presidio del Norte, First Lieutenant Joaquin Peru of Janos, who had been serving on detached duty at Del Norte for over a year, Sergeant Andrés Naranjo, Sergeant Felix Colomo, Cavo Ventura Madrid, Cavo Saturnino Rodriguez, soldado Bernardo Ortega, soldado interpreter Francisco Perez, Antonio Felix Martin de Rivera (at over sixty, the oldest vecino in the area), vecino Pioquinto Carrasco, and carpenter Manuel Marquez. Cordero did not interview the senior officers at the post, including Captain Domingo Díaz and Lieutenant Alberto Maynez, who had been second in command at the time of the Mescaleros' arrival in 1790, but had subsequently been promoted to command of the Fourth Volante. Two other officers, Lieutenant Ventura Montes and Lieutenant Dionisio Valles, were absent on detached duties. See Declaración del Alférez Dn Nicolás Villaroel, and Declaración del Teniente Dn Joaquin Peru, Presidio del Norte, June 23, 1792; Declaración del Sargento Andrés Naranjo; Declaración del Sargento Felix Colomo; Declaración del Cavo Ventura Madrid; Declaración del Cavo Saturnino Rodriguez; Declaración del Soldado Bernardo Ortega; Declaración del Soldado Interprete Francisco Perez; Declaración del Teniente del Vecindario Antonio Felix Martin de Rivera; Declaración del Vecino Pioquinto Carrasco; Declaración del Carpintero Manuel Marquez, all Presidio del Norte, June 25, 1792; all enclosed with Antonio Cordero to Pedro de Nava, Pueblo del Paso, July 20, 1792, AGN, PI, 170.
6. Declaración del Teniente Dn Joaquin Peru, ibid.

7. Declaración del Alférez Dn Nicolás Villaroel, Declaración del Sargento Felix Colomo, Declaración del Cavo Saturnino Rodriguez, ibid.
8. Declaración del Carpintero Manuel Marquez, ibid.
9. Declaración del Alférez Dn Nicolás Villaroel, ibid.
10. The witnesses were captain of militia Francisco Xavier Bernal, captain of militia Miguel de Espinosa, soldado interpreter Juan Pedro Rivera from Presidio San Buenaventura on detached duty, lieutenant of militia Francisco Garcia, Joseph Manuel Telles (at age sixty, one of the oldest vecinos), *Alcalde de Aguas* Francisco Balizan, *Alcalde de Real* Diego Antonio Candelario, the Piro Indian *teniente del pueblo* Juan Antonio Narvaez, and the *Administrador de la Renta de Tabacos, Naipes, y Polvora* Francisco del Barrio. See Declaración del Capitán de Milicia Dn Francisco Xavier Bernal; Declaración del Capitán de Milicia Dn Miguel de Espinosa, both El Paso del Norte, July 13, 1792; Declaración del Soldado Interprete Juan Pedro Rivera; Declaración del Teniente de Milicia Dn Francisco Garcia; Declaracion del Vecino Joseph Manuel Telles; Declaracion del Alcalde de Aguas Francisco Balizan; Declaración del Alcalde de Real Diego Antonio Candelario; Declaración del Teniente del Pueblo de Juan Antonio Narvaez; Declaración del Administrador de la Renta de Tabacos y Polvora, Dn Francisco del Barrio, all El Paso del Norte, July 14, 1792; all enclosed with Antonio Cordero to Pedro de Nava, Pueblo del Paso, July 20, 1792, AGN, PI, 170.
11. Declaración del Capitán de Milicia Dn Francisco Xavier Bernal, Declaración del Administrador de la Renta de Tabacos y Polvora, Dn Francisco del Barrio, ibid.
12. Declaración del Capitán de Milicia Dn Francisco Xavier Bernal, Declaración del Vecino Joseph Manuel Telles, ibid.
13. Declaración del Capitán de Milicia Dn Francisco Xavier Bernal, Declaración del Vecino Joseph Manuel Telles, Declaración del Alcalde de Aguas Francisco Balizan, ibid.
14. Cordero to Uranga, El Paso, July 17, 1792, Uranga, "Distribución por menor de las Armas de fuego, Pólvora, y municiones de Guerra, que he tenido a mi cargo para de la defensa de este Pueblo del Paso, y demás de su Jurisdicción, desde el 20 de Abril de 1788, en que recibí el mando, hasta el día de la fecha de abajo," enclosed with Uranga Cordero, El Paso, July 18, 1792, ibid.
15. Cordero to Nava, Pueblo del Paso, July 20, 1792, ibid.
16. Minor, *Light Gray People*, 89–92.
17. Nava to Campo de Alange, May 30, 1793, AGS, SGU, Indios, Provincias Internas, 7022, 2.
18. Domingo Díaz to Pedro de Nava, Norte, October 23, 1792, AGN, PI 170.
19. Ibid.
20. Durant and Durant, *Age of Napoleon*, 9–74.
21. Santiago, *Jar of Severed Hands*, 181; Revillagigedo to Conde del Campo de Alange, Mexico, February 28, 1793; Nava to Campo de Alange, Chihuahua, April 24, 1793; Revillagigedo to Conde del Campo de Alange, Mexico, April 30, 1793, all in AGS, SGU, Correspondencia de Pedro de Nava, 7045, 6.

22. Santiago, *Jar of Severed Hands*, 181–83.
23. Hendricks and Timmons, *San Elizario*, 33–34.
24. Babcock, *Apache Adaptation*, 175–76. Griffen, *Apaches at War and Peace*, 77–78; Hoja de Servicio of Fernando de Chacón, enclosed with Pedro de Nava to Dn Juan Manuel Albarez, Chihuahua, July 4, 1797, No. 374, El Comandante General del Provincias Internas de N. E Remite ojas de servicios pertenecientes a fín del año de 1796, AGS, SGU, Nueva España, Provincias Internas, 7278, 2.
25. Griffen suggested that "discontent may well have been as much as anything from the accumulation of small irritations of living under new circumstances and not because of major Spanish restrictions." Griffen, *Apaches at War and Peace*, 77.
26. Extracto de hostilidades ocurridas en las Provincias Internas de N. E. y de las operaciones executadas contra los Enemigos. Enclosed with Nava to Conde de Campo de Alange, Chihuahua, April 3, 1794, Indios, Provincias Internas, AGS, SGU 7023, 1.
27. Ibid.
28. Ibid.
29. Ibid.
30. Ibid. Hendricks, "Massacre in the Organ Mountains," 173–74.
31. Extracto de hostilidades ocurridas en las Provincias Internas de N. E. y de las operaciones executadas contra los Enemigos. Chihuahua, June 5, 1794, enclosed with Nava to Conde de Campo de Alange, Chihuahua, June 5; Extracto de hostilidades ocurridas en las Provincias Internas de Nueva España y de las resultas de las operaciones que se han practicado contra los Enemigos. Chihuahua, July 10, 1794, enclosed with Nava to Conde de Campo de Alange, Chihuahua, July 10, 1794, both in AGS, SGU, Indios, Provincias Internas, 7023, 1. Hendricks and Timmons, *San Elizario*, 36.
32. Extracto de hostilidades . . . Chihuahua, July 10, 1794, enclosed with Nava to Conde de Campo de Alange, Chihuahua, July 10, 1794, AGS, SGU, Indios, Provincias Internas, 7023, 1; Manuel Rengel, Hoja de Servicio, December 31, 1794, enclosed with Nava to Conde de Campo de Alange, Chihuahua, August 6, 1795, AGS, SGU, Provincias Internas, Nueva España, 7278, 4; Hendricks and Timmons, *San Elizario*, 36.
33. Extracto de hostilidades ocurridas en las Provincias Internas de Nueva España y de las resultas de las operaciones que se han practicado contra los Enemigos, enclosed with Nava to Conde de Campo de Alange, Chihuahua, September 4, 1794, AGS, SGU, Indios, Provincias Internas, 7024, 1; Nava, Extracto de hostilidades ocurridas en las Provincias Internas de Nueva España y de las resultas de las operaciones que se han practicado contra los Enemigos. Enclosed with Nava to Conde de Campo de Alange, Chihuahua, November 6, 1794, AGS SGU, Indios, Provincias Internas 7023, 1.
34. Nava, Extracto de hostilidades ocurridas en las Provincias Internas de Nueva España y de las resultas de las operaciones que se han practicado contra los Enemigos. Enclosed with Nava to Conde de Campo de Alange, Chihuahua, November 6, 1794, AGS

SGU, Indios, Provincias Internas 7023, 1; Extracto de hostilidades ocurridas en las Provincias Internas de Nueva España y de las resultas de las operaciones que se han practicado contra los Enemigos. Enclosed with Nava to Conde de Campo de Alange, Chihuahua, August 6, 1795, AGS SGU, Indios, Provincias Internas 7024, 1.
35. Santiago, *Jar of Severed Hands*, 183–85, 203.
36. Marichal, *Bankruptcy of Empire*, 11–12, 59–87,104–18,122–41; Marichal and Souto Mantecón, "Silver and Situados" 587–96, 613; Archer, "Bourbon Finances and Military Policy," 325–27, 335–37.
37. Babcock, *Apache Adaptation*, 177–80, 183–84; Babcock, "Turning Apaches into Spaniards," 247–48, 263–67.

Chapter 7. Sparking the Fire

1. Pedro de Nava to Conde del Campo de Alange, Chihuahua, November 3, 1795, No. 230, "El Comandante General de Provincias Internas de Nueva España Remite Extracto de hostilidades," AGS, SGU, Provincias Internas, Indios, 7025, 1. Deeds, *Defiance and Deference*, 81, 139–40. Santa Cruz is the modern Valle de Rosario, about 120 miles south of Chihuahua City.
2. Deeds, *Defiance and Deference*, 186–89. Ortelli, *Trama de una Guerra conveniente*, 113–35, 151–56, 170–71,183–90.
3. Pedro de Nava to Conde del Campo de Alange, Chihuahua, September 1, 1795, No. 217, "El Comandante General de Provincias Internas Refiere hostilidades de Enemigos y sus disposiciones para escarmentarlos"; and Nava to Campo de Alange, Chihuahua, November 3, 1795, No. 230, "El Comandante General de Provincias Internas de Nueva España Remite Extracto de hostilidades," both in AGS, SGU, Provincias Internas, Indios, 7025, 1. Modern-day Bachíniva is about 93 miles west of Chihuahua City and 250 miles south of El Paso.
4. Ibid.; Minor, *Turning Adversity to Advantage*, 85–86.
5. John, "A Cautionary Exercise," 306. Matson and Schroeder, "Cordero's description of the Apache," 342–43.
6. John, "A Cautionary Exercise," 306, 309–10. Blyth, *Chiricahua and Janos*, 73–76. Cordero, "Diario seguido."
7. The details on the Mescaleros' actions surrounding the outbreak of war can be gleaned from Nava to Campo de Alange, Chihuahua, September 1, 1795, No. 217, "El Comandante General de Provincias Internas Refiere hostilidades de Enemigos y sus disposiciones para escarmentarlos;" Nava to Campo de Alange, Chihuahua, November 3, 1795, No. 230, "El Comandante General de Provincias Internas de Nueva España Remite Extracto de hostilidades;" and Cordero, "Diario seguido," all in AGS, SGU, Provincias Internas, Indios, 7025, 1.

Chapter 8. Blood and Suffering

1. Cordero, "Diario seguido"; "Diario—Continuación de las operaciones practicadas por el Teniente Coronel Dn Antonio Cordero con el destacamento de su cargo en cumplimiento de órdenes de su General el Señor Mariscal de Campo Don Pedro

de Nava," enclosed with Cordero to Nava, Campamento de Fr. Cristóbal en el Rio grande del Norte, September 14, 1795 (hereinafter cited as Cordero, "Diario continuación"); both enclosed with Nava to Azanza, Chihuahua, July 5, 1796, AGS, SGU, Provincias Internas, Indios 7025, 1.
2. Cordero, "Diario seguido."
3. Ibid.
4. Ibid.
5. Cordero to Nava, Paso del Rio del Norte, August 27, 1796, AGS, SGU, Provincias Internas, Indios 7025, 1.
6. Cordero, "Diario continuación." Cordero divided his forces at the Paraje de Robledo, present-day Fort Selden, New Mexico. The Paraje de San Diego was about ten miles north of that of Robledo, as the crow flies, and is between Ft. Selden and Rincon, New Mexico.
7. Ibid.
8. Cordero to Nava, Campamento de Fr. Cristóbal en el Rio grande del Norte, September 14, 1795, AGS, SGU, Provincias Internas, Indios 7025, 1.
9. The following account and quotations are from Cordero, "Diario continuación."
10. Parte al Teniente Dn Miguel Mesa, Campamento de Fray Cristóbal, September 14, 1795, AGS, SGU, Provincias Internas, Indios 7025, 1.
11. "Diario—Continuación de las operaciones de Guerra ejecutadas por el Destacamento del cargo del Teniente Coronel Don Antonio Cordero, desde el 13 de Octubre hasta la fecha en cumplimiento de las ordenes de su General el Señor Mariscal de Campo Don Pedro de Nava." (hereinafter cited as Cordero, "Diario—Continuación de las operaciones de Guerra"), enclosed as Oficio 1, Cordero to Nava, Paso, November 21, 1795, enclosed with Nava to Azanza, Chihuahua, July 5, 1796, AGS, SGU, Provincias Internas, Indios 7025, 1.
12. Cordero, "Diario—Continuación de las operaciones de Guerra."
13. Ibid. However, in his cover letter to Nava, Cordero gives a different version, saying that he attacked the second ranchería "belonging to capitancillo Cambalaza, in the Cajon de San Teodoro; and I only managed to take prisoner one Gandul, and wound several, killing a woman and taking all their goods."
14. The following account and quotations are from Cordero, "Diario—Continuación de las operaciones de Guerra."
15. Ibid. According to his diary, Cordero had searched through "the Cerro del Aire . . . Sierra Hueca . . . los Arenales . . . the Tinajas Hondas and the Malpaises, the Cerro Blanco, and then came to the banks of the Rio Grande, finding nothing."
16. Ibid.
17. Cordero to Nava, Campamento de la Loma Alta, November 6, 1795, enclosed with Nava to Azanza, Chihuahua, July 5, 1796, AGS, SGU, Provincias Internas, Indios 7025, 1.
18. Ibid.
19. Ibid.

20. Parte del Teniente Miguel Mesa, El Paso, November 20, 1795, enclosed as Oficio 1 in Cordero to Nava, El Paso, November 21, 1795, AGS, SGU, Provincias Internas, Indios 7025, 1.
21. Cordero to Nava, El Paso, November 21, 1795, AGS, SGU, Provincias Internas, Indios 7025, 1.

Chapter 9. The Cruel Season

1. Certification of Br. Secundrino Muñoz, Cantón de San Andrés, January 11, 1798, enclosed with Joseph Antonio Rengel to Viceroy Marqués de Branciforte, Orizaba, January 10, 1798, AGN, Indiferente de Guerra, 1677.
2. Miguel de Emparan Hoja de Servicio, December 31, 1795, enclosed with Pedro de Nava to Miguel Joseph de Azanza, Quartel de la 1ª Compania Volante en Guajoquilla, August 3, 1796, AGS, SGU, Provincias Internas, Nueva España, 7278, 3.
3. Miguel José de Emparan, Petition for appointment to the vacant colonelcy of the Regiment of the Dragoons of Mexico, Mexico, April 22, 1807, enclosed with Miguel José de Emparan to the King, Mexico, April 22, 1807, AGN, Indiferente de Guerra, 3866.
4. Nava to Campo de Alange, Chihuahua, September 1, 1795, AGS, SGU, Provincias Internas, Indios 7025, 1.
5. Weber, *Bárbaros,* 148–49, 165–66. Babcock, *Apache Adaptation,* 110–11.
6. Parte del Teniente Dn Nicolás de Almansa, Paraje de la Artesa on the Rio del Norte, December 13, 1795 (hereinafter cited as Almansa, "Parte"), enclosed as Oficio 1 in Cordero to Nava, El Paso, December 13, 1795, AGS, SGU, Provincias Internas, Indios 7025, 1.
7. Almansa, "Parte."
8. Ibid.
9. Ibid. Cordero to Nava, El Paso, December 13, 1795, AGS, SGU, Provincias Internas, Indios 7025, 1.
10. Ibid.
11. Ibid.
12. Ibid.
13. Ibid.
14. Cordero to Nava, El Paso, December 13, 1795.
15. Ibid.
16. Ibid.
17. Ibid.
18. Ibid.
19. Nicolás Villaroel to Señor Don Antonio Cordero, Presidio del Norte, December 8, 1795, enclosed as "Otro [Parte] del Teniente Dn Nicolás Villaroel, Numero 2," in the former, AGS, SGU, Provincias Internas, Indios 7025, 1.
20. "Extracto de hostilidades ocurridas en las Provincias Internas de Nueva España y delas resultas de operaciones que se han practicado contra los Enemigos," enclosed

with Nava to Campo de Alange, Chihuahua, February 2, 1796, AGS, SGU, Provincias Internas 7025, 1. TSHA, *Handbook of Texas Online*, "Devils River," accessed August 25, 2017, http://www.tshaonline.org/handbook/online/articles/rnd03.

21. Ibid.; Miguel José de Emparan hoja de servicio for 1795, AGS, SGU, Provincias Internas, Nueva España, 7278, 3. The number of individuals in the rancherías can be calculated using the estimates for Apaches compiled by Griffen and Moorhead. Griffen estimated a ratio of 2.6 individuals per adult male for calculating the size of Mescalero populations based on reported adult males at Presidio del Norte in 1787–1788. Using this calculation and conservatively assuming one adult male per tent, then twenty one tents would yield some fifty five persons in the encampment. Moorhead, on the other hand, used a higher ratio of 3.6, which would yield just more than seventy five individuals. Griffen, *Apaches at War and Peace*, 268.

22. Ibid.

23. Relación de las Despojas que sufrió la Ranchería del Desmolado y Mulato, de resultas del ataque al amanecer del día 24 de Diciembre de 1795, enclosed with Nava to Campo de Alange, Chihuahua, February 2, 1796, AGS, SGU, Provincias Internas 7025, 1.

24. Ibid.; Extracto de hostilidades ocurridas en las Provincias Internas de Nueva España y de las resultas de operaciones que se han practicado contra los Enemigos, enclosed with Nava to Campo de Alange, Chihuahua, February 2, 1796, AGS, SGU, Provincias Internas 7025, 1.

25. Nava to Campo de Alange, Chihuahua, February 2, 1796, AGS, SGU, Provincias Internas 7025, 1.

26. Ibid.

Chapter 10. War in Their Own Lands

1. Nava to Azanza, Valle de San Bartolomé, September 8, 1796, and Nava to Azanza, Villa de Chihuahua, January 31, 1797, enclosing: Numero 1: Prevenciones que han de observar los Comandantes de Compañías y Destacamentos para el Servicio de Campaña, Chihuahua, 19 de Junio de 1793, certified copy by Manuel Merino, Chihuahua, January 5, 1796; Numero 2: Aumento a las Prevenciones para el Servicio de los Destacamentos de Campaña comunicadas en 19 de Junio de 1793, 26 June 1794, certified copy by Manuel Merino, Chihuahua, January 5, 1796; Numero 3: untitled, Chihuahua, March 23, 1795, certified copy by Manuel Merino, Chihuahua, January 5, 1796; Numero 4: Untitled, Nava to Diego de Borica, Chihuahua, July 2, 1792, certified copy by Manuel Merino, Chihuahua, January 5, 1796, AGS, SGU, Indios, Provincias Internas, 7026, 2.

2. Nava to Campo de Alange, Chihuahua, May 3, 1796, AGS, SGU, Provincias Internas, Indios, 7025, 1.

3. Ibid.

4. Ibid.

5. Pedro de Nava to the Señor Governor of Texas [Manuel Muñoz], Chihuahua, May 20, 1796, enclosed with Juan Cortes to Señor Gobernador Dn, Manuel Muñoz, La

Bahía del Espíritu Santo, July 1, 1796, Bexar Archives, UT, Roll 26. The same fight is described by Nava in Extracto de hostilidades ocurridas en las Provincias Internas de Nueva España, y de las resultas de operaciones que se han practicado contra los Indios Enemigos, enclosed with Nava to Azanza, Chihuahua, July 5, 1796, AGS, SGU, Provincias Internas, Indios, 7025, 1.
6. Ibid.
7. Extracto de hostilidades ocurridas en las Provincias Internas de Nueva España, y de las resultas de operaciones que se han practicado contra los Indios Enemigos, enclosed with Nava to Azanza, Chihuahua, July 5, 1796, AGS, SGU, Provincias Internas, Indios, 7025, 1.
8. Ibid.
9. Ibid.
10. Ibid.
11. Diario de las Novedades ocurridas en la Correduría hecha por Dn Juan Ignacio Ramón 1r Teniente y Comandante de esta Contra los Indios Enemigos que se introdujeron en la Provincia de Coahuila colindante a esta del Nuevo Reino de León y es como sigue, enclosed with Igancio Ramón to Lieutenant Colonel Simón de Herrera, Lampazos, May 23, 1796, AGN PI, 63.
12. Nava to Excmo Señor Marqués de Branciforte, Chihuahua, July 16, 1796, AGN PI, 63.
13. Nava to Campo de Alange, Chihuahua, February 2, 1796, and Extracto de hostilidades ocurridas en las Provincias Internas de Nueva España, y de las resultas de operaciones que se han practicado contra los Indios Enemigos, Chihuahua, July 5, 1796, enclosed with Nava to Azanza, Chihuahua, July 5, 1796, AGS, SGU, Provincias Internas, Indios 7025, 1.
14. Nava to Branciforte, Puesto de la 1ª Compañía volante en Guajoquilla, August 3, 1796, AGS, SGU, Provincias Internas, Indios, 7025, 1; Data de lo dado para la manutención de los indios que en collera se remitieron a la ciudad de México; and Data de lo pagado por los fletes de la conducción de las colleras de Apaches que se condujeron a la ciudad de México, both in Cuenta de Real Hacienda del año de 1796, Chihuahua, July 16, 1796, AGI, Guad. 459. The Spaniards had taken sixty-nine captives throughout 1795 from Nueva Vizcaya, New Mexico, and Coahuila, the majority of which may be deduced to have been Mescaleros, with perhaps a few Gileño Chiricahuas as well. The troops captured another twenty-six from Nueva Vizcaya in May and June, for a total of ninety-five. The seventy-nine prisoners in Mateos's collera clearly included these. The list of Mateos's collera specifies no young children or girls under twenty years old, and this is explained by the fact that all of the children were kept in Chihuahua and most likely distributed to Spanish families to be raised as domestic servants; Nava to Dionisio Valle, Chihuahua, October 24, 1796, Janos Collection, University of Texas at Austin, Folder 13, Section 1.
15. Santiago, *Jar of Severed Hands*, 185–86.
16. Nava to Azanza, Valle de San Bartolomé, September 8, 1796, AGS, SGU, Indios, Provincias Internas, 7026, 2.

17. Ibid.
18. Nava to Miguel Joseph de Azanza, Chihuahua, November 7, 1796, AGS, SGU, Correspondencia de Pedro de Nava, 7045, 6.
19. Filiation of Mariano Madrid, enclosed with Extracto de Revista de Inspección of Presidio del Norte, December 5, 1797, AGS, SGU, 7027, 12.
20. Antonio Cordero, Hoja de Servicio, December 31, 1797, Provincias Internas, Nueva España, AGS, SGU, 7278, 1; Antonio Cordero to the King, Monclova, August 14, 1802, AGS, SGU, Antonio Cordero, Correspondencia, 7046, 5.
21. Título de Capitán de la Compañía que se halla vacante en la congregación de Silao correspondiente a la Legión del Príncipe en Dn Manuel Rengel y Camargo, Viceroy Matias de Gálvez, Tacubaya, May 13, 1784, AGN, Indiferente Virreinal, Títulos y Despachos de Guerra, Caja 2738; for the career of José Antonio Rengel, see Rengel to Exmo. Señor Conde del Campo de Alange, Mexico, September 24, 1790, AGS, SGU, José Rengel, Provincias Internas 7045, 5.
22. Manuel Rengel, Hoja de Servicio, Presidio de Carrizal, January 1, 1791, 7278, 8 Provincias Internas, Nueva España.
23. Manuel Rengel, Hoja de Servicio, Presidio de Janos, December 31, 1791, Provincias Internas, Nueva España, AGS, SGU, 7278, 2; Hendricks and Timmons, *San Elizario*, 36.
24. Nava to Miguel Joseph de Azanza, Chihuahua, November 7, 1796, Correspondencia de Pedro de Nava, AGS, SGU, 7045, 6.
25. Nava to Azanza, Chihuahua, January 30, 1797, AGS, SGU, Correspondencia de Pedro de Nava, 7045, 6; Manuel Rengel, Hoja de Servicio, Janos, December 31, 1796, AGS, SGU, Provincias Internas, Nueva España, 7278, 2.
26. Ibid.

Chapter 11. Invasions Real and Imagined

1. Laborda, "La ocupación de la isla de Trinidad." Alonso and Flores, *El Caribe en el Siglo XVIII*, 164–74.
2. Ibid.; *London Gazette,* March 27, 1797, 286.
3. Ibid.
4. Bushnell, "Marqués de Branciforte," 390–400; Archer, *Army in Bourbon Mexico*, 35–37, 82–84.
5. Alonso and Flores, *El Caribe en el Siglo XVIII*, 193–350.
6. Pedro de Nava to Señor Comandante de la Compañía de Janos, Chihuahua, June 12, 1797, and Nava to Janos Commander, Chihuahua, July 14, 1797, both in Janos Microfilm Collection, University of Texas at El Paso (hereinafter cited as JMC, UTEP) Roll 10. Quotations are from Pedro de Nava to Exmo. Sor. Dn Juan Manuel Albarez, Chihuahua, April 4, 1797, AGS, SGU, Indios, Provincias Internas, 7026, 2.
7. Nava to Albarez, Chihuahua, April 4, 1797, AGS, SGU, Indios, Provincias Internas, 7026, 2.
8. Nava to Albarez, Chihuahua, June 6, 1797, AGS, SGU, Indios, Provincias Internas, 7026, 2.

9. Nava to Albarez, Chihuahua, April 4, 1797, AGS, SGU, Indios, Provincias Internas, 7026, 2.
10. Nava to Albarez, Chihuahua, June 6, 1797, AGS, SGU, Indios, Provincias Internas, 7026, 2.
11. Hoja de Servicio of Pedro Nolasco Carrasco, San Carlos de Parras, December 31, 1791, AGS, SGU, Provincias Internas, Nueva España, 7278, 1; Nava to Azanza, Chihuahua, October 3, 1797, AGS, SGU, Provincias Internas, Pensiones y viudad 7028, 1; Antonio Cordero, Extracto de Revista de Inspección . . . Comp. Presidial de la Bábia; Valle de Santa Rosa, December 7, 1797, containing filiations of troopers Blas María Ximenes, José María Fernándes, José María San Miguel, Pablo Maldonado, and Juan Estevan Talamantes, AGS, SGU, Compañía Presidial de La Bábia, 7027, 3.
12. No.1–Noticias de Filadelfia, No. 2–Real Orden, No. 3–Media Filiacion del Hombre sospechoso, all enclosed with Branciforte to Nava, Orizaba, June 22, 1797, Gobernador Provincias Internas sobre expedición de ingleses, AGI, Estado, 37, N.21.
13. Branciforte to Nava, Orizaba, June 22, 1797, AGI, Estado, 37, N.21.
14. Nava to Branciforte, Chihuahua, July 17, 1797, AGI, Estado, 37, N.21.
15. Nava to Exmo. Sor. Príncipe de la Paz, Chihuahua, August 1, 1797, AGI, Estado, 37, N.21. Nasatir, *Borderland in Retreat*, 86–101.
16. Nava to Janos Commander, Chihuahua, June 12, 1797, and Nava to Janos Commander, Chihuahua, July 14, 1797, both in JMC, UTEP, Roll 10.
17. Nava to Janos Commander, Chihuahua, July 1, 1797, JMC, UTEP, Roll 10. Griffen, *Apaches at War and Peace*, 103–4.
18. Nava to Janos Commander, Chihuahua, June 26, 1797, JMC, UTEP, Roll 10.
19. José María de la Riva to Sor. Teniente Gobernador Francisco Xavier Bernal, San Elizario, July 18, 1797, JA, UTEP, Ro1113.
20. Manuel Rengel to Sor. Teniente Gobernador Dn Francisco Xavier Uranga, San Elceario, April 10, 1797; Manuel Rengel to Sor. Dn Xavier Bernal, Tiburcios, May 8, 1797, both in JA, UTEP, Roll 13.
21. Nava to Dn Francisco Xavier Bernal, Passo, Chihuahua, January 3 and February 8, 1797; Nava to [Señor Teniente Gobernador del Pueblo del Paso], Chihuahua, March 9 and April 7, 1797, all JA, UTEP, Roll 13.
22. Manuel Rengel to Señor Justicia del Pueblo del Paso, Tiburcios, June 10, 1797, JA, UTEP, Roll 13.
23. José María de la Riva, to Francisco Xavier Uranga, San Elizario, September 2 and September 7, 1797, both JA, UTEP, Roll 13.
24. Nava to Señor Teniente Gobernador del Pueblo del Paso, Chihuahua, August 9, 1797; Nava to Teniente Justicia Interino del Pueblo del Paso, Chihuahua, June 7, 1797; Manuel Rengel to Francisco Xavier Uranga, Tiburcios, August 1, 1797, all in JA, UTEP, Roll 13.
25. Antonio Cordero, Hoja de servicio, December 31, 1797, AGS, SGU, Provincias Internas, Nueva España, 7278, 1; Nava to Excmo Sor. Dn Juan Manuel Alvarez, Chihuahua, May 2, 1797, and Antonio Cordero to the King, Monclova, 14 August 1802,

both in Antonio Cordero Correspondencia, AGS, SGU, 7046, 5. Nava to Alvarez, Chihuahua, January 9, 1798, AGS, SGU, Provincias Internas, Indios, 7027, 8.
26. Nava to Alvarez, Chihuahua, January 9, 1798, AGS, SGU, Provincias Internas, Indios, 7027, 8. Josef Menchaca, Hoja de Servicio, December 31, 1797, Provincias Internas, Nueva España, AGS, SGU, 7278, 1.
27. Santiago, *Jar of Severed Hands*, 185–86.
28. Manuel Rengel to Señor Teniente Gobernador, San Elceario, November 2, 1797, JA, UTEP, JA, Roll 13.

Chapter 12. The Calamities of War

1. Nava to Alvarez, Chihuahua, April 3, 1798, AGS, SGU, Provincias Internas, Indios, 7027, 8.
2. Zozoya's Hoja de Servicio, Guajoquilla, December 31, 1799, AGS, SGU, Provincias Internas, Nueva España, 7279, 2; Nava to Alvarez, Chihuahua, April 3, 1798, AGS, SGU, Provincias Internas, Indios, 7027, 8.
3. Nava to Alvarez, Chihuahua, April 3, 1798, AGS SGU, Provincias Internas, Indios, 7027, 8.
4. Ibid.
5. Nava to Alvarez, Chihuahua, June 5, 1798, AGS, SGU, Provincias Internas, Indios, 7027, 8.
6. Ibid.
7. Ibid.
8. Ibid.
9. Ibid.
10. Nava to Alvarez, Chihuahua, July 10, 1798, AGS, SGU, Provincias Internas, Nueva España, 7029, 2; Pedro Nolasco Carrasco, Hoja de Servicio, December 31, 1798, Provincias Internas, Nueva España, AGS, SGU, 7279, 3. In his letter to Alvarez, Nava reported the Mescalero casualties as two killed, fourteen prisoners, and sixty horses taken. I have used Carrasco's numbers, as they are first-hand.
11. Nava to Alvarez, Chihuahua, July 10, 1798, AGS, SGU, Provincias Internas, Nueva España, 7029, 2.
12. Nava to Alvarez, Chihuahua, September 4, 1798 (two letters; first quotation from the second letter) AGS, SGU, Provincias Internas, Nueva España, 7029, 2; Antonio Griego, Hoja de Servicio, December 31, 1798, AGS, SGU, Provincias Internas, Nueva España, 7279, 3.
13. Santiago, *Jar of Severed Hands*, 81–86; Nava to Alvarez, Chihuahua, September 4, 1798 (two letters; items from the second letter) AGS, SGU, Provincias Internas, Nueva España, 7029, 2.
14. Nava to Alvarez, Chihuahua, September 4, 1798 (two letters; quotations from the first letter) AGS, SGU, Provincias Internas, Nueva España, 7029, 2.
15. Ibid. (quotations from the second letter).
16. Minor, *Turning Adversity to Advantage*, 129; Miguel Joseph de Azanza to Excmo Sor. D. Juan Manuel Alvarez, Mexico, August 27, 1798, and Azanza to Alvarez, Mexico September 26, 1798, both in AGS, SGU, Provincias Internas, Nueva España, 7029, 2.

17. Nava to Alvarez, Chihuahua, November 6, 1798, AGS, SGU, Provincias Internas, Nueva España, 7029, 2.
18. Lemeé to Azanza, Mexico, October 15, 1798; Azanza to Nava, Mexico, October 17, 1798, AGN, Indiferente de Guerra, 3364.
19. Nava to Azanza, Chihuahua, November 6, 1798, AGN, Indiferente de Guerra, 3364. The two colleras of 1798 contained a total of 147 prisoners. In January through September 1798, the Spaniards had captured 124 Mescaleros, with another thirty-eight voluntarily surrendered, for a total of 162. The numbers of Apache prisoners reported from Sonora totaled eighteen and were most likely Chiricahua or Western Apaches captured in the early part of the year. There were no reported captures of Lipan, Lipiyan, or Jicarilla Apaches during the year. Therefore, it seems certain that while there may have been some Apaches from other groups in the first collera under Lemeé, the second collera under Moreno was exclusively made up of Mescaleros.
20. Azanza to Nava, Mexico, November 24, 1798, and January 16, 1799, AGN, Indiferente de Guerra, 3364.
21. Santiago, "The Flight of Some Weak Women," 51–68; Conrad, "Captive Fates," 261.
22. Nava to Alvarez, Chihuahua, December 4, 1798, AGS, SGU, Provincias Internas, Nueva España, 7029, 2.
23. Azanza to Alvarez, Mexico, October 27, 1798, and November 28, 1798, and January 5, 1799, AGS, SGU, Provincias Internas, Nueva España, 7029, 2.
24. Nava to Alvarez, Chihuahua, April 9, 1799, AGS, SGU, Provincias Internas, Nueva España, 7029, 2.
25. Ibid.
26. Ibid.
27. Nava to Alvarez, Chihuahua, April 9, 1799, AGS, SGU, Provincias Internas, Nueva España, 7029, 2.
28. Nava to Alvarez, Chihuahua, May 7 and June 11, 1799, AGS, SGU, Provincias Internas, Nueva España, 7029, 2.
29. Nava to Alvarez, Chihuahua, September 10, 1799, AGS, SGU, Provincias Internas, Nueva España, 7029, 2.

Chapter 13. Chasing the Shadow of Peace

1. [Francisco Granados], Noticias de lo suministrado a los Apaches de paz enfermos de viruelas de orden de mi Capitán desde hoy 4 de Junio de 1800, Norte, August 13, 1800, enclosed in Blas de Aramburu, Francisco Granados, and Joaquín de Herrera, Comprobantes de gastos de Apaches en el segundo semestre del año de 1800, Norte, July 1—December 30, 1800, AGN, Cárceles y Presidios, Caja 0583; Griffen, *Apaches at War and Peace*, 81, 89, 106.
2. Blas de Aramburu, Francisco Granados, and Joaquín de Herrera, Lista de los Indios de paz en el Presidio del Norte a quienes en esta fecha se les reparte ración para su suministración con arreglo a la instrucción del Señor Comandante General y a los órdenes sobre la materia, Norte, July 1—December 30, 1800, enclosed in Comprobantes de gastos de Apaches en el segundo semestre del año de 1800, AGN, Cárceles y Presidios, Caja 0583.

3. Comprobantes de gastos de Apaches en el segundo semestre del año de 1800, San Elizario, June 30–December 8, 1800; Comprobantes de gastos de apaches establecidos de paz de la primera compañía Volante, Guaxuguilla, 1800; Comprobantes de gastos de apaches establecidos de paz en el Presidio del Príncipe, Coyamé, 1800; Comprobantes de gastos de apaches establecidos de paz en el Presidio de San Carlos de Cerrogordo, San Geronimo, 1800; Comprobantes de gastos de Apaches en el segundo semestre del año de 1800, Norte, July 1–December 30, 1800, all in AGN, Cárceles y Presidios, Caja 0583.
4. Totaling the information in Spanish records over the course of the war yields 728 Mescaleros killed, captured, or surrendered, a casualty rate of 14.56 percent for a population of five thousand, 18.2 percent for a population of four thousand, and 24.2 percent for a population of three thousand. Yet there were surely more individuals that were killed and not recorded by the Spaniards, as well as those that were wounded and escaped, only to succumb later. Finally, the number of those wounded or maimed but who survived must also have been significant.
5. Hendricks and Timmons, *San Elizario*, 37.
6. Joseph Ignacio Carrasco, Geronimo Pantoja, and Joseph María de la Riva, Comprobantes de gastos de Apaches en el segundo semestre del año de 1800, San Elizario, June 30—December 8, 1800, AGN, Cárceles y Presidios, Caja 0583; Griffen, *Apaches at War and Peace*, 72–74, 80, 88–89.
7. No .2 [untitled] Riva, San Elizario, July 2, 1800; Manuel de Ochoa, Apunte del Bastimentos dado a siete Apaches que van a campaña con el Capitán Dn Manuel Ochoa por treinta días y algunas prendas indispensables para su salida, San Elizario, July 29, 1800, both in Comprobantes de gastos de Apaches en el segundo semestre del año de 1800, San Elizario, AGN, Cárceles y Presidios, Caja 0583.
8. Riva, No. 11 [untitled], San Elceario, August 7, 1800; Riva, No. 15 [untitled],San Elizario, August 29, 1800; Ochoa, No. 17 [untitled], San Elizario, August 29, 1800; Riva, No. 23 [untitled], San Elizario, September 15, 1800; Ochoa, No. 37 [untitled], San Elizario, November 11, 1800, all in ibid.
9. Riva, No. 3 [untitled] San Elizario, July 7, 1800; Riva, No. 18 [untitled] San Elizario, September 1, 1800 Riva; No. 21 [untitled] San Elizario, September 11, 1800; Ochoa, No. 29 [untitled] Tiburcios, October 1,1800, all in ibid.
10. Riva, No. 9 [untitled] San Elizario, July 29, 1800; Ochoa, No. 17 [untitled] San Elizario, August 29, 1800, ibid.
11. Riva, No. 18 [untitled], San Elizario, September 1,1800, ibid.; Griffen, *Apaches at War and Peace*, 89, 94; Hendricks and Timmons, *San Elizario*, 37–38, 52.
12. Riva, No. 49 [untitled], San Elizario, December 2, 1800, Comprobantes de gastos de Apaches en el segundo semestre del año de 1800, San Elizario, AGN, Cárceles y Presidios, Caja 0583.
13. Hendricks and Timmons, *San Elizario*, 38.
14. Riva, Cargo de Prisioneros No. 1, San Elizario, September 4, 1800; Ochoa, Cargo de Prisioneros No. 4, San Elizario, October 18, 1800, Comprobantes de gastos de

Apaches en el segundo semestre del año de 1800, San Elizario, AGN, Cárceles y Presidios, Caja 0583.
15. Ochoa, Cargo de Prisioneros No. 2, San Elizario, September 24, 1800; Ochoa, Cargo de Prisioneros No. 3, San Elizario, September 24, 1800, ibid.

Epilogue

1. No. 1297—Acompaña instancia en que solicita que la piedad del Rey le releve del empleo de Comandante General y le permita restituirse a España, Cuartel de la primera Compañía Volante en Guajoquilla, August 3, 1796, Francisco Xavier de Truxillo, listed in Indice de las cartas que dirige al Excmo. Señor. Dn Miguel Joseph de Azanza el Comandante General de las Provincias Internas de Nueva España, AGS, SGU, Correspondencia de Pedro de Nava, 7045, 8.
2. Nasatir, *Borderland in Retreat*, 35–50, 91–102, 115–27.
3. Chipman, *Spanish Texas*, 210–15; Kessell, *Spain in the Southwest*, 329–30.
4. Hendricks and Timmons, *San Elizario*, 38–41. Griffen, *Apaches at War and Peace*, 87–91.
5. Nasatir, *Borderland in Retreat*, 127–40. Weber, *Spanish Frontier*, 289–96.

BIBLIOGRAPHY

Archival Sources

Archivo General de las Indias. Audiencia de Guadalajara. Microfilm copy at Bancroft Library, University of California, Berkeley.
Archivo General de Simancas. Guerra Moderna. Microfilm collection at University of New Mexico, Albuquerque.
Archivo General de Simancas. Secretaría de Estado y del Despacho de Guerra. Portada de PARES, http://pares.mcu.es/.
Archivo General de la Nación, México. Provincias Internas. Microfilm copy at University of New Mexico, Albuquerque, and at University of Texas at El Paso.
Archivo General de la Nación, México. Cárceles y Presidios, Indiferente de Guerra. Provincias Internas, http://www.gob.mex/agn/guiageneral/.
Janos Collection. Benson Latin American Collection. University of Texas, Austin.
Janos Microfilm Collection. University of Texas at El Paso.
Juarez Archives Microfilm Collection. University of Texas at El Paso.

Published Primary Sources

Basso, Keith H., ed. *Western Apache Raiding and Warfare from the Notes of Grenville Goodwin*. Tucson: University of Arizona Press, 1971.
Brinckerhoff, Sidney B., and Odie B. Faulk. *Lancers for the King: A Study of the Frontier Military System of Northern New Spain, With a Translation of the Royal Regulations of 1772*. Phoenix: Arizona Historical Foundation, 1965.

Bringas de Manzaneda, Father Diego Miguel, O.F.M. *Friar Bringas Reports to the King: Methods of Indoctrination on the Frontier of New Spain 1796–97.* Translated and edited by Daniel S. Matson and Bernard L. Fontana. Tucson: University of Arizona Press, 1977.

Cordero y Bustamante, Manuel Antonio de. "Cordero's Description of the Apaches–1796." Translated and edited by Daniel S. Matson and Albert H. Schroeder. *New Mexico Historical Review*, vol. 32 (October 1957): 335–56.

Cortés y de Olarte, José Maria. *Views from the Apache Frontier. Report on the Northern Provinces of New Spain.* Edited by Elizabeth A.H. John. Translated by John Wheat. Norman: University of Oklahoma Press, 1989.

Gálvez, Bernardo de. *Instructions for the Governing of the Interior Provinces of New Spain, 1786.* Edited and translated by Donald E. Worcester. Berkeley, Calif.: Quivira Society, 1951.

Edgeworth, Henry Essex. *Authentic Memoires of the Revolution in France and the Sufferings of the Royal Family*, London: W. Simpkin and R. Marshall, 1817.

Fora, Nicolas de la. *Relación del viaje que hizo a los presidios internas situados en la frontera de la América septentrional, perteneciente al rey de España.* Edited by Vito Alessio Robles. México, D.F.: Editorial Pedro Robredo, 1939.

Hadley, Diana, Thomas H. Naylor, and Mardith K. Schuetz-Miller, eds. *The Presidio and Militia on the Northern Frontier of New Spain. Volume Two, Part Two. The Central Corridor and the Texas Corridor, 1700–1765.* Tucson: University of Arizona Press, 1997.

Jackson, Jack, ed. *Imaginary Kingdom: Texas As Seen by the Rivera and Rubí Military Expeditions, 1727 and 1767.* Austin: Texas State Historical Association, 1995.

Mendoza, Juan Domínguez. *Juan Domínguez de Mendoza, Soldier and Frontiersman of the Spanish Southwest.* Edited by France V. Scholes, Marc Simmons, and José Esquibel. Albuquerque: University of New Mexico, 2012.

O'Conor, Hugo. *The Defenses of Northern New Spain: Hugo O'Conor's Report to Teodoro de Croix, July 22, 1777.* Edited and translated by Donald C. Cutter. Dallas: Southern Methodist University Press, DeGolyer Library, 1994.

Naylor, Thomas H., and Charles W. Polzer, S.J., comps. and eds. *The Presidio and Militia on the Northern Frontier of New Spain, A Documentary History, Volume One: 1570–1700.* Tucson: University of Arizona Press, 1986.

Pike, Zebulon. *The Southwestern Journals of Zebulon Pike 1806–1807.* Edited by Stephen Harding Hart and Archer Butler Hulbert. Albuquerque: University of New Mexico Press, 2006.

Thomas, Alfred Barnaby. *Teodoro de Croix and the Northern Frontier of New Spain, 1776–1783: From the Original Document in the Archives of the Indies, Seville.* Norman: University of Oklahoma Press, 1941.

Secondary Sources

Alonso, Maria M., and Milagros Flores. *El Caribe en el Siglo XVIII y El Ataque Británico a Puerto Rico en 1797.* San Juan, Puerto Rico: Publicaciones Puertorriqueñas, 1998.

Anderson, Gary Clayton. *The Indian Southwest, 1580–1830: Ethnogenesis and Reinvention.* Norman: University of Oklahoma Press, 1999.

Archer, Christon I. *The Army in Bourbon Mexico, 1760–1810.* Albuquerque: University of New Mexico Press, 1977.
———. "Bourbon Finances and Military Policy in New Spain, 1759–1812," *The Americas,* vol. 37, no. 3 (January 1981): 325–27, 335–37.
Babcock, Matthew. *Apache Adaptation to Hispanic Rule.* Cambridge: Cambridge University Press, 2016.
———. "Turning Apaches into Spaniards: North America's Forgotten Indian Reservations," Ph.D. diss., Southern Methodist University, 2008.
Barney, Oscar Cruz. "Derecho Indiano Local: El Reglamento Provisional Para las Milicias del Real de Mazapil de 1787." *Anuario Mexicano de Historia del Derecho,* vol. 22 (2010): 103–18, 125–28.
Bergamini, John D. *The Spanish Bourbons: the History of a Tenacious Dynasty.* New York: Putnam Press, 1974.
Blyth, Lance R. *Chiricahua and Janos: Communities of Violence in the Southwestern Borderlands, 1680–1880.* Lincoln: University of Nebraska Press, 2012.
Bushnell, David. "El Marqués de Branciforte." *Historia Mexicana,* vol. 2, no. 3 (January–March 1953): 390–400.
Carter, William B. *Indian Alliances and the Spanish in the Southwest, 750–1750.* Norman: University of Oklahoma Press, 2009.
Chipman, Donald E. *Spanish Texas 1519-1821.* Austin: University of Texas Press, 1992.
Cloud, William A. "Indian Hot Springs," *Handbook of Texas Online,* accessed August 23, 2017, http://www.tshaonline.org/handbook/online/articles/rpi01.
Conrad, Paul Timothy. "Captive Fates: Displaced American Indians in the Southwest Borderlands, Mexico, and Cuba, 1500–1800." Ph.D. diss., University of Texas at Austin, 2011.
Cook, David Noble, and George W. Lovell, eds. *"Secret Judgements of God." Old World Disease in Colonial Spanish America.* Norman: University of Oklahoma Press, 1992.
Deeds, Susan M. *Defiance and Deference in Mexico's Colonial North: Indians under Spanish Rule in Nueva Vizcaya.* Austin: University of Texas Press, 2003.
Dobyns, Henry F. *Spanish Colonial Tucson: A Demographic History.* Tucson: University of Arizona, 1976.
Dunn, William Edward. "Apache Relations in Texas, 1718–1750." *Texas State Historical Association,* vol. 14 (January 1911): 198–269.
Durant, Will, and Ariel Durant. *The Age of Napoleon.* The Story of Civilization, vol. 11. New York: Simon & Schuster, 1975.
Forbes, Jack D. *Apache, Navaho and Spaniard.* Norman: University of Oklahoma Press, 1994.
Griffen, William B. *Apaches at War and Peace: The Janos Presidio, 1750–1858.* Norman: University of Oklahoma Press, 1998.
———. "The Chiricahua Apache Population Resident at the Janos Presidio, 1792 to 1858." *Journal of the Southwest,* vol. 33, no. 2 (Summer 1991): 191–92.
Hämäläinen, Pekka. *The Comanche Empire.* New Haven, Conn.: Yale University Press, 2008.

Hendricks, Rick, "Massacre in the Organ Mountains: The Death of Manuel Vidal de Lorca." *Password*, vol. 39 (Winter 1994): 169–77.
Hendricks, Rick, and W. H. Timmons. *San Elizario: Spanish Presidio to Texas County Seat*. El Paso: Texas Western Press, 1998.
Hickerson, Nancy Parrott. *The Jumanos: Hunters and Traders of the South Plains*. Austin: University of Texas Press, 1994.
Jacoby, Karl. *Shadows at Dawn: An Apache Massacre and the Violence of History*. New York: Penguin Press, 2008.
Jansen, Andre. *Charles et Théodore de Croix, Deux Gardes Wallons, Vice-Rois de l'Amérique espagnole au XVIIIe siecle*, Paris-Gembloux: Duculot, 1977.
John, Elizabeth A. H. "A Cautionary Exercise in Apache Historiography." *Journal of Arizona History*, vol. 25, no. 3 (Autumn 1984): 301–15.
———. *Storms Brewed in Other Men's Worlds: The Confrontation of Indians, Spanish, and French in the Southwest, 1540–1795*. 2nd ed. Norman: University of Oklahoma Press, 1996.
Jones, Oakah L. "Settlements and Settlers at La Junta de los Rios, 1759-1822." *Journal of Big Bend Studies*, vol. 3 (1991): 43–70.
Kessell, John L. *Spain in the Southwest: A Narrative History of Colonial New Mexico, Arizona, Texas, and California*. Norman: University of Oklahoma Press, 2002.
Laborda, Antonio. "La ocupación de la isla de Trinidad por los británicos en 1797." *Revista de Historia Naval* (February 6, 2007), http://www.todoababor.es/articulos/trinidad_.htm, accessed on July 1, 2016.
Marichal, Carlos. *Bankruptcy of Empire: Mexican Silver and the Wars between Spain, Britain and France, 1760–1810*. Cambridge: Cambridge University Press, 2007.
Marichal, Carlos, and Matilde Souto Mantecón. "Silver and Situados: New Spain and the Financing of the Spanish Empire in the Caribbean in the Eighteenth Century." *Hispanic American Historical Review*, vol. 74, no. 4 (November 1994): 587–96, 613.
McCarty, Kieran. "Bernardo de Gálvez on the Apache Frontier: The Education of a Future Viceroy." *Journal of the Southwest*, vol. 36 (1994): 103–30.
Minor, Nancy McGown. *The Light Gray People: An Ethno-history of the Lipan Apaches of Texas and Northern Mexico*. Lanham, Md.: University Press of America, 2009.
———. *Turning Adversity to Advantage: A History of the Lipan Apaches of Texas and Northern Mexico, 1700–1900*. Lanham, Md.: University Press of America, 2009.
Moorhead, Max L. *The Apache Frontier: Jacobo Ugarte and Spanish-Indian Relations in Northern New Spain, 1769–1791*. Norman: University of Oklahoma Press, 1968.
———. *The Presidio: Bastion of the Spanish Borderlands*. Norman: University of Oklahoma Press, 1975.
Murphy, Dan. *Salinas Pueblo Missions: Abó, Quaria & Gran Quivira*. Tucson, Arizona: Southwest Parks and Monuments Association, 1993.
Nasatir, Abraham P. *Borderland in Retreat: From Spanish Louisiana to the Far Southwest*. Albuquerque: University of New Mexico Press, 1976.
Navarro García, Luis. *Don José de Gálvez y la Comandancia General de las Provincias Internas del Norte de Nueva España*. Sevilla: Escuela de Estudios Hispano-Americanos de Sevilla, 1964.

Nelson, Al B. "Campaigning in the Big Bend of the Rio Grande in 1787." *Southwestern Historical Quarterly*, vol. 39 (January 1936): 200–27.

———. "Juan de Ugalde and Picax-Ande-Ins-Tinsle 1787–1788." *Southwestern Historical Quarterly*, vol. 43 (April 1940): 438–64.

Officer, James E. *Hispanic Arizona, 1536–1856*. Tucson: University of Arizona, 1987.

Opler, Morris E. "The Apachean Culture Pattern and its Origins." In *Southwest*. Edited by Alfonso Ortiz. Volume 10. *Handbook of North American Indians*. Edited by William C. Sturdevant. Washington, D.C.: Smithsonian Institution, 1983.

———. "Chiricahua Apache." In *Southwest*. Edited by Alfonso Ortiz. Volume 10. *Handbook of North American Indians*. Edited by William C. Sturdevant. Washington, D.C.: Smithsonian Institution, 1983.

———. "Mescalero Apache." In *Southwest*. Edited by Alfonso Ortiz. Volume 10. *Handbook of North American Indians*. Edited by William C. Sturdevant. Washington, D.C.: Smithsonian Institution, 1983.

Ortelli, Sara. *Trama de una Guerra conveniente: Nueva Vizcaya y la sombra de los apaches (1748–1790)*. Mexico City: El Colegio de Mexico, 2007.

Pozo Redondo, Felipe del. "Parentesco y Acceso a la Administración Colonial. Funcionarios Canarios en América en los Siglos XVII y XVIII." *Coloquio de Historia Canario-Americano*, Coloquio 10, Numero 1, 1992, Universidad de Las Palmas de Gran Canaria, Biblioteca Universitaria, Memorial Digital de Canarias, http: //mdc.ulpgc.es/cdm/search/collection/coloquios, accessed on July 25, 2016.

Santiago, Mark. "The Flight of Some Weak Women: Apache Prisoners of War in New Spain, a 1799 Incident." *Journal of Arizona History*, vol. 51, no. 1 (Spring 2010): 51–68.

———. *The Jar of Severed Hands: Spanish Deportation of Apache Prisoners of War, 1770–1810*. Norman: University of Oklahoma Press, 2011.

———. *The Red Captain: The Life of Hugo O'Conor, Commandant Inspector of the Interior Provinces of New Spain*. Tucson: Arizona Historical Society, Museum Monograph No. 9, 1994.

Sonnischen, C. L. *The Mescalero Apaches*. Norman: University of Oklahoma Press, 1973.

Sweeney, Edwin R. *Mangas Coloradas: Chief of the Chiricahua Apaches*. Norman: University of Oklahoma Press, 1998.

Tiller, Veronica E. "Jicarilla Apache." In *Southwest*. Edited by Alfonso Ortiz. Volume 10. *Handbook of North American Indians*. Edited by William C. Sturdevant. Washington, D.C.: Smithsonian Institution, 1983.

Timmons, W. H. *El Paso: A Borderlands History*. El Paso: Texas Western Press, 1990.

Timmons, W. H., and Rick Hendricks. *San Elizario: Spanish Presidio to Texas County Seat*. El Paso: Texas Western Press, 1998.

Weber, David J. *Bárbaros: Spaniards and Their Savages in the Age of Enlightenment*. New Haven, Conn.: Yale University Press, 2005.

———. *The Spanish Frontier in North America*. New Haven, Conn.: Yale University Press, 1992.

Weddle, Robert S. *The San Sabá Mission: Spanish Pivot in Texas*. Austin: University of Texas Press, 1988.

INDEX

Abercromby, Ralph, 152
Agua del Cuervo (Nueva Vizcaya), 98, 102
Aguayo, Marqués de San Miguel, 49
Alamogordo, N.Mex., 112
Alange, Conde de Campo, 121
Albuquerque, N.Mex., 38, 86, 189, 192
Alegre, Domingo (Mescalero chief), 43, 52, 63, 207n4
Alegre (or Daban Chu; Mescalero chief), 87; loyalty of to Spaniards, 84, 95; peace negotiations by at El Paso del Norte, 61–62; ranchería of at Presidio del Norte, 64, 79, 127
Almansa, Nicolás de: attack on Mayá's ranchería by, 123–26; role of in Spanish attacks on Mescaleros homeland, 104–5, 107–8, 112, 114
Alonso (Mescalero capitancillo), 43
Alta California, Province of, 47, 85; threat of British invasion of, 157, 159
Alvarez, Juan Manuel, 169, 173–74
American Revolutionary War, 45, 144

Apache Indians, 5, 1, 14–16, 27, 30, 94, 122; as allies of Pueblo Indians, 31; ambush of Spanish soldiers, 14, 105; Bernardo de Gálvez's view of and policies for, 3, 45–46, 50; Comanches as enemy of, 31–32, 141; Cordero's campaigns against, 29, 57–58, 60, 107–10, 221–22n19; Cordero's knowledge of, 21–23, 57; culture and society of, 22, 30, 26, 28, 172; deportation of as prisoners of war, 37, 78, 91, 111, 117, 135, 141–42, 164, 176, 187, 192; at establecimientos de paz, 11, 18, 77, 80; interaction with Spanish by, 26–27; O'Conor's campaigns against, 33–34, 37–39; Ópata Indians as enemies of, 96, 100; origins of, 25, 29; peace with Spanish by, 3–5, 11, 41, 68, 71, 88; raiding by, 11, 22–23, 29–30, 36, 40, 48–50, 67–68, 96; Spanish campaigns against, 7–8, 12, 61–62, 65, 87, 90–91, 128, 144, 167; Spanish identification of, 27; Spanish lack of trust of, 55, 61;

231

Apache Indians (*continued*)
  as Spanish military allies against other Apaches, 22, 41, 44, 52, 104; Spanish policies for peace with, 7, 35, 41, 44–45, 47, 50–51, 65, 70, 74, 195, 197–98; and threat of British invasion, 77, 157
Apaches de paz (peaceful Apaches), 4, 22, 74, 86, 91–92, 144, 171; departure from establecimientos de paz by, 23, 54, 86, 92; keeping peace among, 159–60; as Spanish military auxiliaries, 22, 72, 88, 101, 107–11, 115, 126–28, 169, 190; and threat of British invasion, 158. *See also* Mescaleros de paz
Apodaca, Sebastián Ruiz de, 148–50
Aramburu, Blas de, 78, 80; care of sick Mescaleros de paz by, 184–85; role of in Spanish campaign against Mescaleros, 90, 104–7
Arce, Antonio, 88–89
Arco (Mescalero chief), 63
Arizona, 25, 27–28
Arrieta, José Antonio de, 38
Arrieta (Mescalero chief), 73, 162
Arroyo de la Soledad (Province of Texas), 66
Athabaskan people, 25, 28
Avila, Spain, 70
Azanza, Miguel José de, 133, 177, 179; on Lipans at peace, 174–75, 180–81

Bacoachi, Presidio of, 4
Baja California, 47, 85; threat of British invasion of, 157, 159
"Bald One, the" (Mescalero chief). *See also* Picax-andé-Ynstinclé de Ugalde (Mescalero chief)
Balizan, Francisco, 82, 211n10
Baltimore, Md., 156–57
Barrio, Francisco del, 81, 211n10
Barrio. *See* Nzazen (or Barrio; Mescalero chief)

Bear Mountains (N.Mex.), 208n17
Belen, N.Mex., 86
Bellido, Francisco, 38–39
Bernal, Francisco Xavier, 64, 81, 211n10
Big Bend Country, 36–37; Expedition of Coahuila against Mescaleros in, 142, 153; Manuel Rengel's campaign north of, 145; Mescalero Apaches territory in, 27–29, 31, 140; Spanish campaigns against Mescaleros in, 39, 53, 135–36, 145, 171–72, 181; Volante killed by Spanish in, 186
Bigotes el Bermejo (or Chilitsó; Mescalero capitancillo), 104, 127, 207n4; and peace negotiations at El Paso del Norte, 61–62; and raid into Nueva Vizcaya, 95; ranchería of at Presidio del Norte, 64, 79
Black Range (N.Mex.), 109–10
Bolsón de Mapimí, 134; as base and route for Apache raids, 36, 43, 79, 96–97, 127, 139–40; Spanish campaigns against Apaches in, 37, 53
Bonaparte, Napoleon, 199
Botas (Mescalero chief), 191
Branciforte, Marqués de, 140, 174; actions of against threat of British invasion, 151, 155–59; corruption of, 150; and deportation of Apaches, 141; as viceroy of New Spain, 120
Bucanneti (Mescalero chief), 73
Buena Esperanza, Nuestra Señora de la (Mescalero settlement at Presidio del Norte), 43–44, 52, 61–62
buffalo, 130; Apache hunting of, 26, 29; Comanche follow herds of, 65; impact of drought on, 65; influence on Apaches groups in east, 26; Lipans annual hunt for, 174; Mescaleros annual hunt of, 40, 51–52, 72–73, 84, 115, 127, 142, 198; Mescaleros' use of, 129; Nava's plan to disrupt Mescalero hunt of, 122, 163, 187

Index

Caballero de Croix. *See* Croix, Teodoro de (Caballero de Croix)
Cajon de Jesus Nazereno (Sacramento Mountains, N.Mex.), 112
Cajon de San Teodoro, 215n13
Cajon Sombrio (Sierra Blanca Mountains, N.Mex.), 112
Calabazas Canyon (N.Mex.), 107
California: Neve as governor of, 44; threat of British invasion of, 158–59. *See also* Alta California, Province of; Baja California
Calleja, Felix María de, 156, 158
Cambalza (Mescaleros chief), 95, 215n13
Canada, 85, 155–58, 196
Canary Islands, 11, 69, 169
Candelario, Diego Antonio, 64, 211n10
Cañon de San Sabas (Tex.), 115
Cañon de Ugalde (Tex.), 66
Canoso (Lipan chief), 174
Cape St. Vincent, Battle of (1797), 152
Capitan Mountains (N.Mex.), 114, 126
Caracas, Venezuela, 70; Pedro de Nava in, 11
Carancaguace Indians, 158
Caribbean Sea, 7, 10, 92, 148
Carondelet, Baron de, 156, 196
Carpintero, Manuel, 179
Carrasco, Joseph de, 104
Carrasco, Joseph Manuel, 89
Carrasco, José Ygnacio, 107; role in pursuit and attack of Mescaleros, 18, 108, 110, 112, 114
Carrasco, Pedro Nolasco, 155, 171–72
Carrasco, Pioquinto, 211n5
Castillo de San Juan de Ulúa (Veracruz, Mexico), 156
Castro, Ramón de, 78, 152; as commandant general of Eastern Interior Provinces, 70; conflict with Emparan, 119–20; hostile view of Apaches, 74, 83; struggle to control Apaches, 75, 77

Cavallero y Basve, Joseph, 49
Cerro del Aire Mountains (N.Mex./Tex.), 88, 104, 114, 215n15
Cerro Gordo, Nueva Vizcaya, 188
Cerro Redondo (N.Mex.), 123–25
Cerros Huecos. *See* Hueco Mountains (N.Mex./Tex.)
Chacón, Fernando de, 86, 111, 131–32
Chacón, José María, 148, 150
Chal-coay. *See* Montera Blanca (or Chal-coay; Mescalero chief)
Charles III (king of Spain): policies of toward Apaches, 44, 47; and reformation of economic and military structures of empire, 35, 45, 50
Charles IV (king of Spain), 69, 85, 133, 150, 196; and war with France, 77, 91
Cheguindilé. *See* Volante (or Cheguindilé; Mescalero capitancillo)
Chihuahua, Villa de, Nueva Vizcaya, 12, 42, 45, 61, 80, 128; Apache prisoners of war sent to, 111, 192–93, 218n14; Apaches visit Nava in, 63, 80; Mescalero raiders near, 94; as Nava's headquarters, 14, 74, 115, 117, 131, 133, 159, 169, 173–74; as O'Conor's headquarters, 36
Chihuahua City, Nueva Vizcaya. *See* Chihuahua, Villa de, Nueva Vizcaya
Chilitsó (Mescalero chief). *See* Bigotes el Bermejo (or Chilitsó; Mescalero capitancillo)
Chimeslán (Mescalero chief), 64, 73, 80
Chiquito (Lipan chief), 174
Chiricagui Apaches, 27, 205n7. *See also* Chiricahua Apaches; Gileño Chiricahua Apaches; Mimbreño Chiricahua Apaches
Chiricahua Apaches, 144, 182, 188, 205n7; as allies of rustlers in Nueva Vizcaya, 94; as allies of Spanish against other Apaches, 58, 162; Cordero as peace agent for, 57; deportation of as

Chiricahua Apaches (*continued*) prisoners of war, 221n19; at establecimientos de paz, 22, 54, 70; Nava helps keep peace among, 159–60; and peace with Spaniards, 4, 199; as Spanish military auxiliaries, 87; Spanish military campaigns against in Sonora, 110, 195. *See also* Apache Indians; Gileño Chiricahua Apaches; Mimbreño Chiricahua Apaches

Chiricahua Apaches de paz, 144; as Spanish military allies, 162, 165, 190–91

Chisos Mountains (Tex.), 171

Chiyal-toé (Mescalero), 95, 104

Chu-ul-y-cué (Lipan chief). *See* Pino Blanco (Lipan chief)

Ciénega del Coyamé (Nueva Vizcaya), 208n17

Ciénega de los Olivos, Nueva Vizcaya, 12, 203n7

Ciudad Juárez, Mexico. *See* El Paso del Norte

Cluyé (Mescalero chief), 190

Coahuila, Province of (New Spain), 4, 47, 49, 54, 64, 119, 155, 167, 173; and British invasion, threat of, 156–59; conditions in after war, 195; Cordero as interim governor of, 163, 173; defense against Apache raiders in, 140; deportation of Apache prisoners of war from, 176, 192, 218n14; Emparan's expedition in, 128, 131; Expedition of Coahuila campaigns in, 142–43, 153; as headquarters for Eastern Interior Provinces, 53, 66, 74; Lipans seek peace in, 85, 141; Mescalero and Lipan uprising and raiding in, 36, 42–44, 53, 55–56, 67–68, 77, 97, 127, 139, 159; Spanish military campaigns in, 27, 51, 159–60, 163; troops from in campaigns against Mescaleros, 20, 111, 113, 120–22, 128, 132, 134, 139, 145, 170, 172, 175, 181–82, 187

Colomo, Felix, 79, 211n5

Colonia del Nuevo Santander, Province of. *See* Nuevo Santander, Province of

Comanche Indians, 32; as allies with Spain against Apaches, 32, 66, 121, 141, 187; as allies with Spain against British invasion, 159; attacks on Apaches by, 29, 31–32, 41–42, 51, 61, 65, 89, 131; as enemy of Mescaleros, 67, 71, 83, 188; massacre of Mescaleros by, 39–40; Spanish protect Mescaleros from, 52, 71

Concha, Fernando de la, 86

Copas, Estancia of (Real of Mazapil, Zacatecas), 48

Cordero y Bustamante, Antonio, 72–73, 96, 111, 144, 164, 187; campaigns against Mescalero by, 57–62, 65, 135, 208n16; deporting of Apache prisoners of war by, 117; and establecimientos de paz, 72, 82–83; and Expedition of Coahuila campaigns, 142–43, 145, 153–54, 154, 163, 170–71; as interim governor of Texas, 143; investigation by of Mescaleros de paz aiding Lipans, 78–83; knowledge of and experience with Apaches by, 20–23, 57, 96, 144; pursuit of and attacks on Apaches after ambush of Spanish soldiers, 24, 102–17, 123, 126–28; and Spanish military campaigns against Mescaleros, 132, 174

Cornudas Mountains (N.Mex./Tex.), 88, 104, 114, 126, 136

Coronado, Francisco de Vásquez, 26

Corral de Cuellar (plateau in Mimbres Mountains) (N.Mex.), 108

Cos, Juan de Díos, 178–80

Coyamé, Nueva Vizcaya, 12, 16, 98, 188, 194

Coyotero Apaches, 27. *See also* Apache Indians
Croix, Teodoro de (Caballero de Croix), 61; accomplishments of, 44; as commandant general of Interior Provinces, 40, 45; implementation of peace policy of with Apaches, 41–44, 47
Cuarta Compañía Volante. *See* Fourth Compañía Volante
Cuartel of Pilar de Conchos, 177
Cuba, 45, 92; Apache prisoners of war deported to, 37, 91, 111 117, 135, 141, 164, 192
Cuerno Verde (or Pases-flá; Mescalero chief), 64, 79, 90, 207n4
Cumbre del San Rafael (in Sierra Blanca Mountains, N.Mex.), 112

Daban Chu. *See* Alegre (or Daban Chu; Mescalero capitancillo)
Davis Mountains. *See* Sierra del Mogano (Tex.)
Dayél (Mescalero chief), 79, 171
Desmolado ("Toothless"; Mescalero chief), 129–31
Devils River (Tex.), 129
Diablo Mountains (Tex.), 114
Díaz, Domingo, 64, 211n5; concerns about Picax-andé by, 83–84; illness of, 127–28; and peace negotiations with Mescaleros, 51–53, 63
Doña Ana Ford (N.Mex.), 123
Dragoons of Mexico, Regiment of the, 119
Dragoons of Spain, Regiment of the, 20–21
drought, 65; impact of on Mescaleros and Lipans, 67–68, 77; as reason for Mescaleros seeking peace negotiations, 41–42, 51, 65

Eagle Mountains (Tex.), 116
Eagle Pass, Tex., 142

El Calvo ("the Bald One"; Mescalero chief). *See* Picax-andé-Ynstinclé de Ugalde (Mescalero chief)
El Carpintero (Mescalero chief), 186–87
El Cautivo (Mescalero chief), 192
El Natagé (Mescalero chief), 127, 207n4
El Natajé. *See* El Natagé (Mescalero chief)
El Paso del Norte, N.Mex., 31, 37–38, 57, 81, 86, 100, 106, 210n25; campaigns against Apaches near, 104, 135–36, 161; and Cordero's investigation of Mescaleros de paz aiding Lipans, 80–82; Indian auxiliaries from, 106; Lieutenant Governor Urange at, 18, 62; Mescaleros' and Faraónes' homeland north of, 31, 145; Mescaleros at establecimiento de paz at, 5, 7, 18, 37, 63–64, 70–71, 73, 77–78, 86, 92, 107, 145, 160, 194; Mescaleros in mountains near, 87–88, 95; Mescaleros' raids near, 19, 71–72, 89, 138; military cantonment at, 145, 161; parade of Spanish troops and Indian auxiliaries in, 100–102; peace negotiations with Mescalero at, 60–61, 63, 135; relations between Spanish and Mescalero de paz at, 20, 82, 86; relative quiet during uprising, 162–63; as staging area for campaigns against Apaches, 58, 62, 103–5, 110–11, 123, 126–27
El Pozo (campsite, Real of Mazapil, Zacatecas), 48
El Quemado (Mescalero chief), 207n4
El Valle del Pilón, Nuevo León, 166
Emparan, José Joaquín de, 119
Emparan, Miguel José de, 119; as commander of campaign against Mescaleros, 111, 118–20, 123, 128–29, 132; conflict with Ramón de Castro, 119; impact of assault by on Mescaleros, 130–31; on increase in

Emparan, Miguel José de (*continued*)
raiding in Coahuila, 67–68; peace
negotiations with Lipans by, 68
England. *See* Great Britain
Escageda, José, 112, 114
Espinosa, Miguel de, 211n10
Esquin-yoé (Mescalero chief), 95, 116;
illness and death of, 184–86; ranchería
of at Presidio del Norte, 64, 79
Esquin-Yoé Viguis (Mescalero chief), 113
establecimientos de paz (peace
establishments), 5, 71, 73, 86, 92,
194; Apaches seek peace at, 4, 91;
Chiricahua and Western Apaches
at, 195; and Cordero's investigation
of Mescalero aid to Lipans, 78;
keeping tranquility in, 20, 86, 159–60;
Mescaleros return to after war, 184,
188; movement of Mescaleros in and
out of, 23, 71–72, 95, 191; as Spanish
tactic to control Apaches, 3, 7, 10–11,
74–75, 144–45. *See also* Mescaleros de
paz
Estancia Basin, N.Mex., 31
Expedition of Coahuila, 142, 145, 153, 163

Faraón Apaches, 104, 205n7; Manuel
Rengel campaign against, 59, 145;
O'Conor combat with, 33–34; raiding
of Spaniards by, 30, 72; Spanish
identification of, 27–28; territory
of, 28. *See also* Apache Indians;
Mescalero Apaches
Fernández, Bernardo, 181–82
Fernández, Juan, 12, 16, 204n17;
Mescaleros' ambush of, 17–18
First Compañía Volante, 12; as part of
Expedition of Coahuila, 142; troops
from in campaigns against Apaches,
12–13, 106, 139
First Compañía Volante of Nuevo
Santander, 166
First Flying Company. *See* First
Compañía Volante

Fixed Battalion of Caracas (Venezuela),
70
Flores, Francisco, 155
Flores, Manuel Antonio, 50, 54–55, 59, 65
Florida, 45
Fort Selden, N.Mex., 214n6
Fourth Compañía Volante, 21, 203n7,
211n5; in campaigns against Apaches,
12, 15, 106–7, 112, 139; Cayetano
Limón as member of, 15; as part of
Expedition of Coahuila, 142
France, 199; execution of king of, 76–77;
Indian policies of, 45; Spain's wars
against, 7, 10–11, 85, 91, 150; trade with
Apaches by, 130
Francisco (or Tlayelel; Mescalero chief),
105; in dispute with Nzazen, 72; at El
Paso del Norte establecimientos de
paz, 81; as loyal ally of Spanish, 18–19,
25, 95, 103–4, 127, 191–92; ranchería of
at El Paso del Norte, 64, 73
French Revolution, 77
Friega la Olla (Mescalero chief). *See*
Esquin-yoé (Mescalero chief)
Fuerte (Chiricahua Apache), 191. *See also*
Mangas Coloradas (Chiricahua chief)

Gallinas Mountains (N.Mex.), 208n17
Gálvez, Bernardo de, 49, 96; background
of, 45; impact of death, 50; military
structure of Interior Provinces under,
47; Nava follows maxims of, 198;
policies of toward Apaches, 3, 5,
45–47, 53, 70, 175, 189; view of Apaches
by, 47
Gálvez, Conde de. *See* Gálvez, Bernardo
de
Gálvez, José de, 45
Gálvez, Matías de, 45
García, Francisco, 211n10
García de Texada, Antonio, 12
Gaslán (Mescalero), 95, 104
Gaspar Grande Island (Trinidad), 148
Gibraltar, siege of (1782), 144

Gila River, 27, 39
Gileño Chiricahua Apaches, 23, 57, 205n7; Cordero's campaign against, 110, 117, 126; deportation of as prisoners of war, 218n14; establecimientos de paz for in New Mexico, 86; Mescaleros as Spanish allies against, 43, 63; O'Conor's campaign against, 38; raids by, 40, 106, 189; Spanish campaigns against, 62, 192; Spanish identification of, 27; as Spanish military auxiliaries, 101, 104–5, 107. *See also* Apache Indians; Chiricahua Apaches
Godoy, Manuel, 150, 158–59
Granados, Juan Francisco, 72
Great Britain, 45; invasion of Trinidad by, 148–50; Philip Nolan as agent of, 197; as Spain's ally, 10; Spain's wars against, 7, 35, 144, 150, 152; threat of invasion of New Spain by, 151, 155–58; threat of war with, 8, 40, 44, 164, 196, 198
Griego, Antonio, 154, 172–73; combat with Mescaleros by, 181–82; forwarding of Volante's scalp by, 173–74
Grúa Talamanca, Miguel de la. *See* Branciforte, Marqués de
Guadalajara, audiencia of, 69
Guadalupe Mountains (N.Mex./Tex.), 87; reports of no Mescaleros in, 126; Spanish campaigns against Mescaleros in, 89–90, 114, 128, 136, 138; Zozoya's combat with Mescaleros in, 164, 166–67, 169
Guajoquilla, Presidio of, 176, 188, 194
Guanajuato, Mexico, 144
Güero (Chiricahua chief), 160
Guhlkahéndé Apaches, 28. *See also* Mescalero Apaches
Guipuzcoa, Basque Province, Spain, 119
Gulf coast (Tex.), 38, 156, 158
Gulf of California, 10, 35, 37

Gulf of Mexico, 10, 35; threat of British invasion on coasts of, 156–57
Gutiérrez de la Cueva, Juan, 163

Hacienda de Bonanza (Real of Mazapil, Zacatecas), 49
Hacienda de Carrizal, Nuevo León, 139
Hacienda de Dolores, 132
Hacienda de Encinillas, 132
Hacienda de la Gruñidora (Real de Mazapil, Zacatecas), 48
Halifax, Newfoundland, 156
Harvey, Henry, 149
Havana, Cuba, 37, 91, 111, 135, 141, 164, 177, 192
Hidalgo, Miguel, 200
Horsehead Crossing (Pecos River), 128
Horses and mules, 30; belonging to Mescaleros, 29, 39, 51, 65–67, 69, 97; killing of by Mescaleros in combat, 168; Mescaleros and Lipans stealing of, 14, 48, 56, 67, 77, 139–40, 162, 174; Philip Nolan's procurement of in Texas, 196–97; as rewards for Apaches de paz, 41; Spanish loss of in campaigns, 145, 172; Spanish recovery of during campaigns against Mescaleros, 145, 154, 176, 181–82; of Spanish soldiers, 13, 17, 19, 33–34, 53, 58, 62, 98, 161, 166–67; trading of, 71, 79, 81, 198
Hueco Mountains (N.Mex./Tex.), 87, 104, 114, 126, 136, 215n13

Infantry Regiment of León, 70
Instructions for the Governing of the Interior Provinces of New Spain (Gálvez, 1786), 175, 189; as official Spanish policy for Apaches, 45, 50, 52, 71; strategy of policies in, 3, 47
Instructions of 1786. *See Instructions for the Governing of the Interior Provinces of New Spain* (Gálvez, 1786)

Interior Provinces, Central Division, 47, 144
Interior Provinces, Eastern Division, 4, 70; Apache raids and attacks in, 56, 77–79, 83; campaigns against Mescaleros in, 61, 65; Castro as commandant general of, 74, 119, 152; trading of horses and mules stolen in, 81; Ugalde as commandant general of, 47, 53
Interior Provinces, Western Division, 4, 47, 61, 70, 74, 77
Interior Provinces of New Spain, 12, 21, 47, 50, 119, 130, 159; Cordero's military career in, 21, 57; deportation of Apache prisoners of war from, 141, 175; governance of, 6, 34–36, 40, 44–45, 47, 50, 68–69; impact of Spain's wars on, 85, 92; Mescalero raids and attacks in, 7, 180, 193; Mescalero uprising in, 4, 20, 23, 121, 153; Nava as commandant general of, 10–11, 85; Spanish campaigns against Apaches in, 54, 65, 153, 197; threat of British invasion of, 150, 155–57, 196; threat to from United States, 197, 199
Iticha (Mescalero chief), 73

Jagosum (Mescalero chief), 162
Jasquedegá (Chiricahua chief), 190
Jasquenelté (Chiricahua chief), 190–91
Jicarilla Apaches, 27, 29, 32, 222n19. *See also* Apache Indians
Joagosun (Mescalero chief), 160; request for peace by, 135
Jocome Indians, 27. *See also* Apache Indians
Jornada del Muerto (N.Mex.), 73, 91, 107, 110, 145, 210n25
José Antonio (Lipan chief), 71, 84
Joseph (or Jusnates-dey; Mescalero chief), 104; killing of Lipans by, 84; raids by, 95, 126–27; ranchería of at Presidio del Norte, 63–64, 79, 87

Josnatesdey. *See* Joseph (or Jusnates-dey; Mescalero chief)
Juan Tuerto (Mescalero capitancillo), 43
Jumano Indians, 27. *See also* Apache Indians
Junta de los Ríos, 31, 43
Jusnates-dey. *See* Joseph (or Jusnates-dey; Mescalero chief)

La del Piñon Mountains (N.Mex.), 208n17
Laguna de la Victoria (N.Mex.), 59
Laredo, Nuevo Santander, 56, 174, 181
Las Cruces, N.Mex., 105
Las Salinas (salt deposits), 31
Lemeé, Nicolás, 176–77, 222n19
Licay, Vida (Mescalero Apache de paz), 113
Limón, Cayetano: ambush of by Mescaleros, 17–19, 20, 23–25, 102–3, 106; background of, 14; pursuit of Apache raiders by, 12, 16, 90, 99, 204n17
Limón, Cayetano (elder), 15
Limón, Ygnacio, 15
Lipan Apaches, 27, 94, 222n19; Comanches as enemy of, 32; Cordero's investigation of Mescaleros de paz aiding of, 78, 80–81; influence of Picax-andé over, 83–84; Mescaleros as Spanish allies against, 85, 172; peace negotiations with, 4–5, 41–42, 65, 68, 71, 74, 83, 85–86, 140–41, 199; raids and attacks by, 40, 49–50, 56, 67–68, 70, 77, 95, 119; Spanish campaigns against, 56, 67, 119; Spanish characterization of, 42–43. *See also* Apache Indians
Lipiyan Apaches, 66; disaffection with Mescaleros by, 173–74, 187; identification of by Spanish, 27; Picax-andé as chief of, 54, 78, 80, 83; as prisoners of war, 222n19; and peace

negotiations with Spanish, 169, 173, 181; separation from Mescaleros by, 173; Spanish campaigns against, 163, 170. *See also* Apache Indians; Llanero Apaches

Llanero Apaches, 27, 54, 83, 89, 95, 104, 115. *See also* Apache Indians; Lipiyan Apaches

Llano Estacado, 39; Comanche threat to Mescaleros on, 51, 122; drought in, 65; Mescalero Apache territory in, 28–29, 115; Mescaleros' annual buffalo hunt on, 61, 187–88; Spanish campaign against Mescaleros in, 56, 120

Loma Alta (encampment), 114

Los Pilares (ford on Rio Grande), 16, 204n17

Louisiana, 45, 156; Philip Nolan procures horses to sell in, 196–97; preparations in against British invasion, 85, 156, 158; return of to France, 199; threat of British invasion of, 157; threat to from United States, 196

Louisiana Purchase, 199

Louis XVI (king of France), 85; execution of, 76–77, 91

Madrid, Mariano, 143

Madrid, Nicolás, 107; role of in Spanish campaign against Mescaleros, 110, 112, 136–38

Madrid, Spain, 8, 11, 69, 121, 131, 133, 140, 143, 145, 153–54, 156, 158, 169, 173–74, 180, 183

Madrid, Ventura, 211n5

Magdalena, N.Mex., 58

Magdalena Mountains. *See* Sierra de Magdalena

Málaga, Spain, 144

Mallá. *See* Mayá (or Tucon chujaté; Mescalero chief)

Mangas Coloradas (Chiricahua chief), 191

Manso Indians, 27, 100–101. *See also* Apache Indians

María Louisa (queen of Spain), 150

Marquez, Manuel, 79–80, 211n5

Maselchindé (Mescalero chief), 64, 73, 80, 88, 95

Mateos, Andrés, 141, 218n14

Mayá (or Tucon chujaté; Mescalero chief), 88, 145; Almansa's attack on ranchería of, 123–26, 126; at El Paso del Norte establecimientos de paz, 64, 73, 80, 191; raiding by, 72, 95, 106, 162; renewed threat of attack by, 160–61; Spanish punitive campaign against, 89–90, 164

Maynez, Alberto, 80, 211n5

Medina, Nolasco, 13–14

Medinueta, Pedro de, 38

Melgares, Facundo, 110

Menchaca, Josef, 163–64

Menorca, siege of (1782), 144

Merino, Manuel, 133

Mesa, Miguel, 109; role in Spanish attack on Mescalero homeland, 107, 110, 112, 115–17

Mescalero Apache Reservation, 28

Mescalero Apaches, 7–8, 78, 83, 92, 169, 200, 205n7; Almansa's campaign against, 123–26, 223n4; ambush of Spanish soldiers by, 14, 16–17, 19, 98–99, 131, 136, 155; Comanches as enemy of, 29, 31–32, 39–40; Cordero's campaigns against, 57–60, 62, 115, 123, 127, 163; Cordero's pursuit of into homelands of, 24–25, 102–7, 111–14, 117; and cycle of raiding and Spanish campaigns against, 90, 138–40, 196; and death of Volante, 174; deportation of as Apache prisoners of war, 44, 60 91, 141–42, 164 175–77, 178–80, 187, 192–93, 218n14, 221–22n19; description of items lost by in combat with Emparan, 77; Emparan's campaign

Mescalero Apaches (*continued*)
against, 128–30; at establecimientos de paz, 5, 16, 43, 64, 68, 70–72, 79, 87, 193, Expedition of Coahuila campaigns against, 142–43, 153–54; hunting and gathering by, 71–72; Lipans and Lipiyanes as allies of, 140, 173; looting of dead Spanish soldiers by, 98–99; Madrid's combat with, 136–38; Mesa's campaign against, 115–16; Nava's successful strategy against, 7, 118, 120–23, 134–35, 147, 152, 155, 163, 176, 187, 195; O'Conor's campaign against, 33–34, 37–39; progenitors of, 25, 27–28; raiding and vengeance as part of culture of, 29–30, 196; raiding by, 36, 40, 49–50, 56, 67–68, 97–98, 119, 182; raids in Nueva Vizcaya by, 94–97, 127; reasons for seeking peace by, 51, 64–65; relationship with Spanish, 8–9, 89–90, 190; Rengel's campaigns against, 144–45, 154, 161; results of failed uprising, 147, 193; social structure of, 28, 95; as Spanish allies against other Apaches, 42–44, 63, 79; Spanish continuous campaign, impact on, 8, 67, 134, 171, 173, 182–83; Spanish identification of, 27–28, 73; Spanish military campaigns against, 31, 57, 88–91, 119, 135, 145, 153–54, 159–60, 164–65, 170–72, 175–76, 180–82, 185, 192, 199; Spanish peace negotiations with, 41–44, 51–52, 54–56, 60, 62–65, 86, 88, 207n4, 211n5; Spanish policies for control of, 50, 61; Spanish vecinos trade with, 79–80; surrender of, 164, 169–70; territory of, 28–29, 31; Ugalde's campaign against, 53, 55–56, 65–66; Ugalde's peace negotiations with, 42, 47; uprising of, 4–6, 20, 55, 132; Uranga's experience with, 61–62; Zozoya's combat with, 166–68

Mescaleros de paz, 72, 77, 106, 132, 162, 172, 192, 200, 216n21; Cordero's investigation of for aiding Lipans, 78–83; disloyal members of, 113, 171, 173; dissatisfaction with lifestyle of, 77, 84, 86; at El Paso del Norte, 64, 81–82; involvement of in uprising, 23, 103, 106; movements from establecimiento de paz of, 189–90; at Presidio of San Elizario, 25, 104, 190; raids by, 78, 95, 119; rancherías north of Rio Grande, 16, 87, 192; relationship with Spanish, 72–73, 82, 89, 134; relocation of by Ugalde, 54–55, 92; return to establecimientos de paz, 89–90, 188, 193–94, 198–99; smallpox epidemic among, 184–86; as Spanish auxiliaries and spies against other Apaches, 72–73, 79, 85, 101–2, 107, 190–91

Mexico, 4, 8, 20, 26, 29, 49, 144; Apaches deported to, 91, 135; independence of, 200; Mescalero Apache territory in, 27, 29; Spain's need for silver from, 91–92; threat of British invasion of, 150, 152, 155, 196

Mexico City, New Spain, 21, 40, 70, 92, 119, 150; Apache prisoners deported to, 37, 44, 111, 141, 164, 177–78, 192–93; Branciforte's corruption known in, 150–51; death of Gálvez in, 50

Mier, Nuevo Santander, 56

Miguel (Mescalero Apache), 127

Mimbreño Chiricahua Apaches, 27, 40, 62, 205n7; Cordero as peace agent for, 57; Cordero's pursuit of after ambush of Spanish soldiers, 105–6, 111, 117, 126; establecimientos de paz among, 86; O'Conor's campaign against, 38. *See also* Apache Indians; Chiricahua Apaches

Mimbres Mountains (N.Mex.), 107–8

Mimbres River (N.Mex.), 87, 105

minister of war (Spain), 169, 173–74
Miranda, Francisco, 155
Mission La Purísima Concepción de Quarai, 31
Mission San Buenaventura de las Humanas, 31
Mission San Gregorio de Abó, 31
Mississippi River, 10–11, 130, 155, 196; threat of invasion from, 156–57, 196
Missouri River, 156–57
Mogollon Mountains (N.Mex.), 161
Monclova, Villa de, Coahuila, 119
Montera Blanca (or Chal-coay; Mescalero chief), 95, 127, 207n4; ranchería of at Presidio del Norte, 64, 79
Montes, Ventura, 211n5
Moorhead, Max, 47
Moreno, Valentín, 177–78, 222n19
Moreno, Ventura, 79
Moreno. *See* Pino Blanco (or Moreno; Lipan chief)
Mulatto (Mescalero chief), 129–31
Muñoz, Manuel, 43, 46, 143, 196–97
Múzquiz, Miguel Francisco, 153, 170–71
Múzquiz (Mescalero chief), 176

Nacogdoches, Presidio of (Tex.), 197
Nacogdoches, Tex., 158
Naranjo, Andrés, 211n5
Narvaez, Juan Antonio, 211n10
Natagé Apaches, 83; O'Conor's combat with, 33–34; Spanish identification of, 27–28. *See also* Apache Indians; Mescalero Apaches
Natahéndé Apaches. *See* Natagé Apaches
Nations of the North (Indian groups), 141, 157–58, 187
Navajo Indians, 27
Nava y Porlier, Pedro de, 8, 17, 72, 75, 81, 127, 133, 138–39, 145, 161, 183, 186, 189; accomplishments as commandant general of Interior Provinces, 195–98; and Apaches seeking peace after Spanish campaigns, 88, 164, 169; background and career of, 11, 69–70 and beginning of Mescalero uprising, 14, 18, 20, 23, 102–3, 121; belief in peace policies by, 71, 73–74; as commandant general of Interior Provinces, 7, 85, 198; Cordero's reports on campaigns to, 104–5, 110, 115, 117, 126–27; and creating wedge between Mescaleros and Lipiyanes, 173; deportation of Apache prisoners of war by, 111, 141, 164, 175–77; and Emparan's campaign, 119, 131; and establecimientos de paz, 17, 83, 85–86, 159–60; evaluation of Apache situation in Interior Provinces by, 70, 189; and Expedition of Chihuahua campaigns, 142–43, 145; and investigation of Mescaleros de paz aiding Lipans, 78, 82; lack of trust of Mescalero leaders by, 89–90; peace negotiations with Lipans by, 71, 80, 86, 140–41; reliance on Antonio Cordero by, 57, 163; role in Philip Nolan affair, 196; strategy of continuous campaigns against Mescaleros by, 1, 111, 118, 128, 132, 134–36, 142, 145–46, 153–55, 170–71, 173, 176, 180–82, 187, 193; strategy to disrupt Mescalero encampments and food supplies, 121–22, 152, 163; and threat of British invasion of Interior Provinces, 7–8, 10, 155–59; use of punitive campaigns by, 25, 89, 192; and viceroy of New Spain, 120–21
Nelson, Horatio, 152
Neve, Felipe de, 44–45, 47
New Mexico (modern day), 86, 112, 123
New Mexico, Province of, 25, 30, 58; Apaches in, 26–28; Cordero's campaigns against Mescaleros in, 105, 114–15, 208n16; disruption of

New Mexico, Province of (*continued*)
establecimientos de paz in, 86;
gathering of Mimbreños and Gileños
in, 126; lieutenant governor of, 18, 60,
62, 104; Spanish military campaigns
against Apaches in, 4, 31, 38, 51,
87, 154; threat of Great Britain and
United States to, 85, 156–47, 159, 199;
troops from in campaigns against
Mescaleros, 111, 113, 120–22, 131–32, 134

New Orleans, La., 156–57, 196

New Spain, Viceroyalty of, 3, 49, 70,
167–68; bandits and outlaws in, 180;
Gálvez as viceroy of, 45; military
policy of in northern frontier of, 6,
35; peace on northern frontier, 77;
threat of invasion by Great Britain,
85, 151–52, 155–57

Nitahéndé Apaches, 28. *See also*
Mescalero Apaches

Nolan, Philip, 196–97

Nuestra Señora de la Buena Esperanza.
See Buena Esperanza, Nuestra
Señora de la (Mescalero settlement at
Presidio del Norte)

Nuestra Señora de la Luz Mountains
(Sierra Blanca, N.Mex.), 112

Nueva Vizcaya, Province of, 4, 13, 36,
44–45, 54, 62; campaigns against
Mescaleros in, 144, 159; Chiricahua
Apaches at establecimientos de paz
in, 54, 70; compañías volantes, 15,
100, 106; Cordero's military career
in, 21, 57–58; deportation of Apache
prisoners of war from, 192, 218n14;
Expedition of Coahuila in, 142,
145, 153; Josef Urías from, 11–12;
Mescalero establecimientos de paz
in, 54, 188, 193, 195; Mescalero raids
in, 26, 36, 53, 55, 83, 94, 97, 111, 127,
138–39; Mescaleros at peace in, 44,
199; raids by renegade Indians and
mulattoes in, 49; smallpox epidemic
in, 184; threat of British invasion, 159;
troops from in campaigns against
Mescaleros, 20, 24, 120–22, 132, 134,
154–55, 163–64, 176, 181–82, 187

Nuevo León, Province of, 47, 85, 116,
121, 166; Lipan Apaches at peace in,
5, 174, 180, 195; Mescalero and Lipan
raids in, 4, 56, 77, 97, 139–40, 147,
163; Nava's defense of from British
invasion, 159

Nuevo Reyno de León, Province of. *See*
Nuevo León, Province of

Nuevo Santander, Province of, 47, 166;
under control of viceroy of New
Spain, 85; Lipan Apaches at peace in,
5, 174, 180, 195; Mescalero and Lipan
Apache raids and attacks in, 4, 56, 77,
121; and threat of British invasion, 156,
158–59

Nzazen (or Barrio; Mescalero chief),
73, 88, 95; at El Paso del Norte
establecimientos de paz, 64, 68,
71–72, 80; peace negotiations by at El
Paso del Norte, 60, 62–63, 145; after
Spanish punitive campaign, 89–90

Ochoa, Joseph de, 176

Ochoa, Manuel, 190

O'Conor, Hugo, 35–36, 40; campaigns
against Apaches by, 33–34, 38–39, 41,
121; deportation of Apaches by, 37;
establishment of presidial line by, 37,
71–72

Ojinaga, Mexico, 31. *See also* Junta de los
Ríos

Ojito de Samalyuca, 73

Oñate, Juan de, 26, 28, 30

Ópata Indians: as enemies of Apaches,
96; as part of Spanish campaigns
against Mescaleros, 100, 104, 106,
108; as Spanish military auxiliaries,
123–25, 154, 176

Organ Mountains (N.Mex.): Mescaleros ambush Spanish soldiers in, 88–89; Mescaleros de paz in, 72, 87; Spanish expeditions against Mescaleros in, 104, 106, 112, 123, 126
Ortega, Bernardo, 211n5
Oscuro Mountains (N.Mex.). *See* Sierra Oscura (N.Mex.)
Our Lady of Good Hope (Mescalero settlement). *See* Buena Esperanza, Nuestra Señora de la (Mescalero settlement at Presidio del Norte)

Pacheco y Padilla, Juan Vicente de Güemes. *See* Revillagigedo, Viceroy Second Conde
Paraje de Bachíniva (Nueva Vizcaya), 94
Paraje de Fra Cristóbal (N.Mex.), 107, 110
Paraje de la Artesa, 126
Paraje de los Encinos (Tex.), 154
Paraje de Robledo (N.Mex.), 214n6
Paraje de San Diego (N.Mex.), 105, 208n16, 214n6
Paris, France, 76, 85
Pases-flá. *See* Cuerno Verde (or Pases-flá; Mescalero chief)
Pasqualillo (Apache chief), 160–62, 164
Patule El Grande (Mescalero capitancillo), 43–44, 52, 207n4
Pecos River, 28, 126; Emparan's campaign at, 118, 128–29; massacre of Mescaleros by Comanches at, 39; Spanish campaigns against Mescaleros near, 89, 114, 120, 145, 153, 170, 181
Peña Blanca, Tex., 80
Perez, Francisco, 64, 211n5
Perote, Mexico, 178
Peru, Joaquin, 79, 110, 211n5
Peru, Phelipe, 107, 112
Peru, Viceroyalty of, 44

Picax-andé-Ynstinclé de Ugalde (Mescalero chief), 95, 173; at establecimientos de paz, 80–81; seeks peace, 54, 78, 207n4; as threat to stability of peace, 83–84, 104
Pilares, Presidio of (site of), 114
Pino Blanco (or Moreno; Lipan chief), 80, 83–84, 174
Piro Indians, 71, 80, 211n10; Apaches raid settlement of, 71; as Spanish military auxiliaries, 100–101
Portugal, 70, 152
Presidio, Tex., 31. *See also* Junta de los Ríos
Presidio del Norte, 20, 61, 143, 161; campaigns against Mescaleros from, 90, 176, 181; Cordero's investigation of Mescaleros de paz aiding Lipans at, 78–80, 211n5; Lipans seek peace at, 83, 86; Mescalero establecimiento de paz at, 5, 16, 43, 51–52, 54–55, 64, 68, 70–71, 78–79, 82, 86–87, 128, 132, 171–72, 188, 198, 216n21; Mescalero peace negotiations at, 53–54, 56, 62–64; Mescaleros de paz after war, 187, 193–94, 198; raids and attacks by Mescaleros de paz from, 6, 95, 106, 119; removal of establecimiento de paz from, 92; smallpox epidemic at, 184–86
Presidio del Príncipe, 13, 15–16, 78, 90, 132, 177, 203n7; campaigns against Mescaleros from, 13, 24, 90, 102; Chiricahua Apaches de paz relocate to, 160; First Compañía Volante at, 12; Tovar as commander of, 14; troops from in campaigns against Mescaleros, 104, 125, 138
Presidio de San Agustín del Tucson, 4
Presidio San Eleceario. *See* Presidio San Elizario
Presidio San Elizario, 20, 38, 96, 113, 161, 192; and ambush of Limón and Urías, 18–19, 103; Apache prisoners of war

Presidio San Elizario (*continued*)
sent from, 114, 193; establecimiento de paz at, 101, 190, 198; Mescaleros at establecimiento de paz of, 5, 16, 20, 86, 92, 95, 127, 188, 191, 193–94; Mescaleros de paz of as Spanish auxiliaries and allies, 104–5; as operations base for campaigns against Mescaleros, 25, 89, 112, 114, 116, 136, 153–54; and peace negotiations with Apaches, 63, 88; as ration distribution center for Mescaleros de paz, 86–87; Spanish military campaigns against Mescaleros near, 89, 106; troops from in Spanish campaigns against Mescaleros, 107, 192

Presidio Santa Rosa de Aguaverde, 42, 163, 176, 181; Lipans seek peace at, 68, 141; Mescaleros seek peace at, 169; Zozoya assigned to, 167

Presidio Santiago de Monclova, 139, 153, 167, 170, 174

Primera Compañía Volante. *See* First Compañía Volante

Provincias Internas. *See* Interior Provinces

Pueblo de la Joya, 203n7

Pueblo Indians, 26, 28, 30; as allies to Spanish military against Apaches, 90; Apache raiding of missions of, 31; contact with Apaches by, 26, 31

Pueblo Revolt (1680), 27, 29, 31, 100

Puerto España, Trinidad, 148–49

Puerto Rico, 70, 92, 152

Punta de Lampazos, Nuevo León, 139–40

Puquienete (Mescalero chief), 190

Quencla (Mescalero chief), 72

Querecho Indians, 28. *See* Apache Indians

Quesada, Joseph Valentín, 155

Quitman Mountains (Tex.), 204n18. *See* Sierra de los Ojos Calientes

Rabago, Joseph de, 167

Radium Springs, N.Mex., 208n16

Ramón, Ygnacio, 139–40

Rancho de los Sartuchis (Coahuila), 68

Rancho de San Juan, 132

Rancho de Santa Cruz, 203n7

Rancho Santa Cruz (Nueva Vizcaya), 93

Real de Boca de Leones, Nuevo León, 140

Real de Mazapil, Zacatecas, 48–50, 53

Regiment of the Provincial Dragoons del Príncipe, 144

Regulations for Governing the Interior Provinces of New Spain. *See* Regulations of 1772

Regulations of 1772, 37, 41, 45; adoption of, 35–36

Rengel, José Antonio, 47, 90, 144

Rengel, Manuel, 143, 162; background of, 144; campaign against Mescaleros commanded by, 89, 145–46, 154–55, 160–62; as commander of troops at San Elizario, 153, 164; knowledge of Apaches, 144–45

Revilla, Nuevo Santander, Apaches raids at, 56

Revillagigedo, Viceroy Second Conde, 69, 74, 78, 85, 119–20; and implementation of Instructions of 1786, 65, 70–71; orders Ugalde to end campaigns, 67–68; silver shipped to Spain by, 91–92; support of Pedro de Nava by, 75

Rincon, N.Mex., 208n16, 214n6

Rio Bonito (N.Mex.), 59

Rio Colorado (Tex.), 80

Río Conchos, 12, 20, 31, 43, 93, 160

Río de Balleza (Nueva Vizcaya), 93

Río de Pecos. *See* Pecos River

Río de Sabinas (Coahuila), 54–55

Río de Sacramento (N.Mex.), 113

Río de San Pedro (Tex.), 129

Río de Teria (Coahuila), 155

Index

Rio Grande, 12, 18, 36, 43, 60, 62–64, 114, 126, 142, 160, 162, 210n25; Apache raiding along, 20, 31; Apaches cross for raids, 13, 37, 42, 90, 93–94, 97, 99, 102, 174, 193; as boundary to Mescalero territory, 16, 29, 31, 51–52, 87, 96, 106; and Cordero's pursuit of Apaches, 105, 107, 110, 115, 126, 208n16, 215n13; Expedition of Chihuahua campaigns north of, 143, 153; and Faraón Apaches, 28, 145; as part of presidial line, 35, 37, 43; Spanish military campaigns along or near, 24, 38, 57–58, 115, 123, 128–29, 161, 192; Spanish military campaigns north of against Mescalero, 53–54, 88–90, 104, 120, 135–36, 145, 170, 188
Rio Ruidoso (N.Mex.), 59
Rio Salado (N.Mex.), 58, 208n17
Riva, José María de la, 161
Rivera, Antonio Felix Martin de, 211n5
Rivera, Juan Pedro, 64–65, 211n10
Robledo Mountains (N.Mex.), 72, 105, 161
Rodriguez, Saturnino, 79, 211n5
Royal Military Academy (Avila, Spain), 70
Rubí, Marques de, 35

Sabana Grande ranch (Real de Mazapil, Zacatecas), 48
Sabinal, N.Mex., 86
Sabinal River Canyon (Tex.), 66
Sacramento Mountains (N.Mex.), 88; Cordero's campaigns against Mescaleros in, 57–59, 62, 65, 112–13, 117, 123, 135; Manuel Rengel's pursuit of Mescaleros into, 154; Mescalero Apaches live in, 28, 105; Mescaleros de paz in, 72, 87, 191; Mescaleros hold junta in, 160; Mescaleros live in, 28, 62, 95, 189; O'Conor's campaign against Mescaleros in, 38–39; Spanish campaigns against Mescaleros in, 90, 111, 131, 170, 192
Salinas Pueblos, 30–31. *See also* Mission San Gregorio de Abó; Mission San Buenaventura de Las Humanas; Mission La Purísima Concepción de Quarai
Saltillo, Villa de, Coahuila, 56, 68
San Agustín Springs (N.Mex.), 112, 123
San Andres Mountains (N.Mex.), 57, 112, 123, 126
San Antonio, Real de Mazapil, Zacatecas, 48
San Antonio Bucareli de la Bábia, Presidio of, 155
San Antonio de Bejar, Tex. *See* San Antonio de Bexar, Tex.
San Antonio de Bexar, Tex., 31, 56, 174, 181, 195; Philip Nolan in, 196–97
San Antonio de Chorreras (Nueva Vizcaya), 208n17
San Buenaventura, Presidio of, 54, 104, 123, 138, 211n10; Cordero as commander of, 21; Mescaleros raid near, 138; troops from in Spanish campaigns against Mescaleros, 107, 112–13, 125, 136
San Carlos, Presidio of, 12, 14, 16, 44, 94, 117, 203n7, 204n17
San Carlos de Buenavista, Presidio of, 15
San Carlos de Parras, Coahuila, 155, 171
San Carlos de Parras, Presidio of, 155
San Damaso (Spanish ship), 149
San Diego Crossing (N.Mex.). *See* Paraje de San Diego (N.Mex.)
San Felipe y Santiago Janos, Presidio of, 79, 87, 89, 211n5; Apaches de paz as Spanish military auxiliaries from, 101, 104–5, 109, 162; Chiricahuas de paz at, 144, 159–60, 190; Cordero as commander of, 21–22, 57; establecimientos de paz at, 4, 22; troops from in campaigns against Mescaleros, 104, 160, 211n5

San Fernando de Carrizal, Presidio of, 39, 89, 115, 190
San Francisco de Conchos, Presidio of, Josef Urías from, 11
San Geronimo, Nueva Vizcaya, 194
San Juan, Puerto Rico, 152
San Juan Bautista de Río Grande, Presidio of, 141, 154, 172
San Mateo Mountains (N.Mex.), 160, 189
San Miguel de Bavispe, Presidio of, 100, 104, 106, 108; troops from in attacks on Mescaleros, 116, 125
San Nicolás de la Hoya, Nueva Vizcaya, 93
San Sabá, Tex., 32
San Sabá River (Tex.), 42
Santa Cruz de Tarahumaras, Mission (Nueva Vizcaya), 93
Santa Cruz de Tarahumaras, Nueva Vizcaya, 93, 99
Santa Fe, N.Mex., 27, 31–32, 90, 131
Santa Gertrudis de Altar, Presidio of, 15
Santa Rita del Cobre, N.Mex., 199
Santa Rosa, Presidio of (Santa Rosa de Sacramento), 54–55
Santa Rosa, Real of Mazapil, Zacatecas, 48
Santa Rosa, Villa de, Coahuila, 176
Santo Domingo (island), 156
Second Compañía Volante, 72, 104, 106
Second Company of the Voluntario Cataluña, 178–79
Senecú, N.Mex., 71, 80, 100, 162
Seven Rivers Apaches, 31. *See also* Mescalero Apaches
Seven Years' War (1756–63), 35, 70
Sierra Blanca (N.Mex.), 170–71, 28, 88, 215n13; Cordero's pursuit of Mescaleros in, 112–13; Spanish campaigns against Mescaleros in, 31, 38, 90, 111
Sierra de Guadalupe. *See* Guadalupe Mountains (N.Mex./Tex.)
Sierra de la Cola de la Aguila (Tex.), 116
Sierra de las Petacas, 123. *See* San Andres Mountains (N.Mex.)
Sierra del Carmen (Tex.), 135, 140
Sierra del Carrizo (Nuevo Vizcaya), 13–14, 17, 19, 24, 98, 102
Sierra del Lágrimas (Nueva Vizcaya), 98
Sierra del Mobano (Tex.). *See* Sierra del Mogano
Sierra del Mogano (Tex.), 115–16; combat between Spanish and Apaches in, 33–34; reports of no Mescaleros in, 126–27; Spanish campaigns against Apaches in, 37, 128. *See* Davis Mountains
Sierra de los Ojos Caliente, 16–18, 24, 204n18; Mescaleros gather in, 96–97, 99, 102
Sierra de los Organos. *See* Organ Mountains (N.Mex.)
Sierra de los Taraises, 153
Sierra del Sacramento. *See* Sacramento Mountains
Sierra de Magdalena (N.Mex.), 160, 189
Sierra de San Nicolás (N.Mex.), 112
Sierra de Tamaulipas (Nuevo Santander), 166
Sierra La Sal (N.Mex.), 208n17
Sierra Madre (Nueva Vizcaya), 93–94, 96–97
Sierra Negra (N.Mex.). *See* Black Range (N.Mex.)
Sierra Oscura (N.Mex.), 88, 123
Sierra Rica (Nueva Vizcaya), 171
Siete Rios Apaches. *See also* Mescalero Apaches; Seven Rivers Apaches
Sinaloa, Villa de, 15
smallpox, 184–86
Socorro, Tex., 100
Soldados de Cuera, 167–68
Soledad Canyon (N.Mex.), 112
Sonora, Province of, 15, 26, 47, 51, 100, 111, 106; deportation of Apaches as prisoners of war from, 221n19;

establecimientos de paz in, 4, 70; peace between Spaniards and Apaches in, 195, 199; prevalence of smallpox in, 184; threat of British invasion of, 157, 159; troops from in campaign against Mescaleros, 20, 153, 164, 176

Sotelo, Ignacio, 192

Spain, 20, 36, 69, 70, 134; hostilities with Apaches by, 4–5, 8, 26–27, 30–31, 62; identification and characterization of Apaches by, 27–30, 32, 45, 73; impact of European wars on Interior Provinces, 77, 85, 91–92, 150–52, 199; and independence of Mexico, 155, 200; policies of for dealing with Apaches, 6–7, 35, 37, 41, 44, 46–47, 50, 52, 68, 91; and threat of British invasion of Interior Provinces, 10, 155, 198

Spanish Guards, Regiment of, 69

Spanish military, 8, 57, 37, 40, 49, 67–68, 94, 134; and Apaches as allies against other Apaches, 4, 52, 114; Apaches' killing and looting troops of, 6–7, 98; and description of compañías volantes of Nueva Vizcaya, 100; disproportionate use of force against Apaches by, 90–91; and governing structure of Interior Provinces, 35, 40, 50; impact of campaigns of on Mescaleros, 153–54, 188; use of Indian auxiliaries by, 100–102, 124

Spanish Royal Armada, 119

Spanish Royal Guards, 150

Squielnocten (Mescalero chief), 73

Suma Indians, 27. *See also* Apache Indians

Tagajla (Spanish Indian auxiliary), 112

Tarahumara Indians, 49, 93–94

Telles, Joseph Manuel, 81–82, 211n10

Tercera Compañía Volante. *See* Third Compañía Volante

Texas, Province of, 11, 32, 37, 42, 55, 111, 159; Apache territory in, 25, 27; British and U.S. threats to, 85, 156–59, 199; campaigns against Mescaleros in, 38, 114–15, 145, 153; Cordero as interim governor of, 143, 163; Lipans seek peace in, 5; Mescalero and Lipan raids in, 56, 77; Mescalero territory in, 28–29, 31, 96; O'Conor as governor of, 36; as part of Eastern Interior Provinces, 10, 47; Philip Nolan procures horses in, 196–97; Ugalde's campaigns against Mescaleros and Lipans in, 66

Texas Panhandle, 28–29

Third Compañía Volante, 144, 203n7; as escort to deported Apache prisoners of war, 141; in Spanish campaigns against Mescaleros, 12–13, 106, 139, 142

Tinajas Hondas Mountains (Tex.), 95, 103–4, 106, 215n13

Tiwa Indians, 100–101

Tlayelel. *See* Francisco (or Tlayelel; Mescalero chief)

Tonto Apaches, 27. *See also* Apache Indians

Tovar, José de, 12–14

Tovar, Joseph, 90, 181

Trinidad, Island of (Caribbean), 148–50, 152

Trujillo, Mariano, 192

Tucon chujaté. *See* Mayá (or Tucon chujaté; Mescalero chief)

Tueros, Pedro de, 49

Tularosa Basin, 112

Ugalde, Juan de, 50; ambush of Mescaleros by, 55; campaigns by against Mescaleros and Lipans, 42, 44, 51, 53, 56, 65–66, 70; as commandant general of Eastern Interior Provinces, 47, 69; distrust of Apaches by, 70; impact of campaigns

Ugalde, Juan de (*continued*)
of on Coahuila, 67; orders from Revillagigedo to cease campaigns of, 67–68; peace negotiations with Picaxandé by, 54–55

Ugarte y Loyola, Jacobo, 47, 49, 69; and campaigns against Mescaleros by, 55–59; conflicts with Ugarte by, 50, 54–55; and peace negotiations by Lipans at Presidio of Aguaverde, 68; and peace negotiations with Mescaleros, 51–52, 63, 80; policies of toward Apaches, 50, 70

United States, 11, 199; Philip Nolan as agent of, 197; threat from for New Spain, 7–8, 45, 196, 198; and threat of British invasion of Mexico, 155; trade with Apaches by, 130

Uranga, Francisco Xavier de: and Mescaleros de paz, 20, 71–73, 82; and peace negotiations with Mescaleros, 60–63; role in support of Spanish campaigns against Apaches, 18, 104, 162

Urías, Josef: ambush and killing of by Mescaleros, 13–14, 17, 19–20, 24–25, 98, 106; background of, 11–12; investigation into ambush of, 23, 102–3

Urives, Fermin, 110

Uvalde, Tex., 66

Valdez, Casimiro, 139–40

Valle de Rosario, Chihuahua. *See* Ciénega de los Olivos, Nueva Vizcaya

Valle de Santa Rosa (Coahuila), 74

Valles, Dionisio, 87–88, 211n5

Valley of Fires (N.Mex.), 58

Vargas, Antonio, 18–20, 103

Vargas, Diego de, 31

Venezuela, 11, 70, 152

Venta de la Rinconada, Mexico, 178–79

Veracruz, Mexico, 156; Apaches deported to, 37, 91, 135, 142, 164, 177–79; Mescaleros deported to, 91

Vidal de Lorca, Manuel, 88–89

Viguis (Mescalero chief), 95

Villaroel, Nicolás, 79, 127–28, 211n5

Visenegotean (Mescalero chief), 190

Vívora (Chiricahua chief), 160–61, 190

Volante (or Cheguindilé; Mescalero chief), 95, 207n4; death and scalping of, 172–174; killing of Lipans by, 84, 186; and Mescaleros de paz at Presidio del Norte, 64, 127, 173; peace negotiations by at El Paso del Norte, 61–63; ranchería of at Presidio del Norte, 79, 87

Volante Company of San Carlos de Parras, 155, 171

Waco, Tex., 197

War of the Pyrenees (1793–95), 91, 150

Western Apaches, 182, 195, 221n19

White Mountain Apaches, 27. *See also* Apache Indians

White Sands (N.Mex.), 112, 215n13

White Sands Missile Range (N.Mex.), 123

Wilkinson, James, 197

Xavier (Mescalero Apache), 127–28

Yscané (Mescalero chief), 186

Ysleta, pueblo of (Tex.), 88, 100, 162

Ystlebacinla (Mescalero chief), 191

Yusipeyé (Mescalero chief), 95, 103

Zacatecas, 48–49

Zapato Tuerto, 207n4

Zozoya, Joseph Francisco, 170; background and combat experience of, 166–67; combat with Mescaleros by, 167–69

Zuni, pueblo of (N.Mex.), 126

Zuni Indians, 25, 110

www.ingramcontent.com/pod-product-compliance
Lightning Source LLC
Chambersburg PA
CBHW020750160426
43192CB00006B/291